To Mr. Glenn Hawkes,

As we all work together to build a more peaceful, caring world.

Maurine Doerken

July 26, 1988

CLASSROOM COMBAT

TEACHING and TELEVISION

CLASSROOM COMBAT

TEACHING and TELEVISION

Maurine Doerken

EDUCATIONAL TECHNOLOGY PUBLICATIONS
ENGLEWOOD CLIFFS, NEW JERSEY 07632

Library of Congress Cataloging in Publication Data

Doerken, Maurine.
  Classroom combat, teaching and television.

  Bibliography: p.
  Includes index.
  1. Television and children. 2. Television and youth.
3. Violence in television. 4. Television advertising
and children. 5. Teachers—Attitudes. 6. Television
in education. I. Title.
HQ784.T4D63 1983   305.2'3   82-25125
ISBN 0-87778-186-9

Printed in the United States of America.

Library of Congress Catalog Card Number:
82-25125.

International Standard Book Number:
0-87778-186-9.

First Printing: March, 1983.

Preface

Television has been a commanding force in our society for three decades now, and there are many of us who feel a special form of war is being waged between the rest of the world and that ubiquitous TV image. Nowhere is the metaphor of a battle zone more appropriate than in the classrooms of America, where a daily struggle is under way between teachers and television for the attention—indeed, the minds—of our young people.

Certainly, our fascination over television's power and influence has not diminished with the years; if anything, the desire to understand more about the medium's role in our lives has grown steadily as time has progressed. Research scientists, sociologists, and clinical psychologists have spent countless laboratory hours investigating the impact of television; today, increasingly, educators in the classrooms of America are taking an active part in analyzing and discussing the medium's influence on the thinking of children—the heart of the combat zone.

Those of us who work closely with young people in the classroom find it difficult to ignore the tremendous role that TV plays in the lives of our students, molding much of their thinking and overall behavior. We are confronted with a new form of warfare, a different sort of teaching battle than ever found by the teaching profession. On one side, we see the countless hours young people spend in front of their TV sets; on the other, we lament the diminished impact (or so it seems) of the many hours that children spend in the classroom. There are times today when thoughtful teachers honestly wonder who is going to be the victor: them or TV. Indeed, some teachers would say that TV has already won the war and that attempts at either counterattack or accommodation would be futile, or just plain irrelevant.

It has become quite evident in recent years that two types of learning experiences are being conducted simultaneously: one in the traditional classroom and another at home in front of the TV. In school, our students are required to assimilate a formal curriculum of reading, writing, literature, science, social studies, and other subjects; but the TV set presents *another* vast curriculum: advertisements, programs, personalities, and knowledge which our young people seem to acquire effortlessly while watching their sets. The challenge of the struggle is clear: if teachers are to remain active forces in the education of the young, they must understand more about their remarkable teaching rival and somehow try to come to terms with it. It is with this goal in mind that *Classroom Combat* has been written.

The objective throughout this book is to provide a broad overview of television and how it affects the teacher/TV conflict for the allegiance of our youth: its historical background and present political status; the curriculum TV has taught children over the past three decades; *how* TV teaches; and what the implications of this are for education today and in the future. Every attempt has been made to give a representative sampling and cross-section of information to provide the reader with a variety of expert opinion regarding the subject of commercial television and its present, predominantly adversarial role in our young people's educational careers.

Chapter One, "A Teacher Looks at Television," presents the current position of the medium in contemporary society and defines in part the nature of the battleground we now face. How much TV do we consume? What are our attitudes toward its use? What may we expect of television in the future? Placed against this information is the backdrop of education and general learning, and how they apply to both classroom behavior and learning from TV. This, ultimately, is where the real warfare lies, because it has to do with how we learn and think; what we see and hear; and how we process material. It is in light of this information on educational theory that the rest of *Classroom Combat* should be viewed.

Chapters Two and Three offer in-depth investigations on

violence and advertising, respectively, as these topics represent the main focus of interest, both past and present, in the debate on children and television. Indeed, the controversy over violence on TV has produced heated discussion since the medium's inception and still holds a strong position in the television and teaching theater of war. Similarly, advertising is also becoming a closely scrutinized issue and represents, as far as the industry is concerned, the arena where *the* real fight—for dollars and cents—is conducted. Some of the topics covered in these two chapters include historical information on violence and advertising; current studies analyzing a variety of their effects; and the controversy surrounding possible policy changes and industry regulation.

Aside from the pressures and struggles taking place in violence and advertising, there remain myriad other effects. Chapter Four is an attempt to present those areas of television's influence on young people outside the domains of violence and advertising. So much time and effort have gone into the investigation of the first two topics that often a wide range of behavioral influences from television exposure is overlooked. Fortunately, however, this imbalance is now being rectified, and we are learning more and more how the medium affects numerous aspects of our lives. A collection of surveys and data is provided here that probe, in part, television's influence on children's play; their formal education; and its effects on their sleeping and eating patterns, as well as other health issues.

Chapter Five, "A Look at the Television Industry," represents a shift in tone from the previous four chapters, but is by no means a retreat from the television and teaching battleground. If anything, it is an attempt to place the research regarding TV and children against the reality of television as a business and economic force in our society. Those of us in education may discuss various aspects of the classroom versus TV combat metaphor, but too often, debate rests so heavily on the children themselves and what is happening (or being done) to them that the medium and how it works are passed over as unimportant. This should not be the case. On the contrary: it is vital for those of us in education, as well as other related fields, to have some understanding of how the industry functions; the strategies and motivations behind its maneuvering; and the role it plays as a business in our general economic community. It is extremely important that we have some insight into these areas where television fights its own internal battle of wits, attitudes, and dollar signs. With this in mind, Chapter Five offers a brief look at the television industry in order to place the medium and its impact on young people in cultural and historical perspective. Only through such understanding can meaningful dialogue be established, which hopefully will bring about constructive change.

Chapter Six returns to the theme of teaching and television and the role both will play in tomorrow's world. If, until this point, we have dealt with television primarily in its adversarial role *vis-a-vis* education, we must now make some attempt to negotiate some form of constructive compromise or accommodation between home, TV, school, and children. Teachers cannot retreat from the combat with television, but certainly we should make every attempt to emphasize and manipulate the medium's positive attributes, while educating ourselves and our students about the potentially negative aspects of thoughtless television consumption. Chapter Six, therefore, offers some practical suggestions for using television in the classroom, as well as what young people and parents may do at home. Certain thoughts and ideas are also given for future exploration with respect to teacher education and related fields of research in order to help us better understand what is taking place in our high-technology world. A whole new phase of learning and information dissemination is just beginning to open up, and a tremendous amount of work is needed regarding the position of teachers *vis-a-vis* television, the technology of learning, and how we are to approach the process of education, entertainment, and media literacy in the future.

Though *Classroom Combat* holds particular interest for teachers, administrators, counselors, and other professionals involved with learning and instruction, every attempt has been made to present the information collected here in an accessible, understandable manner. It is my sincere belief that the efforts of research should extend to a wide audience, not just an esoteric few. In this light, concerned parents, businessmen, policy-makers, and other members of the public may find this book interesting, helpful, and informative.

Finally, my personal thanks to the many people who contributed their time and knowledge to the making of this book.

Maurine Doerken
October, 1982

Acknowledgments

Chart p. 39. From "Vicarious Processes: A Case of No Trial Learning" in *Advances in Experimental Social Psychology Vol. 2*, Academic Press © 1965. Reprinted by permission of author and publisher.

Charts pp. 83, 84. From William Melody, *Children's Television: The Economics of Exploitation* © 1973, Yale University Press. Reprinted by permission of publisher.

Charts pp. 31, 144, 145, 151, 152, and 155. Adapted and/or reprinted from *Television and the Lives of Our Children*, by Wilbur Schramm, Jack Lyle, and Edwin B. Parker, with the permission of the publishers, Stanford University Press © 1961, by the Board of Trustees of the Leland Stanford Junior University.

Charts pp. 43, 45, 92, 97, and 202. Reprinted with permission from *The Early Window: Effects of Television on Children and Youth*, by Robert M. Liebert, John M. Neale, and Emily S. Davidson, © 1973, Permagon Press.

Charts pp. 107, 110. Reprinted with permission by Robert B. Choate and the Council on Children, Media, and Merchandising.

Chart p. 139. Reprinted by permission of the publisher from "Crime and Law Enforcement on Prime-Time Television," by Joseph R. Dominick, *Public Opinion Quarterly*, 1973, Vol. 37, pp. 245-246, © 1973, by the Trustees of Columbia University.

Charts pp. 146, 152. From Jack Lyle and Heidi Hoffman, "Children's Use of Television and Other Media," *Television and Social Behavior Vol. IV Television in Day-to-Day Life*. Reprinted with permission by US Government Printing Office.

Chart p. 168. From Robert D. Hess and Harriet Goldman, "Parents' Views of the Effects of Television on Their Children," *Child Development*, Vol. 33, 1962. Reprinted by permission of the author and the Society for Research in Child Psychology, University of Chicago Press.

Outline pp. 251-252. From Marianne Frostig and Phyllis Maslow, *Learning Problems in the Classroom: Prevention and Remediation*, Grune & Stratton, New York, 1973. Reprinted by permission of author and publisher.

With special thanks to the following people and organizations for their contributions, in the form of personal interviews and/or information, to this book.

> Richard Bannerman, Children's Programs, BBC
> Dr. Mary Conley, Child Psychologist
> David Crippens, KCET, Los Angeles
> Chase Dane, Director of Media, Santa Monica Schools
> Charles Firestone, Communications Lawyer, UCLA
> Susan Futterman, Children's Programming, ABC Network
> John Goldhammer, formerly with KABC, Los Angeles
> Jeffrey Lloyd and Jean Johnson, Action for Children's Television
> Alice March, Coalition for Children's Television
> Dr. David Merrill, Department of Instructional Technology, USC
> Dr. Thomas Mintz, Psychiatrist
> Giovanna Nigra-Chacon, formerly with KNBC, Los Angeles
> Frank Orme, National Association for Better Broadcasting
> William Porter, Director of Media, Beverly Hills Schools
> Norman Prescott and Lou Scheimer, Filmation Studios, Reseda, California
> Barbara Reardon, formerly with KNBC, Los Angeles
> Douglas Spellman, Advertiser
> Douglas Wildey, Independent Writer/Cartoonist
> Canadian Radio and Television Commission, Ottawa, Canada
> Director of Television Programs, UNESCO
> Far West Laboratory for Educational Research and Development, San Francisco, California
> Regional Educational Television Advisory Council, LA County
> Société Nationale de Programme France Région FR3
> Société Nationale de Television Française
> US Government Printing Office

Table of Contents

Page

Page

CLASSROOM COMBAT

TEACHING and TELEVISION

To My Students:

It must be remembered that there is nothing more difficult to plan, more uncertain of success, nor more dangerous to manage than the creation of a new order of things. For the initiator has the enmity of all who would profit by the preservation of the old institutions and merely lukewarm defenders in those who would gain by the new ones.

Machiavelli, *The Prince*

I

A Teacher Looks at Television

TUNING IN
Which of the following areas of combat sounds most familiar?

Channel 1
You are an elementary school teacher getting ready for class. As you survey your room, you witness two boys in the corner playing The Hulk and three other children imitating Larry, Moe, and Curly Joe of The Three Stooges. On the other side of the room, some youngsters are in the art center painting pictures of their current TV favorites. Right across from you, Mary is singing a candy commercial; and little Alice exclaims, "Oh! Oh! Spaghettios!" as she accidentally drops her books to the floor.

You think: "Another day begins . . ."

Channel 2
You are a high school instructor waiting for your students (half of whom look like replicas of Charlie's Angels or the Dukes of Hazzard) to enter the room. As you sit at your desk, you overhear the following snatches of conversation:

"Yeah, but did you see that game last night on TV? No? Man, it was great! Homework . . . are you kidding!!?? I wouldn't have missed that game for *anything*."

"Oh, it's this new stuff I saw advertised on TV. You like it? Yeah, it's really great. Makes you look older. Costs a lot, but it's worth it . . ."

"Tired? Yeah, guess so. I stayed up kinda late last night watching this old movie on TV."

You wonder: "Did they manage to squeeze in any *homework*?"

5

Channel 3

You are a physical education teacher or playground supervisor who wavers between confusion and despair. On the one hand, you have a collection of students who kung fu their way about like Bruce Lee. Yet, they also find it virtually impossible to become involved in a game without bull-dozing participants to the ground. On the other side, you have more than a few youngsters who are curiously inept at such childhood activities as jumping, hopping, and skipping.

What is going on? Could too much television be partially responsible?

Channel 4

You are a psychologist, social worker, or counselor who works either privately or with a school district. You are amazed at the number of student/family problems which seem to stem from life with the box. Worries about looks, earning money, and being able to buy things are encountered on a routine basis. Other, more subtle, issues involving self-concepts and interpersonal relationships are also beginning to crop up with greater regularity, and which appear to be TV-related.

You ask yourself: "Don't people *talk* to each other anymore?"

And last but not least:

Channel 5

As a school administrator, it is your responsibility to keep abreast of changes in learning and education. TV has been around for a long time now, but you still feel dissatisfied with the way it is (or is not) being used in your school. You want to learn more about it so you can make a few changes and formulate some good curriculum policies for your students and staff.

You have a few questions:

"Where does TV fit into our learning environment? I know kids watch a lot today, but what is it *really* doing? Is it good? How can I make learning from TV better? If I buy new equipment, will my faculty even know how to use it? What's going to happen with TV in tomorrow's classroom? How can I plan for that change now?"

I could go on. The point is this: if you work with young people today—either as a teacher, administrator, or guidance counselor—you must acknowledge that a battle is being waged in some form or another between you, your students, and TV. Indeed, television has become such an integral part of our lives that a day cannot pass without it touching us in some way. Predominantly through television, our young people now have more avenues of exposure—more areas of ideological combat—than any other time in the history of man. Sounds, images, messages, and words flicker unceasingly over the TV screen and engulf both us and the young in a veritable communications sea. A war is being conducted to win our time and attention, and we must consider the ramifications of this warfare in our schools today.

The tremendous influx of information provided by television and the large amounts of time given to consume it have also formed a new learning curriculum, one which offers serious challenge to traditional classroom education. Without doubt, television has become a major teaching force in our society, especially among the young growing up under its gaze. TV "speaks" to more children and adolescents than most teachers or instructors ever could, and has a far greater influence on shaping behavior and cultural aspirations than do the schools.

The challenge of this situation is clear:

For those of us in education to continue as successful classroom communicators, we must take television and its alternative teaching curriculum into account.

TV IN AMERICA

You may think the previous scenes are overstated, the position of television in society exaggerated. But let's look at some of the facts facing teachers and education today regarding this twentieth century phenomenon.

Vast television consumption itself appears to be a preeminent American activity. We do seem to have cornered the market in this regard. More than any other country in the world, we have become the Land of TV. We Americans now own more television sets than any other nation; some ninety-seven percent of all homes have at least one set, and multiple-set families are not far behind. More U.S. homes have TVs, in fact, than indoor plumbing.[1] Not only do we have color and black-and-white consoles; small, medium, and large sizes; remote-control and manual units; we have even managed to amend the rules of football and baseball to conform to the dictates of station breaks and instant replays. If present viewing statistics are correct, the majority of us have our sets on five to six hours a day. We spend over forty percent of our leisure time communing with the tube, and the typical American male viewer from the age of two to sixty-five will spend some 3,248 days (approximately nine years of his life) looking at that small screen.[2]

And that is not all. Not only do we spend an inordinate amount of time with TV, but our fascination with the medium has filtered into other facets of our lives as well. We have a multitude of magazines about TV stars and soap opera summaries in case we miss a day or two of "Dallas." Our most popular reading matter nationwide for several years running has been *TV Guide*. It actually has the largest circulation of any magazine in this country and many years ago replaced *Life, Look*, and *The Saturday Evening Post* as our most consumed weekly periodical. And how many of us—both students and teachers alike—consult the daily television movie schedule before checking the front-page news? It is obvious that television has long since established a firm beachhead in this country.

TELEVISION AND YOUNG PEOPLE

If the above statistics are hard to believe, the following figures regarding television and young people are even more sobering. For example:

(1) The average American nine to twelve years old will attend 980 hours of school in a year's time and watch 1,340 hours of TV.

(2) By the time this same child graduates from high school, he will have spent roughly 11,000 hours in a classroom and more

than 22,000 hours in front of the tube—almost twice the time he is with a teacher.

(3) Among television's heaviest consumers are preschoolers, but nine out of ten three-year-olds in this country will be well acquainted with Fred Flintstone and Gilligan before they know where their local school is or how to read—maybe even before they learn how to write their own names or where they live.[3]

And that is just a start. Putting the power of television as a teacher/educator into further perspective reveals additional disheartening comparisons. As an electronic general commanding troops of children and young people, it does a miraculous job, one which we must acknowledge with a certain amount of shell-shocked admiration. A high school instructor, for instance, may reach some 150 students in a year's time; an elementary school teacher far fewer. A best-selling hardback will be read by 500,000 to several million people. A record can sell several million copies, and a movie can reach millions, too. But a national network television program in America is considered a *failure* if it is not watched simultaneously by at least twenty million households every single week.[4] Even a 1.0 national rating (considered abysmal by TV programming heads) reaches some 600,000 homes!

Given these figures and statistics, how can our classroom curriculum possibly win in a battle against the one which appears on TV? Can you imagine a teacher, guidance counselor, or school administrator consistently reaching 600,000 students in an entire professional lifetime, let alone every single work week? Obviously, the struggle between teachers and television to reach our young hardly appears to be an even match.

TELEVISION AND LOWERING LITERACY LEVELS

The foregoing numbers must make us pause. Television and its new curriculum have been teaching for over thirty years now and competing with traditional classroom instruction during that time. One might well surmise that constant or even slight exposure could result in a certain amount of learning contamination. After all, it is only common sense to believe that several hours a day for thirty years must have had *some* effect.

When television first appeared on the scene during the late forties and early fifties, it was heralded as education's answer to fighting and winning the war against illiteracy and strengthening capabilities among students. It was looked upon as a new teaching helpmate, one that would inspire students to better understanding and learning. Though many were concerned about the medium, it certainly did not have the adversarial role *vis-a-vis* education that it generally assumes today.

But what is the reality three decades later?

This: *a large number of young people in this country cannot read.* Since World War II and the ascendancy of television, literacy levels in America have declined steadily, and guess who (or what) has received much of the blame? Yes, a former friend, now turned foe: television.

Here is a look at the downward trend:

(1) Scores from the Educational Testing Service's Scholastic Aptitude Test have been going down consistently since 1963.

(2) The Department of Health, Education, and Welfare also reports a constant erosion of skills since 1965, especially verbal skills.

(3) At Temple University, the proportion of freshmen failing the English placement exam has increased more than fifty percent since 1968, and forty percent of the University of California freshmen are now deficient in language skills.

(4) The Association of American Publishers has had to rewrite a special freshmen pamphlet from a twelfth-grade to a ninth-grade level in order for incoming students to understand.

(5) The 1975 Scholastic Aptitude Tests revealed the biggest decline in over two decades.[5] *

Like the Trojan Horse that once held great promise, television for school instruction somehow did not work the way many *hoped* it would. Granted, it has become a powerful teacher, but not in the traditional classroom environment.

Nor are the above illustrations alone in their description of falling student competency. More recently, 1980 statistics com-

*The 1982 testing, finally, has shown a small increase.

piled by the National Assessment of Educational Progress, an agency sponsored by state governments to monitor our educational growth, indicate that twenty-eight percent of today's high school juniors and seniors are illiterate; indeed, they are incapable of comprehending even the most simple literacy test given to them.[6] Appalling and unbelievable as it may seem, the literacy rate of the United States is on a par with that of Burma and Albania. The only *worse* country is Zambia, and apparently, we are heading there fast, too. Numerous other stories have begun to appear with greater and greater regularity, bemoaning the same fate. What is more, this decline encompasses all ethnic groups, all economic classes, both public and private school students, boys and girls alike.

Not very encouraging to say the least, but for anyone who has taught today's young people, these trends will not come as a complete surprise. I recently attended a meeting of junior high school English teachers, and their depressing consensus was that this downward spiral is getting worse and worse. The culprit? More than once, several teachers asked with genuine dismay, "How do we combat television?" "How do we get kids to read and talk again?" "How can we make the curriculum which is presented in class appear more important than that which takes place on TV?" A real struggle is apparent, but most of the teachers are at a loss as to how to wage their end of the tug-of-war. Next to all-out surrender to the tube, *what* can they do?

To say that television is solely responsible for this conflict between students and their success in school would be both unfair and wrong. To be sure, there are many other forms of communication and learning experiences which young people now have. But to deny that television is contributing to this change in traditional teaching and learning behavior cannot be accepted either. There definitely is a trend in education today which indicates that students are losing their ability—or, more importantly, *their desire*—to handle complex matters, sophisticated language, and ideas which demand greater critical analysis. A few thoughts present themselves:

(1) Does television jumble thought patterns in such subtle

ways that our powers of expression and concentration have been altered?

(2) Why should youngsters work hard when TV makes everything look so *easy*?

(3) What is "important" about reading and writing, anyway, if all they will have to do is switch on a set and take in what some TV voice has to say?

TELEVISION AND THE FUTURE

It is evident that the confrontation between teachers, television, and students is a challenging and serious one indeed. But if you think life with the box appears daunting to us now, its current position pales in comparison to how the small screen will be used as an educator/communicator in the decades to come. The skirmish for audience attention will expand tremendously in the not-too-distant future, and we should be prepared for a new kind of learning fight.

Consider this:

Recently, the following excerpt appeared in a popular magazine about video's New Frontiers, and this was the image presented of television:

> The time is Christmas Future, and the man who gives himself everything has just settled down for a long night's viewing. At the flick of a switch, his 84-inch television screen lights up with the opening of "Jaws II."

The article continued:

> This will be coming to him unsevered by commercials on the local pay cable channel. When the movie ends, he digs out the latest selection from Video Disc of the Month Club to continue his fun . . .[7]

Such is the upcoming American Revolution in home entertainment, which will be accompanied by videodiscs, video recorders, home TV courses, video games, and whatever else technology provides us (and today's students) to pursue our pleasure. It would appear from this that television's victory over the classroom teacher is almost a foregone conclusion.

Furthermore, if all that sounds formidable and virtually

impossible to counteract, it is just a glimmer of what we have in store. Not only do we have Video Christmas Future to look forward to, but there will also be M O T H E R (Multiple Output Telecommunication Home End Resource)—or something of similar ilk—seven-foot wall screens which will talk back to us, provide 3-D vision, computer hook-ups to the Library of Congress, worldwide programming via satellites, newspaper printouts, plus channels galore. We can hardly even begin to imagine all that will be available to us at the flick of a switch.

Yet, ask yourself: how can even the finest teacher/educator begin to compete in a contest carried on by seven-foot color wall screens, complete with unlimited selection? The battle, if we can even call it that, between classroom and television curriculum appears awesome indeed. But, it is precisely this world in which our students will be living and learning, the world which we must prepare ourselves and them for today.

PARENTS AND TV

Not only must we educators contend with how our students approach TV and its importance in our lives in the near future, but we have other problems as well. How are we to confront parents and their attitudes toward television? How are we to deal with what takes place in the home and the way parents cope with the medium *vis-a-vis* their children? This adds yet another dimension to our struggle.

Despite the discouraging figures in the preceding sections, it seems many grown-ups today have wholeheartedly embraced television as a substitute teacher, surrogate babysitter, and part-time friend for their children. Though parents should be responsible for monitoring their children's consumption and what they are exposed to through the eyes of television, it seems many youngsters are now permitted to watch and watch and watch with no supervision or intervention whatsoever. Either many parents are not aware of the potential conflict taking place between the culture of the classroom and what they learn from the tube, or they simply have given up their side and surrendered to the box.

Other parents may allow their children unrestricted usage because they themselves watch a lot of TV, and perhaps they have not stopped to consider what influence television's curriculum may be having on their offspring. Obviously, all this does not make our job in the classroom any easier.

Here are but a few examples of how many adults perceive television and allow it to speak unrestrictedly to their young. These sentiments further delineate the nature of our battle zone between children and TV.

(1) Well, TV keeps them quiet. They're not apt to go running all over the place.

(2) TV takes some of the burden off me teaching them games.

(3) Kids have a chance to look at the good and the bad and decide for themselves.

(4) TV increases their vocabulary and their general knowledge.

(5) Children learn to express themselves at an early age.

(6) TV has given them a desire to stay at home and not be out where I do not know where they are, getting into trouble.

(7) You mean TV is bad for kids?[8]

Naturally, not all grown-ups hold these views. There are many parents today who are very concerned about television and who *do* try to exert some sort of control over the medium. But often they find it hard. The war between themselves and TV to hold children's attention is not an easy one to win by any means. I heard one mother talk of her three-year-old boy, a TV addict as she described him, who would get out of bed at 2 o'clock in the morning to plug in the set so he could watch. Short of getting rid of the unit altogether, this mother was at a total loss trying to monitor her son's *mania* for TV. In some cases, parents may have rules for using television, but frequently, their children get home from school before they return from work. And, with no one around to say "no," on goes the set. Other parents may have guidelines for viewing, but what happens when their children go to a friend's house? And who wouldn't be sympathetic toward the working parent who allows his or her youngsters to watch Saturday morning cartoons in order to get a little extra sleep?

Clearly, complete control of the medium is not always possible. Nevertheless, it is against these parental attitudes and our culture's general acceptance of the box that teachers and educators must function today and formulate their own strategies for dealing with the tube.

TEACHERS AND TV

What about instructors themselves? It is easy for us to cite statistics galore about the way American society approaches TV, what it is doing to our charges, how intimidating our TV future looks, or the way parents cope with television in the home. But how many of us involved in education today really *think* about TV and the way it is affecting our jobs and the position of learning among our students? How many of us are truly engaged in thoughtful planning regarding the teaching/TV conflict? What weapons are we using to save our eroding position toward today's young?

Like many Americans, I never gave television much thought at all . . . *until I started to teach*. But the first year I was in the classroom, I was amazed at the amount of television-related talk that infested the conversations of all my students. I truly felt as if I were a stranger in a strange land, even though I was one of the original tube initiates and had watched my fair share of TV as a child. Yet, my students would discuss television characters, sing commercial jingles while doing their work, compare their own lives to TV, and play-act TV personalities at recess. At times, it seemed as if *no life existed outside the TV world*. The scenes provided at the beginning of this chapter are all too close to everyday reality in the classroom, and it is a rather chilling thought that our position as mentors to the upcoming generations has been so successfully usurped by an inanimate object.

This does not mean, however, that all teachers and administrators are aware of television's tremendous pull or the seriousness of our present position, especially those in schools today who have grown up with TV. Once, for example, when I was working in a junior high school, I listened to a group of colleagues—all of whom were college graduates, several with Masters Degrees and more than a few years teaching experience—spend a forty-five-minute lunch break challenging each other on TV "trivia." I was quite impressed with their vast stores of information. Here were people who had actually watched *more* TV than I had as a child! But it also puzzled and disturbed me that Nixon's first interview with David Frost, which had been screened the night before, was dismissed as "unimportant" in favor of "What was the emblem on the SKY BIRD plane?" (That one stumped everybody.) Mistakenly, I had thought the interview might have offered some meaty conversation among staff and students. But if teachers can spend that much time thinking and talking about TV, imagine what their *students* are doing!

This illustration only accentuates the problem we professionals face in dealing with television and how we are to function as instructors in a rapidly changing technological society. We must become more aware of this situation within ourselves and more importantly within our students, because we may be just as guilty of consuming television in an unthinking manner as they. The TV user in us may be perfectly content to discuss TV trivia all day, but the teacher and classroom communicator should cringe at the thought of how often our young people may be doing precisely the same thing. Rather, we should be discussing ways of promoting *our* side of the TV/classroom battle.

TELEVISION AND LEARNING THEORY

I have spoken of television material as a vast new form of learning curriculum which is affecting the total process of education and human communication. The following chapters will analyze specifically what that curriculum has been over the past thirty years and in what kind of battlefields we are currently engaged. But, first, it is necessary to give some idea how learning from television and learning in the classroom differ. It is vitally important for those of us in teaching and education to have some idea of the changes that are occurring in traditional learning behavior. Otherwise, we will be at a loss to understand the implications of the combat over ideas and learning we see taking place. What follows, therefore, is a brief look at some key areas in the issue of television and learning and how they apply to situations we come up against almost daily in the classroom.

Active and Passive Learning

Traditionally, people involved with teaching and education have stressed the active nature of learning. If a child wants to play the guitar, he has to practice. If he wants to read, he must pick up a book and make an effort. If he wants to get 100 percent on a spelling test, he must study. And a high school English essay will not get written unless the student takes pen in hand.

Yet, there is another form of learning, called passive learning, which is equally effective and which involves little or no effort on the part of the individual. A person, whether young or old, may gather in painlessly any number of ideas and values simply by watching others. Passive learning is easy, readily responsive to animated stimuli, and characterized by a lack of resistance to what is presented—conditions which are all apparent while watching TV.

Now, many children may actively resist certain classroom activities, but how many teachers have met a child who actively resists TV? Yet, much of what is taught by the medium involves this type of learning, especially among younger viewers. It is very difficult to evaluate this area because material acquired passively while a youngster watches peacefully in front of a set is usually unrelated to immediate needs. He can pick up just about *anything* from the screen. The special quality about passive learning is an absence of resistance to what is presented.

This holds important implications for the classroom and underscores the difficulty of our present struggle. It means that passively learned items have a distinct advantage over many things taught in school. Since the viewer is in a relaxed state, he is more open to what appears before him on the set. There is no threat of failure or ridicule, and effective communication can take place without direct contact or words being exchanged in person. The individual simply watches and assimilates data—whether he consciously chooses to do so or not.

This contrast between passive and active learning involves a distinction between relaxation and excitement: two very different aspects of interest. Obviously, motivation in action or attitude is the desired result in both instances, but divergent means are used to achieve this end. Most of what we educators know about motivation and learning is based on what excites and stimulates, but little is known about what relaxes and how this affects the acquisition of information and the process of education and communication as a whole.[9]

Voluntary and Involuntary Learning

This difference in the way we acquire information has also been described as voluntary versus involuntary learning. In the classroom, for example, a child's learning generally is active and voluntary; he must seek out and pursue certain facts and knowledge. Learning from television, however, as we know it and approach it today generally is passive and involuntary. In other words, the child is not necessarily seeking anything, but that does not mean he cannot learn a great deal. On the contrary: if all learning were solely active or voluntary, we would have several problems. First of all, it is impossible to attend actively and consciously to every given task at all times. The body system itself could not function without an intricate series of automatic, unconscious reflexes, such as heartbeat and breathing. Also, if learning were based solely upon active, high-level interest, there would be no such thing as subliminal suggestion or hypnosis, which works upon the individual when he is relaxed and not intently involved.

Classroom instruction usually stresses voluntary participation, whereas involuntary learning stresses yielding and persuasion. While in the latter learning condition, the individual is encouraged to accept the viewpoint of the persuaders, not necessarily to think for himself. Learning in the classroom, by way of contrast, attempts to stimulate the individual to clarify his own point of view and sense of self based upon the facts he has gathered, not merely to accept the opinion of others. Two very different goals are in mind and represent a conflict of learning interest.

Alpha and Beta Brain Waves

Experiments have been performed which analyze how the brain operates during different learning conditions and how these changes in perception apply specifically to TV.

In a study of market research techniques, for example, a woman was shown several commercials, and her brain waves were monitored. She registered more slow brain wave patterns (Alpha waves, associated with relaxation) than high ones (Beta waves, associated with stimulation and involvement) while watching the TV ads. When the woman *read* the ads, however, her involvement increased. In fact, the investigation revealed that the amplitude of the print-induced waves was about five times that of the TV-induced ones.[10] In other words, the woman was more aroused, alert, and active while reading the advertisements than while seeing them on TV.

What is particularly significant about the brain wave research is that the effect of TV-watching appears to be independent of content *per se*. It may be that it is inherent in the physical properties of the television image, as shown on the cathode ray tube screen. In its physical properties, the make-up of TV image is qualitatively very different from, say, a motion picture image as shown on a theater screen, and it is very different from viewing real-life scenes. The implications of this research are quite startling. It may be that changing TV content for the better, while an important and worthwhile goal, will not alleviate many of the major problems caused by TV-viewing, since these may be inherent in the very nature of the medium itself.

This does not mean, however, that the television-received messages were any less effective simply because the subject responded differently to the two forms of presentation. Communication and learning can be *very* successful when a person's attention is involuntary rather than voluntary. As a matter of fact, this relaxed TV state, which involves slower brain wave patterns, may set up a very responsive mood for teaching via the screen.

Images and impressions may enter the mind at the out-of-awareness level of consciousness and remain for some time. With Alpha wave increases and Beta wave decreases, some very real learning differences may occur. Teachers in particular need to know more about alterations in brain wave patterns due to television exposure and how this type of learning affects our actions with today's students. If we are involved in a fight to preserve the ability to *think,* then we had better understand more about *how* the mind apprehends information under different learning conditions, and especially from TV.

The Sleeper Effect and Deferred Imitation

In conjunction with the concept of passive, involuntary, or incidental learning (these terms are used interchangeably), there is something called the sleeper effect. As the name implies, the sleeper effect means that a number of communications may have a stronger long-term than short-term impact. What a viewer picks up from the screen may go beyond that which is first presented and may strengthen in time, especially if what he sees is repeated over and over again. The viewer may not act or think any differently immediately following the initial presentation, but nevertheless may have been influenced, and he will demonstrate a change in behavior at some future date.

Jean Piaget, the renowned Swiss child psychologist and educator, calls this delayed learning deferred imitation. He explains it in this manner:

> The first reproduction of the model does not necessarily occur when the model is present, but may do so when it has been absent for some considerable time . . .[11]

He gives the following example of deferred imitation (also called deferred learning) based upon observations of his own daughter:

> J. had a visit from a little boy of 18 months whom she used to see from time to time, and who, in the course of the afternoon, got into a terrible temper. He screamed as he tried to get out of a playpen and pushed it backwards, stamping his feet. I stood watching him in amazement, never before having witnessed such a scene. The next day, J. herself screamed in her playpen and tried to move it, stamping her foot several times. The imitation of the whole scene was most striking.[12]

Naturally, deferred learning and the sleeper effect do not apply solely to TV. As Piaget's daughter so clearly demonstrates, a child can observe the actions of others and reenact them at a later date. But the number of models now available from the TV screen far surpasses those from real life. There are, for instance, only a few teachers in a child's lifetime, but countless television models every week. Again, the contest in terms of numbers is hardly an even match.

Through television's influence, we can see how important observation is in a child's learning and how this observed learning can reveal itself at a later time. Seeds of communication may be planted without manifesting themselves immediately, and whole realms of behavior may be stored for future use. Furthermore, with very young children, up to the age of seven or eight, this sort of imitation is not necessarily conscious; they can confuse their own activity or point of view with that of others. In the classroom, if this kind of unaware imitation occurs, the conscientious teacher usually takes note of it and encourages the child to think for himself. But when unaware imitation occurs from observing television, there frequently is no one around to see what the child picks up from the screen. Whether the learning is positive or negative, it goes unnoticed.

Once more, we teachers must be sensitive to the *way* children learn from television in order to work this to our own advantage. Since we are promised even more screen-delivered programs and information in the future, we had better understand as much as possible about the way these systems affect learning and the assimilation of data.

Piagetian Developmental Sequence

Another important aspect to discuss in relationship to television and children is Piaget's concept of developmental stages within the young.

Piaget believes that all children learn in distinct stages, starting from the time they are born and continuing into adulthood. These phases generally fall between birth and two; two and seven; seven and eleven; then eleven and sixteen or seventeen. (See Appendix

A.) At each level, thought and activity become more sophisticated and require greater *voluntary* learning behaviors.

Without going into what each level encompasses, it must be stressed that the first two are the most crucial in setting the tone and tenor of an individual's life. The foundations for learning are laid in these tremendously important preschool years between birth and the age of five. Cognitive, physical, and emotional development may be permanently hampered or enhanced during this time when children are so vulnerable to the outside world. It all depends upon the type and kind of experiences they do or do not have. It is only toward the end of stage two that an individual becomes capable of distinguishing between other opinions, learning to recognize his own actions as unique, and resisting suggestion.

This early vulnerability is extremely important for educators to bear in mind when considering television's part in teaching the young, for they are doubly susceptible to the medium's informal curriculum during these early years. Indeed, for many preschoolers, TV may represent the only learning curriculum they have, and we must be sensitive to its vast potential for influencing their future behavior through observation and imitation.

Accommodation and Assimilation

Related to Piaget's developmental stages in children is his concept of accommodation and assimilation. Accommodation, according to Piaget, is an out-going process of imitation and learning how to adapt to reality. Assimilation, on the other hand, is an in-taking process of play and using what one has learned for his own purpose and pleasure. These two actions represent a method of giving out and taking in which becomes more intricate through the various stages of growth. In effect, an individual's entire development can be described as a dynamic equilibrium or a rhythmic modulation between these two types of behavior.

This concept of accommodation and assimilation raises numerous questions in relationship to learning from television:

(1) Does watching too much TV, especially during early childhood, change the inherent pattern of accommodation and assimilation which is so vital to optimum learning?

(2) Are growing rhythms themselves either accelerated or inhibited due to immoderate television exposure?

(3) Is a child's physical development unduly impeded from life with the box?

(4) Is the delicate synchronization of the young somehow altered by watching TV?

(5) How might the various stages of sensory, emotional, and cognitive development be affected by excessive viewing?

These questions are particularly relevant for American society because our young people, as the previous statistics indicate, now consume more TV than any other country in the world. We have a real problem on our hands when it comes to teaching, TV, and children. Yet, these same questions apply to any culture which has television and which relies upon it as a primary means of communication and information dispersal. Moreover, these questions will increase in importance as television becomes more widely distributed and used around the globe.

Formal/Informal/Technical Learning

There is a final aspect which should be mentioned regarding traditional styles of learning and how they are affected by television exposure.

In his book, *The Silent Language*, Edward Hall writes that all cultures have three basic types of learning: formal, informal, and technical. Formal communication involves rules and is usually binary in nature: yes/no, right/wrong, permissible/prohibited, and so forth. To a large extent, this type of learning has always been the domain of the home first and schools and religious institutions second. On the other side, informal learning stresses the importance of model and imitation and generally is characterized by unconscious behavior—very similar to passive/involuntary learning and deferred imitation. This is the kind of learning style generally promoted by TV. Technical communication, in contrast, involves specialized skills and knowledge, such as engineering or physics, and is voluntary in nature. The learner must actively pursue a given task or goal. Traditionally, schools have been concerned with this kind of learning. One can see, therefore, how the informal domain, represented by hours of television viewing, could pose a serious challenge to the formal and technical modes of instruction.

Patterning

There are other points to consider in relationship to formal, informal, and technical learning and how they apply to TV.

In the case of formal learning, for example, the individual tries, makes a mistake, and is corrected. There is a specific learning pattern or procedure involved, which entails a dialogue between people. The parent warns his child not to touch the hot stove; the child goes ahead and touches the stove anyway; the youngster then cries and is admonished by the parent. At least he knows what not to do next time. The teacher presents a lesson; the students listen and then do some follow-through assignment. The teacher checks their work and gives some form of comment.

With informal learning, however, the individual generally relies on models and imitation without necessarily receiving any feedback about what he acquires. Patterning can still occur, but there is no two-way participation involved. The child watches his mother cooking and then pretends to cook along with her, regardless of whether or not she is aware of her child's imitation. A child sees a favorite cartoon character and mimics his actions afterwards. But the cartoon character certainly has no knowledge of how it is affecting the child; and the child may be unaware that he is learning behaviors from the animated figure.

This concept of patterning has great relevancy to television, where actors and their programs affect millions of people they never even see. This absence of awareness allows for a high degree of influence because much of the material presented is assimilated unconsciously. It is very similar to incidental/involuntary acquisition of information. In such informal learning situations, copying generally is not deliberate, simply because the model does not take part in the process except as an object of emulation.

Of these three types of learning, Hall believes the informal area has the greatest power in patterning and directing behavior precisely because the participants are not aware of what is happening. He writes:

> Mishandling the informal can often lead to serious difficulties, which are apt to become aggravated since the participants in an informal situation are not fully conscious of what is going on.[13]

In the past, relatives and friends were a child's primary sources of informal learning patterns. Yet, since the advent of television, there has been a terrific shift in this area of the human communication chain. In many respects, television's curriculum has taken over the domain of informal learning in our society. Now a great number of models for behavioral patterning come from TV, not from live models in the home, school, or real life.

Again: how has this change in favor of informal learning patterns from television affected a child's growth and educational progress? If a youngster is accustomed to the informal/passive learning style of TV, with its increased Alpha levels, will he be able to change over to the formal/technical/active learning style required in most classrooms? More importantly, will he *want* to? School and district administrators might wonder if they should modify their expectations and requirements in order to accommodate this change in their pupils.

It is of vast importance that we try to comprehend this alteration in the way we communicate and receive information. With the rapid growth of television and related video technology, educators will have to reevaluate their role in the formal, informal, and technical domains. We may have to revamp many of our teaching strategies and educational practices in order to confront this situation in a constructive manner. Classroom instructors in particular are affected by this shift because the way we have been trained to perceive and understand education may be out of date now that television has ushered in a new era of learning and patterning behaviors. Yet, if we are to remain successful formal and technical communicators, we must learn to appreciate and to cope with this informal teaching giant.

THOUGHTS TO CONSIDER

Increasingly, people involved with learning and education are questioning television's position and function in society, but concern on a large scale is still relatively scant. Why? Why indeed when we read such staggering statistics as children watching up to five hours a day? Why when we see how successful the medium is when it comes to capturing children's attention and occupying their time? Why when we watch how closely the business community and commercial interests pander to the child audience, or have glimpses of even more television in the future?

Part of this lack of concern may be due to the fact that more than half of all research ever conducted on the process of human communication has become available only within the last few decades.[14] For all practical purposes, how the media affect us is a relatively new field, just opening up, and not much of this information has yet filtered down to the general public or to the vast majority of classroom teachers and school administrators.

In addition, attitudes have changed about television. At first, most people generally believed TV had no real impact or influence; but this view has been reversed. Now we are learning more and more, as the following chapters will demonstrate, how *much* television modifies our thoughts and how it has revolutionized communication in our society, both in and out of the formal school environment.

Finally, since television and the economic forces behind it are such volatile enterprises, it is difficult to keep pace with them or to put them into cultural perspective. This, however, should no longer be the case. TV has become a way of life in the United States, and one of the most crucial dialogues which needs to take place in American education today and in the future concerns just this topic.

Before turning to the evidence gathered in the following pages, I want to share a statement which was written as television began its phenomenal rise. Teachers, educators, administrators, school social workers, and guidance counselors alike should ask whether this evaluation is still pertinent today, for it illustrates in part the classroom combat we now face.

> The agitated voices of public interest have quickly and character-
> istically subsided. But the problem [of TV and its effects] . . . is
> still with us. Here are the children and there is the television, and
> whether we publicize the grim fact or not, the two new worlds

[of TV and real life] are locked in irrevocable embrace, destined
to spin through the years of growing up into tomorrow's
questionable maturity. *What are the important facts about these
twentieth century twins?*[1][5] [italics added]

What *are* the facts concerning these twentieth century twins?
The post-World War II generations in America have become a new
breed, possessing a vast analogue of fantasy, trivia, and truth, all
communicated to them by years of living with TV. The children
we teach today are second- and third-wave twins, and those of us
involved in education must accept the fact that there is no
returning to a non-TV world. In a very real sense, whether we
appreciate the full extent of the medium's influence, we must
recognize that we are engaged in a special form of learning warfare
and that our youngsters have a split vision of life. They have had
two teaching curriculums, not just one. They possess two views of
experience: one provided from their day-to-day lives and one
provided to them by TV. Whether television's curriculum is *more*
influential may be open to some debate, but its existence cannot
be denied, and its impact on learning and education should be
seriously explored.

We must ask ourselves the following:

(1) What has television's curriculum taught over the past
thirty years?

(2) What are the implications for television as an instructional tool, both now and in the decades to come?

(3) Which twin will have a greater pull on education and
communication, on feelings and thought processes: personal
life experience or the world of TV?

(4) How will our jobs as professionals change because of
life with the box?

This book will take a step toward exploring some of these
issues.

II

Television and Violence

The arena of combat between educators and television which has drawn the most intense interest is the impact of TV violence on children. This represents by far the most extensive field of investigation done to date. More studies have been conducted on this aspect of the medium's teaching power than all others combined, and there is now a plethora of information available supporting widely divergent points of view. Unfortunately, few of these studies ever reach the classroom teacher or administrator, and even when they do make their way into school, they are often pushed aside or ignored because of their obtuse language and form.

Yet in a society whose citizens have more privately-owned handguns than any other country in the world and whose murder rate is steadily on the rise, the question of violence and young people is an extremely important issue. We should examine the role television may be playing as a potential source of informal learning contributing to this spirit of aggression. Television violence forms a substantial part of the medium's curriculum and represents a real battleground of instruction over children's actions and attitudes. If the hostile or antagonistic behavior we see manifested today in many young people stems even in part from television exposure, then we need to discuss what we as educators can do about it.

Before providing a brief chronicle of violence on American television, I want to stress again that any negative influence from TV violence (or television as a whole, for that matter) is generally achieved *over an extended period of time with consistency and repetition as key factors.* This represents basic learning theory: presentation followed by reiteration. An individual who watches only sporadic images of violence, unless he is severely ill or psychotic, is less likely to be adversely affected than one who has watched such presentations over and over again.

But the fact is that westerns, crime programs, and shootings have filled this country's airwaves for more than thirty years now, and in some cases, this type of antisocial instruction has been more uniform than many children's formal education. When one also considers the concept of passive/incidental learning and how easily young people in particular are manipulated under this learning condition, the possibility of potential negative influence is stronger still. For the child who watches hours of action drama daily, it is not unlikely that some sort of message from all the violence would seep in.

VIOLENCE ON AMERICAN TELEVISION: A PERSPECTIVE

To give some idea how relentless this sort of informal television warfare has been, here are a few surveys done over the past three decades concerning violence on American TV.

As early as 1950, when the medium was just getting started, the National Listener's Council analyzed one week of Los Angeles programming and discovered the following:

One Week of Los Angeles Programming/Circa 1950
91 murders
7 stagecoach hold-ups
3 kidnappings
15 to 20 people killed by an explosion
2 suicides
10 thefts
4 burglaries
2 cases of arson
1 case of blackmail
ALSO: numerous incidents of assault and battery, brawls and drunkenness, and crooked judges, sheriffs, and juries.

1

This was only the beginning! The fifties witnessed a steady escalation in conflict and action on TV. By 1960, American TV violence looked something like this:

---

100 Hours American Viewing Time/Circa 1960
12 murders
16 major gun fights
21 persons shot (not fatally)
21 other violent incidents ranging from shooting at but missing people to shooting up a town
37 hand-to-hand fights:
     15 fist fights
     15 sluggings
     1 attempted murder with a pitchfork
     2 strangulations
     a fight taking place in water
     a case of gagging and tying a woman to a bed
1 stabbing in the back with a butcher knife
4 attempted suicides (3 successful)
4 people falling or being pushed over cliffs
1 psychotic on the loose and raving in an airplane
2 mob scenes (one mob hangs the wrong man)
1 horse grinding a man under its hooves
ALSO: a great deal of miscellaneous violence, including a hired killer, two robberies, a woman killed by falling from a train, a tidal wave, an earthquake, and a guillotining.

---

[2]

Not only was there a greater quantity of violence on the screen, but more people were watching it as well. More sets were available in more homes, and parents had accepted television as a leisure-time activity for themselves and their children. A breakdown of the major networks, one independent, and one educational channel during the '60s reveals that cartoons, westerns, and crime shows—generally the most violent TV offerings—comprised over forty percent of the total programming schedule.[3] By the late '60s, the National Association for Better Radio and TV estimated that the average American child between five and fifteen years of age watched the destruction of more than 13,400 people on his home screen. This number was later amended to about 18,000, and represented a ninety percent increase in action drama since 1952.[4]

Several years later, between 1967 and 1972, George Gerbner, Professor at the Annenberg School of Communication, University of Pennsylvania, performed an extensive survey assessing violence on American TV. Gerbner found no substantial changes in the actual frequency of TV crime, even though the networks had promised reductions. Leading characters involved in violence declined, but those victimized rose to new heights. There was no major change in the percentage of programs containing violence nor the number of violent scenes. Gerbner found that children's cartoons in particular showed even greater amounts of aggressive content than adult drama. When he performed a similar study a few years later, Gerbner found the networks had lowered aggression somewhat; nevertheless, it still occurred in more than two-thirds of all prime-time shows and in nine out of ten weekend children's programs.[5]

In 1974, another survey was conducted, at the University of Washington, which revealed comparable findings. Programs were monitored on each of the three networks from sign-on to sign-off, and it was found that violent episodes occurred at the rate of about seven per hour throughout the day, seven days a week.[6] Only a few years later, two Stanford researchers set up another rating system to judge once again violence on American TV. They devised a special scorecard with a range from two for verbal abuse to fifty for murder, and programs to be marked were chosen randomly from *TV Guide*. Of the ten shows watched, the top prize went to "The Super Cops," a CBS Friday Night Movie, which received a violence rating of 975 points.

The "Super Cops" scorecard is shown on the following page.

These examples represent only a fraction of the total number of aggressive-content studies performed to date.

To say at this point that American television has been loaded with violence is a rather obvious understatement. The more

---

Mills and Kilbridge Violence Index/1977
3 shootings
4 attempted shootings
3 other displays of guns
1 shooting of a phone booth
5 fights
1 display of a corpse
1 purse snatching
ALSO: several scenes of a building being destroyed, with police rookies chasing drug dealers through it, plus various other assaults.

7

---

important observation is that American TV has been so consistently violent since its very inception. Many eyes have seen countless acts of aggression over television's past thirty years. The present generation of American youth has witnessed more violence, both real and fantasy, than perhaps any other group in the history of man. When one adds up all the westerns, "Lone Rangers," "Star Treks," spy shows, and cartoons, not to mention the Kennedy assassinations, Lee Harvey Oswald's "live" assassination, Martin Luther King's assassination, and last, but surely not least, the entire Vietnam War, the list becomes impressive indeed. As one writer put it:

> A visitor from another planet watching United States television
> for a week might conclude that viewers were being brainwashed
> by a cunning conspiracy determined to harness the nation—with
> special attention to the young—for war.[8]

If repetition and consistency are two of the most important conditions for effective learning, and if passive/low involvement situations influence the observer as much as the research indicates, the question teachers must address is not whether there has been an impact from TV violence, but *how much* and *of what kind*.

EARLY RESEARCH ON TELEVISION VIOLENCE

Let us investigate some of the research analyzing this continuing saga of visual mayhem.

By the late forties, we Americans were already calling TV a member of the family, and by 1954 we were spending over $3 billion yearly for sets, services, and power. During 1954 alone, more TVs were produced and marketed than automobiles; and no parallel can be found in any major industry for the rate at which this medium grew. Television literally mushroomed across the land. It hit the American home like a whirlwind, and so many people were busy being fascinated by the box that few took time to wonder what it might be *doing* to them.

1947	10,000 sets in the United States
1949	1 million
1950	3 million
1951	13 million
1955	35 million

One of the first people in this country who did question the role of TV violence in relationship to young people was Eleanor Maccoby, and she provides some interesting thoughts for us regarding its potential impact on children. Maccoby believes that externally-controlled fantasies, such as those provided by TV, may increase motivation and produce frustration. In effect, children could learn to seek out TV action drama simply because it is so *exciting* and unlike their own lives. Yet, habitual exposure might also increase a child's desire for "thrills" and stimulate the search for higher and higher levels of excitement. It is possible that this energy might then be released later in undesirable ways. In other words, if a child grows accustomed to a heightened level of excitement and wants his activity at that level, subsequent behavior could become disruptive if that level declines. The child might become restless or bored until he does something to restore the excitement to which he has grown accustomed. As Maccoby writes:

> If television *does* increase the level of excitement significantly, a
> mild form of addiction might take place; parents and teachers

could get the child's interest only by making things they want to present to him as exciting as the stories he is accustomed to seeing over television.[9]

Twenty-five years later, how many teachers have to make alterations in their instructional presentations in order to cope with their students' need for viewer "thrills"?

Another massive TV study performed during the fifties was headed by Hilde Himmelweit, A.N. Oppenheim, and Pamela Vince, in Great Britain. Their survey regarding the impact of TV on English children offers additional insight into the question of aggression in particular.

Regarding violent content, they write:

> ... One would expect that in the crime and detective series the constant display of aggression by both the criminal and the upholder of the law would also make an impact on those children sensitive to such cues.[10]

They found that television entertainment did indeed bring about changes in a child's outlooks and values, even though programs did not set out to do this deliberately. This is a prime example of incidental learning: even though the children were not in a formal school setting, they still were being taught a great deal. The British investigators also felt impact occurred under the following circumstances:

(1) when the values presented on television recur from program to program;

(2) when attitudes are presented in dramatic form so they evoke primarily emotional reactions rather than cognitive ones;

(3) when the viewer tends to be uncritical and attached to the medium; and

(4) when the viewer does not receive another set of values from parents or friends, providing a standard against which to judge television material.[11]

One assumes from this that violent TV presentations could have a substantial influence. They certainly are shown with great consistency. They appeal to the emotions rather than the intellect, and a large number of children receive little or no formal instruction contradicting what they view. They simply are allowed to watch and accept informally what they see. Again, this has great implications for the classroom. How much incidental information regarding violence do children pick up and bring with them to school? How long does it take for aggressive seeds from accumulated exposure to flower?

Another point Himmelweit, Oppenheim, and Vince bring out is that shooting *as a game* may be carried over into reality. If the aggression on TV is too stylized, children may not be disturbed by the gun fights they see portrayed, and consequently fail to learn that hand weapons have very real, very serious effects. They write:

> Shooting, first in westerns and later in crime and detective stories, has become so much a game that this play attitude enters into [the children's] evaluation of the real situation, even though books, play, and talk at home must have given them some general idea of the tragedy of war and fighting.[12]

This lack of fear or concern may be due to the fact that much of the violence on television is not a true portrayal of violence in real life. It has been cleaned up or "sanitized" so it will not unduly disturb viewers. Yet, this kind of non-gory violence may actually tend to promote, rather than inhibit, later aggression because the *real consequences* are not shown. Pain and suffering are portrayed but not really felt or internalized by the viewer. Another point to consider is that the distinction between the good guys and bad guys is slim. Violence on TV is perpetrated by *both* and often is shown as a legitimate means of attaining one's goals. Consequently, the ability to distinguish between right and wrong regarding the use of violence may be slowed down by the stream of fictional aggression the child sees. Aggressiveness instead receives implicit sanction; it becomes the normal way of dealing with problems and conflict. Violent programs may alter a child's view, making antisocial behavior appear acceptable, especially if the child is inclined to the expression of hostile feelings anyway or receives no formal training from home. The British conclude:

> It is suggested that crime and violence programs increase tension and anxiety, increase maladjustment and delinquent behavior, teach children techniques of crime, blunt their sensitivity to suffering and related to this, suggest to them that conflict is best solved by aggression.[13]

LATER STUDIES

Moving from some of the 1950s' research, we find that by 1960 television had become a fully accepted part of American society. The expenditure on electricity to run sets in one year amounted to some $500 million, and the public was lapping up "Bonanza" while turning more and more to color TV. Indeed, so thoroughly had the medium been integrated into our lives that researchers wanting to conduct surveys on its impact had to go into Canada to find children who had not yet been exposed. Clearly, American kids had become ensconced members of the first TV wave.

Yet, because television had become a way of life, more and more people began to question its function and influence, and the sixties brought with them a new wave of studies and interest in TV. Numerous books and articles began to appear, delving into what that other member of the family was doing to us, and the primary focus was the potential impact of television aggression.

Most of the surveys and investigations conducted during this period involve similar experimental procedures. Groups of people—either preschoolers, elementary school children, adolescents, or adults—were selected and divided into at least two groups. One group would see an aggressive film and then be tested for increased antisocial behavior, while the other (usually referred to as the controls) watched nonaggressive material. The results of the two samples would then be gathered and differences compared. Most studies of this type usually took place in laboratory settings over a relatively short time, but other experimental techniques included long-term field studies in which viewing behavior was examined over extended periods outside a laboratory environment.

Included here are surveys of different age groups because the general consistency of results is significant and worth noting. Bear in mind, however, that the younger the viewer, the more susceptible he is to influence because the developing mind is so open to impressions, both good and bad. The extent to which an individual responds to TV violence naturally depends upon a variety of factors, including viewing time, show preference, educational background, family influence, moral training, and so on. But the general similarity of results in all these studies is impressive and one which professional educators should take into account.

Albert Bandura

Albert Bandura of Stanford University was one of the leaders in assessing the impact of televised violence during the sixties. His extensive work in this area represents some of the core research regarding observational learning from TV and how it influences the behavior of young children.

Bandura has found that children do incorporate new responses simply by watching others and that these responses can last over an extended period of time. He has performed many experiments in which children who watched aggressive adult models later performed twice as much aggression as those who had not seen such models, and these results occurred in a number of different experimental situations.

In one study, for example, Bandura took preschool children and divided them into several groups. Some of the children saw films where an actor behaved aggressively with a large plastic doll and was either rewarded or punished for his actions. The children who saw the model-punished version were less aggressive than those in the other two groups. But when they were offered rewards for reproducing the negative behavior, the previous results were wiped out. An equal amount of learning had taken place among all.[14] This is another example of incidental/deferred learning, for even though some of the youngsters did not perform the aggressive actions during the first viewing, they still had "learned" the negative behaviors. In fact, a number of them later described the model's aggressiveness with considerable accuracy.

In another experiment, Bandura selected preschool boys and girls and again divided them into several groups: real-life aggressive models, filmed models, and cartoon models. Following exposure in various films, the children were mildly frustrated and tested for what they had learned in a different setting. Children who saw the real-life models and filmed models showed no real difference in total negative behavior. The filmed model seemed to have as much power as the live one in influencing the children's actions. Of the three experimental situations, Bandura discovered that exposure to humans behaving aggressively on film rather than from real life was the most potent—a disturbing finding. This means children could actually learn *more* harm from violent TV figures than real people. The youngsters in his film groups performed more total aggression than the rest of the students, and they also engaged in more aggressive gun play. As the chart below indicates, those who viewed the aggressive film and cartoon models demonstrated nearly *double* the negative behavior as those who were not exposed.

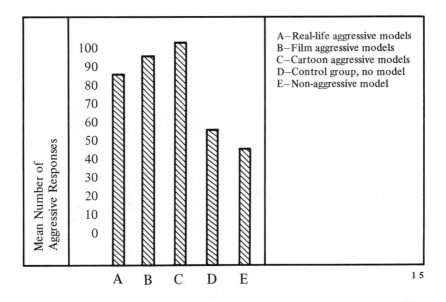

A—Real-life aggressive models
B—Film aggressive models
C—Cartoon aggressive models
D—Control group, no model
E—Non-aggressive model

Mean Number of Aggressive Responses

A   B   C   D   E

15

Still not satisfied, Bandura and colleagues tried yet again. They separated preschoolers into different groups and once again tested for the impact of aggressive TV. Children in the aggression-rewarded situation saw a film with "Rocky" and "Johnny," where Johnny is playing with some toys. Rocky asks if he may join in but is turned away. A fight ensues in which Rocky beats up Johnny. In the final scene, Rocky is the victor, for he exits with all the loot—cookies, 7-UP, and toys. (The model-punished version is similar, but Johnny emerges as the winner.)

Results indicate that the children who saw the model-rewarded film showed more aggressive behavior and liked to copy Rocky. Interestingly enough, however, the majority described his behavior in negative terms. The fact that Rocky got all the riches was the primary attraction, not whether his actions were right or wrong. The following illustration provides graphic proof of what children can say and then do:

> The classic example of how children will incorporate into their own behavior . . . objectionable but successful modeling . . . was offered by the girl who voiced considerable disapproval during the exposure session of Rocky's having appropriated Johnny's toys. Nevertheless, at the conclusion of the experimental period—during which time she exhibited much of Rocky's aggressive behavior—the girl turned to the experimenter and asked, "Do you have a sack here?" (for carrying away all the toys)[16]

This is an excellent example of passive/out-of-awareness learning. The child was not conscious of being influenced at the time of exposure. She disapproved of the aggression, yet she reproduced the negative behavior anyway. Bandura writes:

> . . . [children] did not resolve the conflict by enhancing the attractiveness of aggression; rather they were highly derogatory of Johnny. They criticized him for his inability to control Rocky, for his miserliness, and described him as 'sulky, selfish, mean, and sort of dumb.' In the aggressive model-punished condition, where Johnny provided more justification for censure since he not only refused to share his possessions but also walloped Rocky, negative evaluations were totally absent while Rocky remained the bad boy.[17]

In the children's eyes, *successful* villainry outweighed all else, and the implications of this in relationship to television and classroom instruction are vastly important. Today, the TV screen provides numerous models for children to copy, many of which are not positive. If a child watches a great deal of action/adventure drama before he enters school, how does the teacher begin to undo or cope with all the potentially negative social learning? Learning which has taken place involuntarily and informally and which may be difficult to break? How many teachers today or district psychologists and social workers are experiencing social retardation in their students, and how much of this is due to excessive television exposure?

It should also be pointed out that the children used in Bandura's various experiments were not deviants responding to aggression because they were abnormal. They were average children in nursery school, and one can hardly say that negative social learning is confined to deviant children only. Given the right circumstances, or lack of adult correction, even the quiet and relatively polite child can respond aggressively, especially if he or she sees classmates doing so. If no one explains formally to a child why such actions are unacceptable, he simply learns informally that they are permissible.

Other Studies with Preschoolers

Though Bandura's work represents a major portion of the research regarding TV violence and young children, there have been numerous other experiments conducted during the sixties and later which corroborate his views. In one study, for instance, nursery school children were shown aggressive cartoons or something less arousing in nature. Afterwards, each child was given the opportunity of playing with two mechanical toys. One was quite ordinary, but the other caused one doll to strike another. The children who watched the aggressive cartoons played with the "fight" doll much more than the other youngsters. Both groups made the same number of responses, but the difference was in the time each spent with the punching toy.[18]

In another study with preschoolers, similar results again were obtained. Youngsters were paired off and placed in two groups, then exposed to either aggressive or nonaggressive programs. Each group saw two hours a day over an eleven-day period, and the television material was randomly chosen from Saturday morning children's programs. Behavior was recorded immediately after viewing and compared to behavior during a prior ten-day period. Once more, the children who viewed the aggressive programs showed significantly greater aggressive activity. While no pair's score differed by more than three points at the end of the control period, variances as great as twenty-eight were observed at the end of the experimental session.[19] What other conclusion could the investigators draw than that television contributed to this change?

At this point, it is important to emphasize that negative actions which appear on television are often highly effective even though supposedly *wrong*. The villain may get caught during the last thirty seconds before the final commercial, but for the rest of the program, he is frequently portrayed as resourceful, clever, and efficient. When one works with small children or adolescents, usually immediate rewards are more influential than delayed punishment in regulating behavior. Consequently, the final demise of the bad guy on TV may have a very weak inhibiting factor. It is quite possible for children to rationalize that they will not get caught and go right ahead and copy the negative model. In addition, children and teenagers respond to scenes of high action, emotion, and conflict. They recall images that resemble familiar surroundings or circumstances, and television certainly provides many instances of both. When these two conditions—delayed punishment and high adventure—are present, there is an even greater chance that young people will be negatively affected by what they see. One social scientist writes:

> Everything [we] know about human learning and remembering tells us that [this] carnage is being observed and remembered by the audience. If children can remember and reproduce fourteen to fifteen sequences of behavior from one amateurish five-minute film, how much do they remember from hour after hour of professionally produced TV?[20]

Again, viewing the aggression does not guarantee that the viewer will behave likewise, but it raises the *possibility* he will. The combination of passive/informal learning from TV coupled with a corresponding lack of active/formal training from others makes this possibility even stronger. It is important that those of us involved with young people become aware of these forces and how they may be affecting our students, both in the classroom environment and out.

Studies with Elementary School Children and Adolescents

There are many critics, however, who argue that studies on the impact of televised aggression involving preschoolers are not reliable because young children are so apt to imitate what they see anyway. The old adage "Monkey see, monkey do" is often cited. But the following studies with elementary school children and adolescents indicate that age does not have that much to do with negative influences from television exposure. A remarkable degree of uniformity is apparent in the reports below.

In one study, elementary school boys and girls viewed excerpts from actual television programs containing aggressive and nonaggressive content. They were then given the chance of hurting an ostensible child victim—similar to the experiment involving preschoolers and the bar-pressing device. The children were instructed that they could either push a green button, which would make the handle next door easier to turn and help another child, or they could push the red button, which would make the handle feel hot and hurt the other youngster. The handles were labeled "help" and "hurt," so the experimental child would know exactly which was which, and his choice would be deliberate, not random. The chart below summarizes the findings.

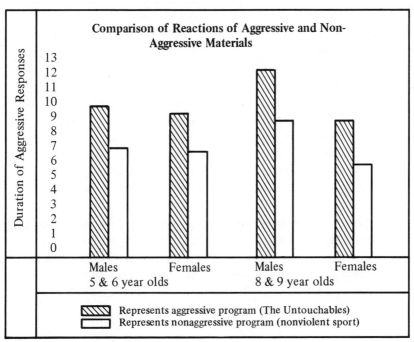

These results emerged even though the aggressive sequences were very brief, and the children were not mildly frustrated, as in some of Bandura's studies. Nationally broadcast materials were used rather than laboratory films specifically prepared for the experiment, and there was also the clear possibility of helping the other child. In addition, each child was carefully instructed that a brief depression of the hurt button would create only slight pain, while longer depressions would cause more. The investigators write:

> This fact, coupled with the finding that the overall average duration of such responses was more than 75 percent *longer* in the aggressive group, suggests clearly that the primary effect of exposure to the aggressive program was that of reducing the subjects' restraints against inflicting severe discomfort on a peer victim.[22]

All the children were then placed in a free-play situation, and the frequency of their aggressive responses recorded. Again, results indicate that the children who were exposed to the aggressive program engaged in higher levels of aggressiveness, particularly among the young boys. Even after a very brief exposure and observation, the children acquired numerous negative behaviors and often reproduced them with great accuracy.

In yet another study, two sociologists obtained similar results. They found that youngsters in three groups who reported some preference for violent programs were more aggressive than those who cited nonviolent shows as their favorites. A breakdown of their findings is shown on the following page. As the chart indicates, there appears to be a definite negative influence from exposure to televised violence.

It is possible, of course, that the children who watched the more violent programs were attracted to aggression prior to exposure and may not have been influenced solely by the programs themselves. For such children, however, action drama and crime shows only reinforce negative social inclinations because the net result is less gentleness and feeling on a human plane.

Over 800 elementary school students participated in another study on the effects of viewing violence, and again researchers found what others had: that exposure to aggressive TV content

Offense	Amount of Violence in Four Favorite Shows			
	Almost None	**Some**	**Much**	**Great Deal**
1. Gotten into serious fight at work or school	25%	30%	33%	37%
2. Gotten something by telling a person something bad would happen to him if he did not give it	15%	19%	20%	18%
3. Hurt someone badly enough to need bandages or a doctor	17%	23%	21%	28%
4. Hit an instructor or supervisor	6%	7%	7%	11%
5. Hit father	5%	8%	8%	8%
6. Hit mother	3%	3%	4%	4%
7. Taking part in a fight where a bunch of friends are against another bunch	9%	23%	24%	28%
8. Used a knife or gun or some other item to get something from a person	2%	4%	3%	8%

[23]

was associated with greater approval of violence and a willingness to use it in real life. The investigators here note:

> For relatively average children from average environments, continued exposure to violence is positively related to acceptance of aggression as a mode of behavior. When the home environment also tends to ignore the child's development of aggressive attitudes [i.e., lack of formal education], this relationship is even more substantial and perhaps more critical.[24]

In a somewhat different survey, additional information was gathered from children's responses in certain hypothetical situations. The youngsters in this study ranged from kindergarten through twelfth grade, and all were instructed that they could handle their troubles by using one of the following methods:

(1) physical aggression,

(2) verbal aggression,

(3) escaping the situation, and

(4) coping in a positive manner (which included telling an adult).[25]

Results show that those who watched violent programs were likelier to select physical aggression as the way to solve their problems. The researchers comment:

> Whatever analysis was performed, the amount of violence in the program affected the amount of aggression subsequently chosen. Nothing else about the program—the context in which the violence was presented, etc.—seemed to influence the aggression.[26]

The children simply learned to think of aggression as a positive means of coping with their problems and incorporated it into their own actions.

It must be remembered that TV aggression itself may not be held completely accountable for making these children more aggressive. In all probability, some of the youngsters with the highest antisocial scores in these investigations were aggressively oriented prior to exposure. Indeed, such young people may seek out violent TV simply because it strikes some inner chord or corresponds to some personal need rather than the aggression itself making them behave in an objectionable way. But, in these cases, the programs act as a strengthening agent. They only underscore pre-existing negative social learning or encourage youngsters to give vent to hostile feelings. In effect, those who need this kind of reinforcement the least may be getting it the most. On the other hand, children who are not antisocial by nature or maladjusted to begin with may simply pick up negative behaviors in an informal manner without giving much thought to the reasons behind them. The violence is perceived as fun, exciting, or effective, so they decide to try it out at a later time. Either way, the influence from such programs is not good.

LONG-TERM FIELD STUDIES

Opponents of the view that watching TV violence affects behavior in negative ways have other objections. They argue that experiments of a few hours or a few days—the kind I have been describing—are not substantial enough proof that there is indeed a relationship between watching aggression and then performing it. The following long-term field studies, however, provide a very different view. One experiment discussed here covers a few months, another six years, and the last one spans a ten-year period; and each of these investigations offers similar results. They all indicate a connection between exposure to violence on TV and later aggressive tendencies.

The first study involves young children who were shown an aggressive and nonaggressive film. Their responses were recorded immediately after exposure and again six months later. Although the level of imitation was lower in the second testing, those who saw the aggressive film were still more aggressive than the controls.[27] These results were supported by yet another sampling. Children were shown a different film in which the model performed a number of aggressive acts, and after an interval of two months, they were given the opportunity of recreating the responses they had seen. Retention tests given at this point showed that sixty percent of the aggressive responses were recalled. A final test conducted after eight months revealed that forty percent of the behaviors were still remembered.[28] It seems the passage of time had little effect in reducing the subjects' negative actions. On the contrary: the antisocial learning was merely stored for later retrieval. Again, these are prime examples of deferred learning and the sleeper effect. The children in these experiments accumulated numerous negative behaviors but were not consciously aware they were doing so at the time of exposure.

A more recent long-term field study conducted by William Belson of the London School of Economics supports the above findings. Belson investigated 1,565 boys ranging from twelve to seventeen and concluded that watching TV violence has very definite negative effects. He writes:

The evidence is very strongly supportive of the hypothesis that

long-term exposure to violence increases the degree to which boys
engage in violence of a serious kind.[29]

Those who watched screen violence over long periods committed
fifty percent more rape and other "mayhem" than those who
viewed limited amounts. This increased antisocial behavior also
applied to less serious offenses, such as swearing and the use of
bad language, aggressiveness in sports, and threatening others.

Belson divided his subjects into two groups: the experimentals
(whom he referred to as qualifiers) and the controls. There were
no substantial differences in these groups regarding family size,
physical development, or emotional stability. So Belson concluded
that the qualifiers committed a significantly greater number of
aggressive acts because of their exposure to violent TV.

Belson also tested the reverse: that the qualifiers watched
violent programs more often because they were more violent to
begin with. The boys were split into two groups—violent and less
violent—and were then matched with variables known to go with
high exposure to violent TV; i.e., fathers leaving school early, boys
in puberty, boys from working-class families, etc. But Belson
found no difference between the two groups. What he did find was
that some forms of TV violence, such as real-life crime drama,
produced greater violence on the part of the viewers. Belson
decided that constant exposure to violence breaks down an
individual's inhibitions against using aggression because changes
take place on the unconscious level. Consequently, his recommendations call for "a major cutback in the total amount of
violence being presented."[30]

Finally, four investigators conducted a ten-year field study in
which they tested the theory that a child's preference for violent
viewing at age eight was related to his aggressive behavior ten years
later. The sample used in this survey included 900 third-grade
boys, who were studied again in the eighth and twelfth grades. A
total of 427 students from the original group was questioned at
the end of the ten-year period, and extensive interviews with
parents, the boys, and their peers formed much of the information
collected and analyzed in this study.

Results show a significant relationship between the boys'

choices of violent television in the third grade and their peer-rated aggression after high school. The researchers here believe that the liking for violent TV at age eight contributed to the development of these aggressive habits. They found the more the student preferred violent programs in the third grade, the more aggressive was the boy's behavior both at that time and ten years later. It also turned out that early television habits were actually *more* influential than later viewing patterns because a liking for violent TV at age nineteen was not necessarily related to current aggressiveness.[31]

These findings only support in long-term field studies what others have tested in laboratory settings. The data suggest that early viewing patterns are very important in a child's development-al sequence. In educational terms, we know that the first few years of a child's life are the most important because he is more open to impressions then than at any other time. Both his wonder and his gullibility are at their highest. Yet, it is precisely during this period that a child may be the most susceptible to the negative influence of violent television or television as a whole.

1972 SURGEON GENERAL'S REPORT

Probably the most extensive study done in the United States regarding the impact of media violence is *Television and Social Behavior*, a special report prepared by the Surgeon General's Office.[32] Because this survey covers a spectrum of information and draws upon numerous experts in the field of human behavior, its findings merit careful examination. It is the largest single source regarding television aggression and young people we have available today.

Background Information

Before going into the specific findings of the *Surgeon General's Report*, some background information leading up to its publica-tion may be helpful. Though the Report itself did not appear until the early 1970s, it represents over twenty years' interest in the subject of television violence. U.S. government involvement began as early as the fifties, when Estes Kefauver headed a number of special Senate investigations into aggressive TV content. The first such hearings were in 1952 and 1954, and the Committee's conclusion *even at that time* was that there is a negative effect on society when crime and violence are presented in large doses. Kefauver's Committee concluded that television crime programs were potentially more harmful to young people than motion pictures, radio, and comic books combined. They also declared:

> Attending a movie requires money and the physical effort of leaving the home. So an average child's exposure to films in the theater tends to be limited to a few hours a week. Comic books demand strong imaginary projections. Also, they must be sought out and purchased. But television, available at the flick of a knob and combining visual and audible aspects into a "life" story, has a greater impact upon its child audience.[33]

The concern which Kefauver initiated did not abate, and the sixties ushered in a new wave of governmental interest in the topic. In 1961, Senator Thomas Dodd headed another Senate Subcommittee look into television and juvenile delinquency. He reported that excerpts from violent shows which he and committee members watched had a cumulative audience of over 66 million children and adolescents. In an average week, there could be over 200 million exposures of young people to violent scenes, and some 130 million of these might be viewed by children under the age of twelve.[34] Dodd's Committee admitted this would mean that a large number of young children might be saturated with violent media content before they were able to read, perhaps even to speak, depending upon their viewing habits. But before Dodd could bring his findings to the general public, he was "persuaded" by broadcasting lobbyists to drop the investigation. He did, and the topic remained dormant for a few more years.

By the late sixties, people once again became anxious about media aggression, particularly after the turmoil and assassinations during the decade, and the Eisenhower Commission was formed to probe this issue further. After its fact-gathering, the Commission stated that a constant diet of antisocial behavior on television had a negative effect on individual character and attitudes by "fostering moral and social values unacceptable in a civilized society." The Eisenhower Commission also stated it was a matter of concern that when other institutions, such as the home and religious organizations, were losing their power as social teachers that television was emphasizing aggressive styles of life. It also cautioned that television's concentration on violence and law enforcement might actually cause greater and greater social unrest.[35]

Finally, picking up the cause that Kefauver and others had pursued during the fifties and sixties, Senator John Pastore and Welfare Secretary Robert Finch requested a massive study on the impact of television violence to be conducted by the Surgeon General's Office. To help guide the Surgeon General in the preparation of the research, a Scientific Advisory Committee was formed which covered a wide spectrum of experience and expertise.[36]

Some qualifications, however, must be made regarding the choice of Advisory members themselves. The Committee included the research director of NBC, a former research executive of CBS, and two active consultants to CBS. So there was a definite bias at the onset of the investigation favoring television interests. Furthermore, industry members on the Advisory Committee were given a veto power over other committee membership. As one writer declares:

> The idea that an industry should not only be represented directly in a scholarly inquiry into its activities, but should also exercise a veto over the membership of the investigating panel, is too stupid and scandalous to escape commentary.[37]

Several social scientists already doing research into violent media impact, some of whom I have mentioned, were not invited to be on the Committee. (In its final report, the Advisory Committee apologized and labeled the veto power given to the industry members a "serious error.")

Another occurrence which makes us question what truly went on behind-the-scenes was the lack of coverage given by the news media. A psychologist and assistant director for the National Institute of Mental Health asked a network reporter why the opening day's testimony was almost completely ignored on the evening news. He was told that "word had come from New York not to put much emphasis on the hearings."[38] Moreover, *The New York Times* and *Broadcasting* magazine declared "TV Violence Held Unharmful to Youth" and "Violence on Air and in Life: NO CLEAR LINK." Yet, these headlines contradict the findings of the experts! Considering the million-dollar budget given for the Report, plus an additional $800,000 for administrative and publishing costs, and the dubious selection of Committee members, it makes one wonder why the project was attempted in the first place. And when the Report finally did appear, it was written in a language virtually unintelligible even to the careful reader.

The Surgeon General's Findings

Obviously, there was much behind-the-scenes politicking and maneuvering, which did a great deal to nullify the Report's findings. The primary thrust of the investigation involves experiments on the effects of violence in films and on television. Two different kinds of influence are explored: imitation (copying) and instigation (being incited to use violence). Some twenty documented experiments are given which support the view that seeing violence increases the likelihood of aggressive behavior.[39] Though these effects are not for the majority, the writers of the Report still cite a "modest relationship" between TV violence and antisocial actions.*

The Report states that the amount of television violence viewed may be less important than subtler matters, such as what the medium says about that violence, whether it condones or disapproves of aggressiveness, whether the violence is committed by sympathetic characters, and so on. The investigators also believe that the attitude of permissiveness toward the use of violence might have significant long-range implications. Again, repetition and basic learning theory are involved because the more

---

*Interestingly enough, a subsequent Pastore hearing on the Report's conclusions revealed that the majority of non-network participants felt the data sufficiently strong to warrant a "causal relationship" between TV aggression and violence in society. It was the network representatives on the Advisory Committee who exerted power over the summary by requesting the "modest" findings.

an individual is exposed to a certain style of life or behavior—
especially in an informal, passive manner—the more likely he is to
assimilate it into his own actions and thoughts. The Report points
out that most people think of violence as being quick, brutal, and
physical, but it does not have to be. The slow, habitual quality of
television violence may be just as damaging in the long run,
perhaps even more so. The Report argues that aggression can be
almost imperceptible. In effect, television violence could be a form
of slow mental disintegration.[40]

Echoing Piaget, the Surgeon General's study also stresses the
importance of early childhood in setting the foundation for
life-long patterns of behavior and learning. Attitudes and values as
well as habits of thinking and reacting are set during these early
years. What a child learns between the ages of one and five may be
more important than what he learns in grade school, high school,
and even college. The Report states:

> A young child's reaction to television is potentially quite
> different from that of an adult. A child has only a limited range
> of past experience and does not have a well-established set of
> conceptual categories for clarifying his experiences. A three- or
> four-year-old's thinking functions at the level of free association;
> he has not reached the stage of cognitive development where he
> can classify, sort, select, and organize. Naturally, some bright
> youngsters will be able to do these things, but most three- to
> five-year-olds viewing television are often unable to follow the
> theme of even a simple story or to understand the relatively
> complex motivations for, and consequences of, behavior demon-
> strated by TV actors.[41]

The Report mentions Bandura's pioneering studies on aggression and his findings that young people can imitate what they
observe on TV. As a matter of fact, the 1972 study states that
children mimicking film-mediated aggression is one of the best
documented findings in the literature. Again, to quote the paper:

> Psychologists generally consider quite convincing the evidence
> that children can readily learn many kinds of behavior, including
> aggressive actions, by . . . watching those behaviors being modeled
> by persons in their presence, on film, or on television . . . There is
> little doubt that by displaying forms of aggression or modes of
> criminal and violent behaviors, the media are "teaching" and
> people are "learning."[42]

The study gives these general conclusions regarding violent media presentations on young children:

(1) Aggression depicted on television can immediately or shortly thereafter induce mimicking or copying by children.

(2) Under certain circumstances, TV violence can instigate increased aggressive behavior among its younger viewers.[43]

The *Surgeon General's Report* relies more on surveys than experiments for information concerning the influence of violent TV on adolescents. The major categories investigated in this area include:

(1) time spent viewing,

(2) preference for violent programs, and

(3) total amount of violent programs viewed.

It was found that the third category had by far the largest effect. Boys who watched a great deal of violent TV were more likely to approve of aggression as a means to an end. This was also true for adolescent girls, though not to the same degree as with the boys. Influence was accomplished in several ways: either identifying with a violent character, learning aggressive techniques, or developing attitudes favorable to the use of violence. As with the younger children, the Report admits a modest relationship between adolescent aggressiveness and watching TV.

To be sure: the evidence for both young children and teenagers does not imply uniformly adverse effects. Televised violence may lead to increased antisocial activity in certain subgroups of youngsters who are already predisposed to such tendencies, and such subgroups could be either large or small. But even a group of several million children would be considerable. As one person states:

> Our present knowledge suggests that the group of children adversely affected by media may include a notable proportion of those youngsters who are for one reason or another often frustrated, and those who are maladjusted in various ways ... If depictions of crime and violence have an unhealthy effect upon even 1 percent of the nation's children, it becomes socially important to inquire whether and how the situation can be rectified.[44]

Aftermath

Unfortunately, the 1972 government report did not get the public attention many had hoped it would. This was partly due to misrepresentation by the news media, partly from public apathy, and partly from the jungle-like language of the Report itself. Jesse Steinfield, who resigned from the Surgeon General's Office in 1973, commented:

> These studies...make it clear to me that the relationship between televised violence and antisocial behavior is sufficiently proved to warrant immediate remedial action. Indeed, the time has come to be blunt: we can no longer tolerate the present high level of televised violence that is put before children in American homes.[45]

During 1974, Senators Pastore and [Howard] Baker continued additional hearings into the impact of violent media content, but again nothing happened. Even though similar evidence was discussed, the Federal Communications Commission did not make any policy decision regarding network programming. This is very ironic, however, in light of an earlier FCC document which concluded that without pressure the broadcasting industry would most likely take the easy way out by writing off its child audience as "captive viewers."[46]

Several years later, Congressional interest still has not abated. The House Subcommittee on Communications recently issued another report regarding its findings on American "vid gore." But, again, the final conclusions were softer on the networks than previous drafts—very similar to what happened to the Surgeon General's original findings. *Variety* reported that the dissenters attacked the report as "clearing the webs [networks] from responsibility." Furthermore, the Congressmen who objected declared:

> The adopted report spread the blame for violence on television away from the networks to such an extent that it reaches the meaningless conclusion that we are all [viewers, licensees, advertisers, producers] to blame for the excessive levels of violence on television—thereby implicitly stating that no one is really to be held accountable.[47]

These Congressmen believe there is a real connection between violence on television and aggressive behavior in life and that

industry self-regulation has not been effective in curtailing the
level of antisocial acts. They further declare:

> The report implicitly tells the American people that with respect
> to the issue of violence on television, there is no need to worry,
> everything is under control, the networks know best how to
> handle the situation, and there is little else that needs to be done.
> We reject these conclusions.[48]

Finally, the most recent governmental effort to investigate the
relationship between television violence and aggression comes
from the National Institute of Mental Health (NIMH). Their
report, which reviews ten years of scientific research since the
original Surgeon General's study, adds strong support to the
contention that violence on TV does indeed lead to aggressive
behavior among children and adolescents. Whether based upon
laboratory experiments or field studies, the Institute states that
the evidence accumulated over the past decade is "overwhelming"
that violence on television and aggression are positively correlated.
They write:

> Recent research confirms the earlier findings of a causal relation-
> ship between viewing television violence and aggressive behav-
> ior . . . The scientific support for the causal relationship derives
> from the convergence of findings from many studies, the great
> majority of which demonstrate a positive relationship between
> television violence and later aggressive behavior.[49]

The Report even cites long-term field studies conducted in
other countries which confirm a positive relationship between TV
violence and subsequent aggression in both boys and girls. So
strong is this finding, in fact, that the Institute says the research
question has now moved from asking whether or not there is an
effect to seeking explanations for it. Like the Surgeon General's
Office, the National Institute of Mental Health agrees that the
long-term, erosive effects of viewing violence may be the most
damaging, and actually concludes its report by declaring that "a
causal link between TV violence and aggressive behavior now
seems obvious."[50]

DESENSITIZATION TO VIOLENCE

The general surveys, laboratory experiments, and field studies reviewed thus far are concerned primarily with two aspects of violence viewing: imitation and instigation. There is a third area, however, which also merits attention in our discussion of television and young children. This is desensitization, which means a lessening of feeling or responsiveness on the part of viewers. Many people are beginning to believe that prolonged exposure to television violence may actually blunt the audience's sensitivity and produce a blasé attitude toward the use of aggression and the suffering of others. The attitude, "Oh, it happens everyday," sets in where the viewer may not become upset by scenes of violence in real life.

People in the medical profession have expressed particular concern over this problem of desensitization from habitual TV exposure. *The Journal of the American Medical Association* states that watching crime and horror programs can produce a callousness to the pain of others and a diminishing of sympathy and compassion.[51] Prolonged exposure to brutality may also result in a numbness or indifference to one's fellow man. As recently as 1977, AMA President, Dr. Richard Palmer, declared:

> TV violence is a mental health problem and an environmental issue. If the programming a child is exposed to consists largely of violent content, then his perception of the real world may be significantly distorted and his psychological development may be adversely affected.[52]

The AMA has become increasingly vocal about this issue of desensitization because the potential of a growing insensitivity among the young presents very real medical problems, as well as a cause for concern among teachers and educators.

A series of experiments has actually been conducted investigating this type of television influence. In one study, for example, TV monitors were placed in classrooms so the children could watch either their teacher or the television image. Generally, the students chose to watch the screen rather than the person. When someone else came into the room and started to aggravate the teacher as part of the experiment, the youngsters *still* chose to watch the set. They would not look at the struggling people, nor did they try to interfere. They merely sat and watched the screen, which removed the violence from its real, immediate context.[53]

Perhaps the most well-known incident of this kind concerns Kitty Genovese, a woman who was raped and murdered in a New York apartment complex while people heard her screams. Even though over forty individuals were aware of her plight, no one came to her aid. She simply was left to die.

This event inspired a laboratory investigation regarding emotional blunting from excessive television exposure. Boys with histories of high and low TV consumption were selected and divided into two groups on the basis of their viewing habits. One group watched TV four hours or less per week for the preceding two years, while the other watched twenty-five hours or more each week for the same time period. The boys were then exposed to nonviolent sports films, and their pulse and blood pressure were taken before and during exposure. The investigators in this experiment believed the boys' pulse and heart beat would increase if they were disturbed by the violence they witnessed on the screen.

Though there were no significant differences before and after the neutral presentation, remarkable changes occurred when both groups saw the violent film. The low-exposure group was more aroused emotionally and physiologically according to pulse and blood pressure counts.[54] This suggests that desensitization or a habituation to violence had set in for the high-exposure group because they were less aroused by what they saw. (This relates to Eleanor Maccoby's belief in a potential addiction problem for higher and higher levels of thrills.) The researchers in this study conclude:

> If one combines the effects of desensitization . . . with the effects of modeling, which provide the explicit mechanics for committing violence, it may not be surprising to see not only major increases in acts of personal aggression in our society but also a growing attitude of indifference and unconcern for the victims.[55]

Habituation to violence, not just among young people, but society as a whole, could be the result. The Surgeon General's Report states:

> It is conceivable that prolonged exposure of large populations to television violence may have very little immediate effects on the crime rate, but that such exposure may interact with other

influences in society (such as weakening parental authority) to produce increased casualness about violence which permits citizens to regard with indifference actual suffering in their own or other societies and to reflect that indifference in major political and economic decisions.[56]

The problem of desensitization has also been the focus of a recent *Newsweek* investigation on TV and children. In one study, for instance, several hundred fifth graders were asked to act as babysitters for a group of younger children. Their instructions were to go for adult help if their charges started to fight or misbehave. It was found that older children who had previously seen a violent film were slower to call for aid than those babysitters who had not seen the film. The investigators believe that the group who witnessed the aggressive program was less disturbed by the disruptive behavior of the younger children. They simply were not bothered by it and did not feel the need to seek grown-up help. As one perceptive eleven-year-old boy said:

> You see so much violence that it's meaningless. If I saw someone really get killed, it wouldn't be a big deal. I guess I'm turning into a hard rock . . .[57]

Is a new wave of callousness growing among the young? There is indeed evidence that emotional detachment and a lack of feeling are beginning to manifest themselves more and more, especially among the juvenile delinquent element. A psychiatrist working with Brooklyn Family Court has described today's youth offenders as showing "a total lack of guilt and lack of respect for life. To them, another person is a thing—they are wild organisms who cannot allow anyone to stand in their way."[58] It seems that more young people are robbing and raping, mugging and murdering than ever before. A special *Time* article on youth crime states:

> . . . a new remorseless juvenile seems to have been born, and there is no more terrifying figure in America today . . . Since 1960, juvenile crime has risen twice as fast as that of adults.[59]

Time describes these juveniles as hardened people, even though very young. In court, they often laugh, scratch, yawn, or even fall asleep while their crimes are being read. As one twelve-year-old juvenile remarked:

> I was young, and I knew I wasn't gonna get no big time. So, you know, what's to worry? If you're doin' wrong, do it while you're young, because you won't do that much time.

Another boy, fifteen, admitted why he shot a "dude":

> It wasn't nothing. I didn't think about it. If I had to kill him, I just had to kill him. That's the way I look at it, 'cause I was young.

When another boy was sentenced to fifteen years to life for shooting someone, the prosecutor said, "He showed no awareness or conscience or remorse. He grinned like crazy."

Nor are the boys alone; it seems that girls, too, are becoming just as hard. One Chicago police lieutenant describes today's female delinquents as a new, frightening breed. He reports, "This is the first time I've encountered young girls this tough." Between 1970 and 1975, the arrest rate for girls under eighteen climbed forty percent versus twenty-four percent for boys, and by 1975, eleven percent of all juveniles apprehended for violent crimes were female.[60]

How much impact has fictional TV violence had on this trend? Are young people developing a taste for aggression? Are they learning an informal language of violence from their years with TV? How much of this negative learning is being brought into the classroom? The antisocial behavior described in *Time* cannot come from television only. Environment, families, and schools, among other things, play a significant role in influencing a child's development. But there has been so much violence on television in this country over such a long period of time that it is not unreasonable to assume some correlation exists. This is particularly true when one considers that the violence on TV seldom reveals the real suffering of the victim. On the contrary: aggression often looks attractive, possibly even "fun." (The *Time* article actually cites one youth who admitted that mugging was "like a game.")

The evidence presented here clearly suggests a relationship between violence on the screen and real life and a lessening of feeling among heavy viewers. Moreover, of the three possible effects of exposure to violent TV—imitation, instigation, and desensitization—the last is probably the most unsettling. A child who commits an aggressive or antisocial act and then experiences a feeling of guilt or sorrow is not as serious a problem as the child who commits random destruction and then grins or brags about his actions. As long as the child shows some concern or feeling, there is hope. But if that human fellow feeling has been blunted, stunted, or perhaps even lost, then the chances for rehabilitation are slim.

The problem which presents itself is this: how many teachers and administrators take the time to discuss these issues among themselves or with their students? Yet, the need for this kind of dialogue is extremely important because it affects the work we do every day. If we do not engage in this ideological warfare with TV, then many of our teaching tactics will simply be ineffective or, even worse, completely lost on our students.

DESENSITIZATION AND THE PROBLEM OF FEAR

There are other points to consider in relationship to the problem of desensitization. Though viewers may become inured to seeing violence on TV or even using it in real life, they can yet harbor feelings of fear that such violence may be used against them. George Gerbner believes excessive violence on TV may give viewers what he calls a "mean-world syndrome."[61] In other words, they see the aggressive TV content and take it as an indication that the world in general is a hostile and unpleasant place. Or, they may even become fearful of life itself and going outside. Indeed, Gerbner has discovered that people who watch over four hours of TV each day do in fact think the world is more dangerous than light viewers, and he has data which support this view. As recently as 1978, in compiling another violence index, he found that among heavy viewers of police and crime shows, twenty-nine percent felt so threatened and uneasy that they purchased guns, and even nineteen percent of the light viewers took similar precautions.[62] Heavy viewers were also more likely to buy locks and dogs for security, and one in ten believed there was a chance of being attacked in the streets. The chances, however, of this happening in reality are closer to one in one hundred.

Nor is Professor Gerbner alone in his feelings. A recent study conducted by the Foundation for Child Development shows that nearly two-thirds of the sample (2,200 seven- to eleven-year-olds) expressed an unexpected fear of the outside world even though they were happy about their family lives. These children reported they were "afraid somebody bad might get them," and thirty-five percent believed someone would hurt them when they went outside to play. The same percentage said they were frightened by violent programs on TV.[63]

A recent *Newsweek* essay also discusses the same sort of trend. A young man hitchhiking across the U.S. reported how much fear and suspicion he encountered as he walked from coast to coast. Most Americans were incredulous he had not been robbed, mugged, molested, threatened, and/or attacked during his journey. They were even more shocked to discover he did not carry a knife or gun for protection against all the "loonies and dope fiends" around.[64] And even the contemporary novel, *Blind Date*, makes the point that fear, guns, and television are the only things that truly bind us Americans together. We should ask ourselves how much truth there is in this assessment and how much of this fear or unease may be infiltrating our students.

THE CATHARSIS THEORY: AN OPPOSING VIEW

The bulk of evidence at this point suggests that viewing violent media content on television has a decidedly negative effect on many of its young viewers. Indeed, it would appear that the data not only suggest this but in many ways confirm it. Classroom experience shows that if an individual lets aggressive behavior, such as hitting, punching, or abusive language go unquestioned, he can count on others joining in. Human nature mimics life, and if life is made up of violent images—whether real or from TV—chances are good that human actions will imitate that violence. Common sense begs this observation. There are, however, opposing views on this subject.

Some researchers argue that watching fantasy aggression may actually help reduce subsequent violent behavior. They believe that dramatic scenes allow the audience to purge its feelings of fear and anger, thereby relieving frustration and aggression rather than increasing them. The foremost proponents of this hypothesis, known as the catharsis theory, are Seymour Feshbach and Robert Singer. They believe the mass media in general serve to stimulate fantasy, which in turn satisfies some emotional need by reducing drive and arousal. For instance, if a viewer sees a nagging boss or wife being punished, he may feel less desire to punish them in his own life. In this sense, the fantasy aggression works to drain off (or cathart) the viewer's own aggressive feelings.

During the sixties, Feshbach and Singer conducted several investigations to test their theory. In one study, they used 400 boys from schools in California and New York. Three of these were private schools catering to upper-middle-class students; the other four were homes for boys who lacked adequate care or who were experiencing adjustment problems. These boys were divided into two groups—one watched aggressive television programs; the other nonaggressive—and each student was asked to watch at least six hours of television per week for six weeks.

Feshbach and Singer employed a number of measurement devices, but the most important scale used was a behavior rating sheet. It consisted of twenty-six items, nineteen of which related to aggression. Results indicate that the boys in the nonaggressive program group were more aggressive than boys in the other situation, both in aggression toward peers and authority. On a week-by-week basis, boys who saw the nonaggressive programs behaved worse than those watching the other TV shows.

But contradictory information was also received, and considerable qualifications were attached to the original findings.[65] The above results held for boys only in the homes for those experiencing problems. Opposite results were obtained from boys in the private schools. In that context, boys in the nonaggressive group declined significantly in aggressive behavior, while those in the aggressive group showed increases. Sometime later, Feshbach stated that the depiction of violence on TV was not necessarily an instruction on how to do it and that people usually suspended disbelief while reading or watching fiction. They still would know the difference between fantasy and real life.[66]

Do people *really* know the difference all the time, especially youngsters? What about the child who believes the commercial sales pitch or the monster in the horror show? What about the 250,000 letters sent to Marcus Welby (written by adults, no less) asking for medical advice?[67] Or the numerous letters received by the United Nations from young people wishing to join U.N.C.L.E.?[68] That people can always separate fantasy and reality is an amazing thing for a professor of psychology to say! If anyone, he should know how often people, especially youngsters and teenagers, confound the two: reality drifting into fantasy and then back again.

Feshbach has also warned against jumping "to a common sense conclusion" on this question of TV violence, but common sense is a sorely needed commodity in this debate. It *is* common sense to suggest that if an individual watches large amounts of certain behaviors—violent or otherwise—he will incorporate at least some of what he sees into his own learning repertoire. Common sense indicates that watching violence will not lessen, drain off, or cathart aggressive tendencies. On the contrary: it should heighten an individual's potential for aggression. Again, this is basic learning theory: observation, repetition, and imitation.

RETESTING THE CATHARSIS THEORY

Other researchers have also questioned the catharsis theory and have cast considerable doubt on the Feshbach/Singer hypothesis. W.D. Wells, working for the *Surgeon General's Report*, performed a similar study in which he tried to substantiate the theory that watching aggression relieves anxiety. He found that boys who watched television programs with no action and adventure were somewhat more aggressive verbally than those who watched a heavy diet of aggression. But he felt this stemmed from complaints about the shows the experimental subjects were required to watch. What Wells actually discovered was significantly greater physical aggression among the boys who viewed violent television, and he saw this as a tendency for action/adventure shows to promote such behavior. He found no evidence to support a catharsis interpretation.[69]

Alberta Siegel of Stanford University, another sociologist

involved with television and children, also conducted a study in which she tested the possibility that violent content drains off antisocial drives. She had pairs of nursery school children see both an aggressive and nonaggressive film and then monitored the children's behavior as they played. According to the catharsis theory, the youngsters viewing the aggressive cartoon should have been less aggressive later on, but Siegel found this was not the case at all. The children who viewed the violent programs were more aggressive after watching than the nonaggressive group.[70]

Finally, Albert Bandura believes the research provides a great deal of opposing evidence. Vicarious participation in antisocial activities can modify the observer's behavior but not necessarily by draining off aroused emotions. As he so aptly comments:

> It is highly improbable that even advocates [of the catharsis theory] would recommend community programs in which sexually aroused adolescents are shown libidinous movies at drive-in theaters as a means of reducing sexual behavior; that famished persons are presented displays of gourmands dining on culinary treats in order to alleviate hunger pangs; and that assaultive gangs are regularly shown films of assailants flogging their antagonists in an attempt to diminish aggressive behavior. Such procedures would undoubtedly have strong instigative rather than reducive consequences.[71]

Indeed, the experiments discussed earlier indicate that people who see movie or TV violence do not discharge their anger through vicarious participation; rather they usually feel freer to attack their tormentors. Observed aggression has little, if any, effect in reducing hostile inclinations unless the consequences of violence are graphically shown. As one sociologist writes:

> Our experiments cast considerable doubt on the possibility of a cathartic purge of anger through the observation of filmed violence. At the very least, the findings indicate that such a catharsis does not occur as readily as many authorities have thought.[72]

It is more logical to assume that an individual's aggressive tendencies will remain in spite of any satisfaction he may get from filmed violence. There is not sufficient evidence to support the belief that negative impulses are noticeably lowered by watching aggression on TV. Fantasy violence may be pleasurable to the observer, especially if he sees himself in the role of hero or protagonist. But this does not necessarily mean that his own aggressiveness will be reduced.

SPECIFIC EXAMPLES OF IMITATION AND INSTIGATION

One of the chief complaints made about violent-television research is that it comes from academics dealing with select children in special laboratory settings. Critics ask, "How can the conclusions of these sociologists and behaviorists count?" "How can they predict what a child will do when he is left to his own devices and away from TV?" Anyone who has worked closely with young people will know that they can, by nature, be quite aggressive; however, they can also be encouraged to bring out much internal goodness with patience and understanding. Yet, this natural aggressive energy in many cases is only augmented by what they observe on TV, which they frequently take to be a reflection of society at large. Perhaps those who are critical of the negative-impact view should go out onto a school playground and watch typical children at play. They might be surprised by all the hitting, punching, and pushing going on. Or, perhaps they should listen to chattering, arguing students as they pass through the halls.

It seems that many children today would rather fight or quarrel than try to discuss problems and work things out in a nonaggressive manner. Naturally, this is not all that different from children going to school in a pre-TV era, for there have always been squabbles in school as in real life, and they will continue. But it is the *degree* to which both physical and verbal aggression are apparent that is so disturbing. Teachers in urban school centers today may spend a large portion of their time untangling emotional outbursts. This does not necessarily mean that they are poor teachers, but simply that there are too many leaks in the dam for them to handle. And I, for one, would not be surprised if television has contributed substantially to this trend. How many other teachers and educators share this view?

Again, though, these are merely my own observations. Perhaps a few documented examples of how television violence has affected young people will prove more convincing to those who question the medium's influence. First of all, these comments made by parents:

(1) He drives the family crazy with this "bang-bang! bang-bang!" from early Saturday morning until late Sunday night.

(2) He tries to imitate and repeat certain words. He talks about guns and gangs, usually saying "Stick 'em up!"

(3) It's not healthy the way my son plays. All day it's machine guns, murder, and gangs. You can't tell me kids don't get those ideas from TV . . .

(4) A father expressed concern that among his son's first words were gun, kill, and kill Mommy.[73]

Or these examples:

(1) A nine-year-old boy was afraid to show his father his report card because of all the bad marks. The boy told his father they should give his teacher a box of poisoned candy for Christmas. The boy's comment, "It's easy . . . they did it on television last week. A man wanted to kill his wife, so he gave her candy with poison in it, and she didn't know who did it."

(2) A six-year-old boy asked his father, a policeman, for bullets because his little sister "wouldn't die for real" when he tried to shoot her "the way they did when Hopalong Cassidy killed them."

(3) A housemaid caught a seven-year-old boy sprinkling ground glass into the family stew because he wanted to see if it worked the way it did on TV.[74]

Or these:

(1) Several boys, eleven through fourteen, pried open a coffin, removed the head from the corpse, took it to their club house, and stuck a candle in it. They got the idea from a TV horror show.

(2) After seeing John Kennedy get shot, Oswald, King, and Robert Kennedy, a group of youngsters developed a Shoot the President game.[75]

Then these examples:

  (1) In 1964, a nineteen-year-old Marine on leave reported that after watching a horror movie on television, 'something came over him,' which incited him to kill his father, mother, and sister with a hatchet.

  (2) In 1973, Boston police blamed a TV movie for a murder in their city in which a gang of youths poured gasoline over a woman and set her ablaze. The murder method was featured in an ABC movie. During the same month, three teenagers reenacted the scene in Miami, Florida.[76]

And these items:

  (1) A five-year-old put his fist through a window, imitating "Kung Fu."

  (2) In one teacher's classroom, children now play Spider-man, Bionic Woman, and Six Million Dollar Man instead of doctor, nurse, or fireman.

  (3) A Los Angeles judge sentenced two boys to long jail terms after they held up a bank and kept twenty-five people hostage for seven hours. The holdup was patterned after an episode of "Adam-12" the young boys had seen two weeks earlier.[77]

Or these examples:

  (1) In March, 1973, CBS aired "The Marcus-Nelson Murders." Later that month, a young woman was raped and murdered, and the homicide detective on duty said the crime scene looked exactly like the one on TV. A seventeen-year-old pleaded guilty to the murder and admitted he had reenacted the whole film.

  (2) In Columbus, Ohio, a fourteen-year-old killed his younger brother when trying to reproduce a scene from "Dirty Harry" he had seen on TV. The fourteen-year-old did not realize that the bullet coming from his father's gun was "for real" because he had "just been playing."

  (3) Brenda Spicer, a sixteen-year-old school girl, was apprehended in January, 1979, for killing two people and wounding eight with a gun. It was reported that Brenda liked watching violent TV programs and seeing people get shot.[78]

TV ON TRIAL

The above examples indicate that the combat zone between children and television violence is a real and serious one indeed. Yet they are by no means alone in illustrating the gravity of the present situation. The possibility that viewing TV aggression may affect youth crime has received additional notoriety in several cases now in court.

In September, 1974, for example, NBC aired a movie called "Born Innocent," a drama about a juvenile detention home in which a young girl was sexually molested with a plumber's tool. Only four days later, several children, aged nine to fifteen, seized two girls on a public beach and replayed the scene with beer bottles. Three of the assailants admitted to police they had seen the movie on TV. This incident resulted in a $22 million damage suit against NBC. A petition was filed by the mother on behalf of her daughter, Valerie, who was only nine years old when the incident occurred. The mother believes there was a direct relationship between the screening of the movie and what happened to her daughter. NBC was sued for criminal negligence, as this particular movie was aired in the early evening hours when more children were likely to be watching. The mother feels this was a gross violation of NBC's responsibility to the younger viewing public.

A more recent and widely publicized lawsuit concerning violence on TV involved a fifteen-year-old boy named Ronny Zamora. Ronny and some of his friends robbed and shot an eighty-three-year-old woman, took $415 and her car, then treated themselves to a weekend at Disney World. The boy's attorney claimed that Ronny was "suffering from and acted under the influence of prolonged, intense, involuntary, subliminal television intoxication," which finally resulted in insanity.[79] The lawyer said Ronny had lost all perspective on right and wrong because of his heavy diet of TV shows such as "Kojak," "Police Woman," and films about the Charles Manson murders.

Previous to the crime, Ronny had been disciplined from watching so many violent programs. A week before the murder/robbery, his parents actually sent him to a psychologist because they were so concerned about their son's behavior, but obviously it was too late. Ronny eventually was convicted and sentenced to life in prison with no possibility of parole for twenty-five years and to a fifty-three-year sentence on charges of burglary and assault. This decision occurred despite testimony by psychiatrists that Zamora's vast exposure to TV violence had become a pacifier to him which resulted in an emotionally disturbed child. After the court's verdict, Ronny's parents held a press conference in an appeal for more funds to meet their mounting legal costs.

Mr. Zamora's only comment at the time: "There are other Ronnys out there." How many Ronnys are sitting in our classrooms today?

TV CRIME AND CRIMINALS IN REAL LIFE

Finally, the most graphic evidence of how television violence can affect aggressive behavior comes from Grant Hendrick, a convicted felon who is serving a life sentence at Marquette Maximum Security Prison.

Hendrick conducted a survey of 208 of the 688 inmates and received some startling results.[80] He writes:

> I asked them ... whether or not their criminal activities [had] ever been influenced by what they saw on TV. A surprising nine out of ten told me that they had actually learned new tricks and improved their criminal expertise by watching crime programs. Four out of ten said that they had attempted specific crimes they saw on television crime dramas ...

Another prisoner told Hendrick he had learned how to hotwire cars at the age of fourteen by watching a TV show. The same man, who is now thirty-four, admitted:

> TV has taught me how to steal cars, how to break into establishments, how to go about robbing people, even how to roll a drunk ... Once, after watching "Hawaii Five-0," I robbed a gas station. The show showed me how to do it. Nowadays, I watch TV in my house [cell] from 4 pm until midnight. I just sit back and take notes. I see 'em doing it this way or that way, and I tell myself that I'll do it the same when I get out. You could probably pick any ten guys in here, and they'd tell you the same thing. Everybody's picking up on what's on TV ...

Nor are Hendrick's findings unique. A Justice Department survey of two correctional institutions reveals that almost all of the prisoners who were questioned listed as their favorite programs such offerings as "The Untouchables," "Thriller," and "Route 66." As in Hendrick's study, most of these convicts admitted they watched three to five hours of violent television each day.[81]

If convicts are admitting that they have been influenced by television, what are we to do when the industry says "no clear link"? What can all the critics say against these numerous illustrations? Are they merely fluke occurrences, or is something going on which is much more significant and pervasive than many of us realize? Naturally, no one can predict what an individual will do after seeing something on television—or in real life, for that matter—but this does not mean there is no influence. These examples show that people, both young and old, may pick up any number of schemes and ideas from watching aggressive behavior on the TV screen. Those of us involved in the field of education should be concerned with how much action/adventure TV our students may be consuming and how this may be affecting their behavior in school.

INDUSTRY ATTITUDES TOWARD VIOLENCE

The question which now raises itself is not whether TV aggression has an impact, but why violence is used so extensively as a theme in American programs. After all, there are many other aspects of life which could act as subject matter for TV. Why do the makers of these programs so limit their view? To answer this, a brief look at some of the arguments used by the industry may be useful; for they will shed some light on how the business perceives young people and its audience as a whole.

In the early 1970s, for example, two independent researchers decided to investigate this preoccupation with violence on American TV, and the responses they received from industry members are revealing. Generally, they found little concern even among program censors regarding the impact of violence and its importance as a social issue. On the contrary: most of those questioned did not believe the young actually formed a substantial portion of their viewing audience. Rather, they believed that television would lose its "credibility" if violence were removed from the air and that most people simply would not accept TV without it. Other responses included:

(1) In drama, conflict was essential and usually became equated with violent conflict.

(2) In TV, where swift resolution of problems was felt necessary, violence was looked upon as being a convenient means of bringing this about.

(3) Mortal danger was considered the best theme because it was easier to recognize and respond to.

(4) Violence was seen as a highly saleable program commodity.

(5) Any serious cutback in the presentation of violence would hurt these programs in foreign markets.[82]

Writers admitted they relied on a limited number of themes in order to conform to industry desires; i.e., producing a saleable product. Nor were many of those interviewed familiar with the research on the effects of televised violence, and even those who had read some did not consider it important for making program decisions. When asked about the work of social scientists, a typical comment was:

We laugh at them. I don't see how the work accomplished so far by social scientists is of any practical value.[83]

As far as the academic information went, most programmers basically ignored it. One director admitted:

People [in the TV business] are not motivated by any great social conscience. They are motivated, however, by what will be acceptable and what will sell.[84]

When asked their opinions regarding the critics of TV violence, industry members again provided a variety of defenses:

(1) Children could learn to distinguish television violence and action from reality, thereby acquiring the proper social sanctions regarding the use of violence.

(2) The attitudes of adults and society toward violence were far more important in influencing children than TV.

(3) TV could trigger a disturbed viewer, but such individuals would be affected anyway, and TV could not possibly cater to only a small minority.

(4) By harping on TV, public attention was being diverted from more fundamental issues and causes of violence.

(5) Many producers and writers found aggression distasteful and did not want to instruct anyone in the use of gratuitous violence. Yet they filmed it anyway.

(6) The catharsis theory applied to aggression on TV.[85]

Etc.

As can be seen, quite an assortment of excuses and justifications.

There were also those who felt violence was necessary because of the very conditions under which we view TV; in other words, that violence is best suited to television because of the way we watch and approach the medium. As one person commented:

> Producers . . . believe that violence is necessary because the reception conditions under which people view TV reduce their ability to concentrate. Since programs are viewed with only partial attention, they must be free of intellect-taxing analyses of life's complex problems.[86]

Another producer continued in the same vein:

> There will always be a market for action drama on TV. Television is viewed with only part of your attention; therefore, the style of a television drama has to be simpler, less involved, more forceful. It cannot be subtle . . . because the conditions under which people view television reduce their acuity and discrimination.[87]

Perhaps we viewers, young and old alike, really are nothing more than a collection of docile onlookers incapable of acuity and discrimination. But I suspect the following statements regarding the use of TV violence are closer to the truth:

> . . . a television executive in America once told me that if the material the television audience sees is too demanding emotionally . . . it means they're not going to be able to sit and watch all night, which is the desideratum (so they can see the commercials). So give them formula drama, straight, vigorous action stuff. Like junk food, you can eat lots of it because it contains no nourishment . . . This is why there is so much violence on TV—it's the easiest type of show to pull off. . . .
>
> The so-called action shows have at their core a vacuum which can only be filled by violence. They are not about real questions;

they are not about real people; they are not about real situations. The only possible controversy is through violence, and therefore, the supply of violence on TV will remain constant as long as there is a constant number of so-called action shows. They have nowhere else to go.

. . . there are so many commercial breaks in a typical show that the only way to hold up the whole teetering structure is through continual jolts of violence. Constant impact is looked for . . . Violence is prevalent in these series because they can be written no other way. Subtlety of theme and character, which are the ordinary tools of a writer, are not required and, in any case, they're quite beyond any person working on the series.[88]

The violence is there because that is what the programming heads think the audience can handle. It is easier to do; it maintains interest while building toward the commercials. This in turn encourages advertiser support and money-making potential. Period.

Of course, not everyone in Hollywood and New York, the prime media centers, regards the public in this manner. There are writers, producers, and directors who are as concerned about the question of violence as consumer action groups, parents, teachers, and educators. Several hundred actors and writers actually signed a statement published in *Variety* and other trade papers which declared, "We will no longer lend our talents in any way to add to the creation of a climate of murder."[89] And the comment below suggests that there are those in the industry who *do* care about what is happening to the audience as well as to the Nielsens:

Wouldn't we perhaps discover that the public is as intelligent as any of us? I have an idea that the public would support an honest story, told well, without violence, and dealing with problems with which they could identify.[90]

There is also some indication that certain sponsors and advertisers have stopped buying time on shows which contain heavy doses of violence. They simply do not want to advertise their products in between gun fights and murders. The president of one company has withdrawn over $2 million of his firm's commercials from violent offerings. He declared:

If one TV show featuring a bizarre crime has a one in 10,000 chance of giving some lunatic a new murderous idea, think of

what twenty shows do to the odds! Do we value life so little in
this country that we put the entertainment of many above the
life of one?[9][1]

An interesting question, certainly. Within eighteen months of
taking this stand, the company president received some 100,000
letters supporting his position. Other corporations have also taken
similar steps and are withdrawing support from overly violent
programs. The only trouble is that these people are working
against the mainstream of the broadcasting business as much as the
general public. Change from within—if any—will come slowly and
with difficulty.

What we educators must appreciate here is the tone and
conscience at work behind the TV screen. In general, there is little
genuine concern over the impact of violence, and it is this kind of
attitude that we must try to understand and counteract in our
fight to reclaim children from TV.

IN PERSPECTIVE: RELATED ISSUES

Where does this leave us?

Clearly, the overview presented here of violence on American
television suggests that a number of viewers, especially the young,
may be affected in a variety of negative ways. Indeed, it is difficult
going over the various data and information without coming to
this conclusion.

Yet, there are still those who insist that all the violence on
television is but a reflection, a mirror of our society, which at the
same time does not exert any great influence on us. It is no doubt
true that some of the aggression we see on TV is there because we
do seem to be a nation preoccupied with a rough-and-ready spirit.
But this does not mean we are unaffected or do not respond in
some way to what we see. To say that many of us—especially the
young—are not influenced by the considerable doses of violence
mirrored on TV simply does not make sense. One of the most
fundamental parts of learning is responding to what we see. This,
coupled with the fact that informally acquired material can exert a
strong, long-term influence, makes the problem of violence on

television that much more pressing for parents, teachers, and educators alike.

There are other points to consider as well in relationship to the problem of television violence and its effect on viewers. For instance: most of the studies reviewed in the preceding pages conclude that the violence exhibited by the experimental subjects stems from *direct* exposure to violent TV. In many cases, this very well appears to be true, but there are also more subtle aspects of influence to be explored. What the majority of these studies prove is that children can imitate and/or be instigated to aggression by watching certain models, and this they can do with or without TV. Some societies are quite violent without the aid of the box. This does not mean, however, that television cannot foster violence in ways different to what most of these studies imply.

It may not be aggressive content alone which makes viewers more violent but other contributing factors as well. Perhaps television itself stimulates a general dissatisfaction by promoting glamorous settings and life styles. TV advertising in particular may create feelings of resentment among those who cannot afford "The Good Life" offered by the screen. Perhaps the constant switching back and forth between scenes somehow agitates viewers, which later manifests itself in antisocial ways. Violent actions among heavy viewers may stem from the fact that while watching so much television they have less opportunity for learning about themselves and others through direct experience. Their subsequent hostility and aggressiveness could arise from this lack of personal contact with others. This human void may then be filled with aggressive TV heroes and private eyes as models for behavior, especially among children and adolescents who have no parents or teachers who will take the time to talk with them about feelings and other ways of dealing with their problems. As Alfred Whitehead once said, the making of an epoch is settled by the ideal which the young set before themselves for imitation. If this is true, *what ideal are we setting before the young*? Violent television models whose effect on youngsters could be extensive and profound? This is hardly encouraging.

Of course, it would be unrealistic to ignore the fact that

violence and aggression have always been around or that passions flare up and strike out in life. The violence we see in a presentation of *Macbeth* or in a documentary on war or civil rights has social merit. At least we see what the consequences of real violence and brutality are. From this perspective, seeing violence has its positive side, for it can broaden understanding of the human condition in a way unlike many others.

Yet violence or aggression which honestly reflects real human emotion and conflict is not the same type of cliché violence which presently dominates the American TV screen. The use of violence made to a formula or violence that is an item to be packaged for sale is not a balanced presentation of human strife. This type of mental violence may be much more significant than instances of imitation or instigation to aggression fostered by specific TV shows. Jean Piaget once said that blows call for blows and gentleness moves us to gentleness, and anyone working closely with young people appreciates this fact about life and human behavior because it has to do with respect for individual beings.

But how often does television concern itself with this kind of respect? What harm is being done to individual consciousness by being exposed so frequently to prefabricated images of hostility? Marshall McLuhan writes that the visual media—TV and movies in particular—are a new kind of literacy which *by their very nature* release human energy and aggressiveness when different people confront each other "eye to eye."[9][2] This hostility may stem from the fear of meeting someone or something new; but if McLuhan is right, then we are only compounding the problem by concentrating so heavily on violent fantasy presentations.

Obviously, no one, whether he is a member of the television industry, a consumer action group, parent, or teacher, can deny that one of the most important lessons an individual can learn is the value and uniqueness of human life. Certainly, it is madness to allow a youngster to watch five or six hours of television a day, and the industry cannot be held accountable for this abdication of parental responsibility. This, however, should not relieve the industry of liability for what it broadcasts. The blame in this case is two-fold. We may be raising a generation of rather unfeeling, uncaring people, simply because parents have not taken the time to interact with their own children and teach them nonviolent means of coping. And the broadcast industry has been less than eager to listen to the findings of the school scientists and to alter its programming. There have been fluctuations in the levels of TV violence over recent years, but we seem to be entering another proviolence era. Programmers for the 1981/82 season unlocked the gun cabinets in a new wave of private eyes, bounty hunters, and FBIs; action drama continues to dominate the screen.

Yet, even if this were not the case, even if the current network season revealed substantially lowered levels of aggression, it would hardly help to alleviate the damage which has already occurred from years of past exposure. Though we cannot abandon our battle against gratuitous violence, we must be wary that our counterattack is not worse than what we wish to prevent. Though the material presented in this chapter *does* suggest a negative effect from excessive violence, it would be unfortunate to see public reaction go too far in the opposite direction.

There has been considerable support among some groups, the PTA, for example, to encourage the production and consumption of more bland, i.e., specifically nonviolent, programming. Yet, would this necessarily be an effective alternative? To advocate that young people should watch so-called "safe" or uncontroversial presentations might help to alleviate the immediate problem of their exposure to excessive violence on TV. But it leaves unanswered the question of how to present honest, realistic portrayals of life. We must remind ourselves that many young people today are quite sophisticated. They have been exposed to many adult issues and topics. Offering either extreme on television—violence on the one hand or blandness on the other—does injustice to young people and their right to receive a balanced view.

Because of this, we need to radically rethink programming philosophies and TV-watching behaviors. This is something we must discuss openly and freely with students in the classroom and their parents at home, at faculty meetings, and with school planning committees. We must emphasize that it is not just a question of outside forces wanting to censor or limit the amount of violence itself so there are fewer car chases, punch-outs, or gun fights per show. This would be a naive view, because man from earliest times has responded to conflict, and social high-mindedness is never going to alter this fact about human nature. But a part of our compromise with the TV industry could be to enlarge the base of dramatic presentations so that it includes more than action/adventure formula crank-outs. This would not infringe upon those people's rights who wish to make such programs, but it would provide a broader spectrum of experience from which to choose, as well as providing wider viewer choice. It would also increase opportunities for new talent and creative expression. Again, it is not a question of censorship but one of balance, that of presenting aggression and conflict in a variety of forms. There might even be less likelihood of the violence seen on most American TV influencing viewers if the market were expanded to include a wide range of program options.

Obviously, the solutions to this particular battle are not easy, and diversity of opinion must be guarded. Yet, the evidence collected here points to some real problems which warrant real social and educational concern. Furthermore, the question of violence on television and related issues, such as desensitization and fear, are matters of international importance because American programs are being shown around the world. And as more countries get television, they too will have to confront these problems. It may be one thing for us to pollute our own airwaves with shootings and murder, but foreign countries perhaps should think twice before they do the same. Finland and Spain have already taken action to stop the importation of violent American telefilms; and William Belson, as mentioned earlier, has urged Britain to cut down on her American TV imports. Furthermore, the First German TV Network has removed such programs as "Kojak" and "Mission: Impossible" from the air, and the Australian Senate Committee on Education and Arts has also recommended less violence on TV, especially children's programs.[93] How many other countries will follow suit? And how will this sort of trend affect the world TV market which the American television industry wishes to protect?

I leave the reader one last example of how TV can influence its viewers:

Orangutan, TV Fan, Dies: Kojak Made Him Violent
An orangutan named Alexander, who loved watching TV, has died at Edinburgh Zoo at the age of 28. He was found slumped in his cage a few feet from his TV set. Television was installed in his cage, presumably to help him forget his homeland in Borneo, but some animal lovers complained that television was doing him harm, especially programs like "Kojak" and "Starsky and Hutch." *When Alexander viewed TV cops in action, he hurled objects about his cage* (italics added).

94

If violent TV shows can affect Alexander, imagine what they may be doing to our students!

III

To Buy or Not to Buy:
Children and Advertising

CARTOON

> A little boy at school, standing next to his teacher with his
> hand over his heart. The teacher's comment: "Very good,
> Bobby, but that wasn't the Gettysburg Address. It was a
> cereal commercial."

A second major theater of war between teachers, children, and
television is the realm of advertising. Consumer education via
the TV screen represents one of the medium's most potent
teaching weapons, and in most instances, overpowers our efforts in
the classroom to instruct children about products and their
consumption. Madison Avenue has artillery in the form of
sophisticated commercials, all aimed at winning children of various
ages into numerous product camps. A tremendous battle is being
conducted for viewer attention, because billions of consumer
dollars are at stake. What are we doing in schools today that even
begins to compare to this kind of sophisticated TV campaign? If
violence represents one facet of television's teaching curriculum,
then advertising to children clearly symbolizes continuous assault,
reinforcement, and follow-through.

Commercials galore exist on station after station across the
entire land. Indeed, an American viewer can hardly turn on his set
today without being painfully aware of all the sales pitches being
thrown out at him. And though some may question the medium's
power to influence people in the realm of antisocial behavior, no
one can deny its success when it comes to pushing *products*.

Though we are all affected by this barrage of messages, we should be doubly concerned about what children and adolescents are learning from this informal television input. The exposure that young people now have to the materialistic values espoused by TV, above and beyond the more mundane and trivial allegiance to specific products, may have far greater impact on their thinking and behavior than many of us appreciate. After nearly thirty years, what might we expect to emerge from this aspect of television exposure? How does all the "buy me" syndrome affect a young person's views on consumerism, materialism, and more broadly *life itself*? How much advertising does he ignore, and how much does he incorporate into his own actions and beliefs? Next to amusement and entertainment, commercials both reflect and affect our entire culture, for they operate on the assumption that human wants and needs—particularly those of children—are inexhaustible. And if Madison Avenue is so interested in children, perhaps we in the classroom should analyze *why*.

EVOLUTION OF COMMERCIALS ON TV FOR CHILDREN

Before reviewing some of the information regarding commercials and children, some explanation is called for on how TV advertisements directed toward youngsters came about in the first place. The United States is one of the few countries in the world which allows widespread television advertising to children, and the genesis of this is an integral part of the medium's early development. It also provides an interesting portrait of what is considered important in our society, and what attitudes we are battling against in schools today.

In the late forties and early fifties, there was a great deal of interest in providing good programming as a means of selling sets. Though many people were already planning to use television as a product promoter, it could obviously never be used as such unless people bought units for their homes. Offering quality programs, therefore, was a way of encouraging the public at large to purchase TVs. In 1951, NBC, CBS, ABC, and the now defunct DuMont networks actually aired twenty-seven hours a week of children's programming during time periods when youngsters were most likely to watch (usually late afternoon and early evening). What is more, many of these programs were shown *without commercials* because it was a way of attracting adult attention to the new medium. By doing this, it was felt that more adults would buy sets, not specifically for their children, but with the idea that children, too, could benefit from this new household appliance.

By the mid-fifties, the sale of television sets had risen sharply, and a shift in emphasis occurred from audience development to efficient advertising. The eyeballs were there in front of the sets; all the advertisers had to do was decide what they wanted to sell to the people attached to those eyeballs. Yet, at this time, the child still was not considered an important marketing agent in product consumption. Ads were directed primarily toward adults.

Advertising Strategy in the Early Fifties

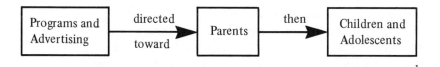

Programs and Advertising — directed toward → Parents — then → Children and Adolescents

[1]

During the mid-fifties, however, attitudes toward advertising began to change. In 1954, the first Disney show was aired, and the popularity of the show made advertisers take notice. Here was a whole new market waiting to be explored! Prior to the Disney era, children's shows were looked upon as an unprofitable activity, but Disney changed this view. Children, in fact, offered a substantial market for producers, networks, advertisers, and stations alike. In 1955, the networks provided twenty-two hours of children's programming, and in 1956, the combined network total of children's shows amounted to thirty-seven hours a week. New economic motivations then began to encourage more program production. By 1957, the TV boom was on, and a different pattern began to emerge. Rather than going to the parent, commercials were aimed directly at the child audience, thus bypassing "the middleman."

Advertising Strategy in the Late Fifties

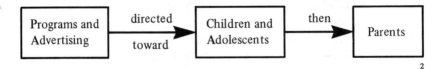

This basic format was used until the early sixties without much change. By then, however, Nielsen rating numbers indicated that Saturday morning might be a very profitable time period in which to concentrate children's programs and commercials. On Saturday, for example, an advertiser could reach 1,000 children by spending only $1 on network weekend shows, whereas that same dollar would reach only 286 children on weekdays and only 133 during prime time.[3] So Saturday morning became the main target for children's advertisements and represented a further shift toward consolidation. In effect, the ad men and network people could make more money and spend less by concentrating their firepower on the weekend, and that was good strategic sense.

This practice has continued until the present with only one or two minor changes. Now Saturday morning children's programs and advertisements are organized along a system called routining. This means that the early morning shows are aimed at younger children (three to seven), and later morning programs are directed toward the older youth audience. One can see a continuing progression of specialization in relationship to children's advertising. The fifties brought about a change in commercial interest from parent to child. The sixties ushered in the concept of Saturday morning "kidvid" and the routining of children's ads and programs. Now shows and commercials have become staggered for maximum impact and profit return. As one author writes:

> Over the past quarter century, we have seen the perceived role of the · child [in America] change from one of relatively little influence over programming and family purchase decisions to one of major influence. Also, we are seeing a continuously developing awareness on the part of advertisers, market researchers, and broadcasters of the unique vulnerabilities of children to advertising and the potential role of children as lobbyists for the advertiser in the home.[4]

THE STORY OF MATTEL

One of the most successful warriors in the fight to capture children's money and attention is Mattel, the toy manufacturer. In many respects, they have been the industry prototype for those who followed, and their development is a key one in the story of children's television commercials.[5]

Until the mid-fifties, cereal companies were the main firms doing advertising on TV to children, and this was primarily on local, not network, programs. The advertising on these live shows consisted of the star promoting products in person. Stand-up actors would give away the items they plugged on their programs as prizes to games played by the child audience. Not what one would call advertising sophistication by today's standards; nevertheless, it was a start.

But attitudes and feelings were beginning to change in the home, and these changes came to be reflected in advertising on TV to young people. When World War II ended, men returned from the war who wanted to start families and get back into careers and business. Naturally, there was a sense of great relief. The Depression and War had ended, and times were changing. These men wanted "The Better Life" for themselves and for their children, because many had grown up during the thirties and remembered their own deprived childhoods. Yet, after the War, they entered an era of relative affluence. They could live in a house; they did not have to stay in an apartment. They could have backyards and a place for their children to play. The attitude developed that parents wanted to get more for themselves and give more to their children than they had been able to have when they were growing up. So the timing for advertising on TV to kids was quite ripe. Advertisers recognized a growing market and accepted the outlook in the home of *giving to the kids*.

The only network then that believed there was any real opportunity for children's programming on a big scale was ABC. Consequently, they got Walt Disney to develop a daily program for young people called "The Mickey Mouse Club." ABC then started to sell Mickey, and the advertising agency for Mattel was offered a spot on the show. The agency went to Mattel—then a small west coast manufacturing company—and said they felt Mattel should take advantage of this option. They believed TV had the potential for reaching more children than ever before, and there was a real opportunity for a toy company to develop its influence in an area where there were virtually no nationally known names. Of course, there was no guarantee for the agency or for Mattel that a TV campaign would work; however, there was a hunch that the times were right for this sort of thing. Mattel decided to take the gamble and signed up. In September, 1955, they went on the air via Mickey and friends with two commercials: one for a musical toy and one for something called a "burp" gun.

In comparison to many of today's efforts, these commercials were very low key. The power of television to reach people and influence behavior simply was not understood as well as it is today. Yet, for Mattel, these ads were a bold venture. Their commercials appeared at the start of the new fall season and continued into October, which is usually a fairly good toy merchandising month. But nothing happened. The people at Mattel were worried, since no real demand was being received at the factory, and this pattern continued into November. Between six weeks and two months elapsed and still nothing. After the Thanksgiving holiday, however, things started to pick up. Mattel factories began to receive sacks of mail requesting merchandise. There was greater demand than there was supply, and orders came in from all over the country which could not be filled.

The advertising agency and Mattel had not appreciated what could happen if something took off very quickly. The toy manufacturing system was structured so that the agency and Mattel were dealing through manufacturers' representatives. These representatives then dealt with jobbers (the wholesalers), and jobbers exerted considerable influence on the toy business because they had all the salesmen. Finally, the salesmen then had to go out and call on the retailers. So there was a chain of communication that had to be worked through *after* the children had seen the initial commercial and responded to it. If the warehouses were out, the jobber then had to contact the manufacturing representative: the representative then had to go to the factory and ask for more shipments, and so on. (This particular pattern, though greatly accelerated today, is still part of the problem the industry faces in responding quickly to trends and consumer desires. Now, however, this delay can be anticipated, whereas at the time Mattel was doing this, nothing could be second-guessed.)

Between Thanksgiving and Christmas, 1955, things began to take off. Mattel sold a million burp guns (at $4 each), and nobody had ever sold a million of *anything* before in such a short span of time. By the end of the year, everything was gone. Not a single burp gun part was left. Not even President Eisenhower could get one for his son, David. Naturally, all this was completely unexpected and met with more than a little surprise. (Mattel actually sent out a letter of apology to the toy trade saying, "Who would have dreamed Mickey Mouse had THAT much strength?!")

By the next year, Mattel was beginning to understand the basic sales pattern of marketing to children: reach the child, the child tells the parent, and the parent goes to the store—with or without the child—and buys the product. Many times the parent would accept the product without question because the item sounded good and his child wanted it. In other cases, if the product were a little too expensive or if the parent were skeptical, then a certain amount of advertising could be directed toward him as well.

Mattel went to the 1956 Annual Toy Fair with some filmed commercials to show potential buyers. They believed this "thing" with TV was no fluke, and they did more business in advance than ever before. The rest of the industry, however, was still doubtful. How could toy companies sell on a fifty-two-week-a-year basis? It just was not done. The business had *always* been very seasonal, and the pros believed that a person could not sell much merchandise during the first nine months of the year.

All this is hindsight, of course, because new products are now introduced almost daily. Each one requires its own strategy, and each is sold as a separate item. Quotas and dollar volume are assessed; each product is studied individually and compared with what else is on the market. All this is done with great speed, for if a manufacturer or ad agency does not move quickly, probably he will be copied. Products are introduced in a staggered manner starting in January, and sales are now only a function of when the product can be made available to the public. And this is just what Mattel did. They helped flatten out the buying curve; and though there still is a peak at Christmas, they created a longer buying period. They were able to change a selling ratio of eighty percent/twenty percent (eighty percent being sold during the last three months of the year and twenty percent for the remainder) to sixty percent/forty percent, and this was significant.

The Barbie Doll Phenomenon

Mattel has developed any number of products and toys for children, but it might be of interest to look more closely at one of their *most* successful items: the Barbie Doll. Hers is a unique story indeed.[6]

By the early 1970s, Mattel had grown into a $320 million business with the nearest competitor in the field being only one-fourth as large. It had become the biggest toy manufacturer in the world by a considerable margin. Its greatest profit-maker, which has not been paralleled by any other product for children, is Barbie. In her career, Barbie has sold at least $500 million worth of merchandise in some fifty-five countries around the world. She has been almost universally accepted, and there has never been anything quite like her (it) in the toy/show business.

Barbie was developed by the original Mattel people. They had a daughter named Barbie who was interested in paper dolls, so they decided to create a fashion-model doll, a doll that could be dressed and undressed and dressed again, like a paper doll. During the mid- and late-fifties, there really was only one type of doll, the baby doll. So the concept of a fashion-model doll was quite new and different. Barbie would be a companion doll, a friend, not simply a baby to be mothered. The Mattel people imagined she would represent an imaginary projection of the young child into a more adult role. They market-tested Barbie and found that mothers did not like the doll, but young girls loved her. The mothers felt, however, that if the child wanted the doll that much, it could not be all that bad. Mattel decided to market the doll, largely via TV, despite parental reaction.

All this was in 1958/59, and Mattel knew right away that they had a "hit" (a "razor/razor blade" idea in the language of the ad agencies). Naturally, there was a rash of copying by competitors, but Mattel was first and was able to protect the unique Barbie image. In effect, Mattel created a whole new area of merchandising, the fashion doll, which we still have today. Barbie was so popular that *Life, Look, Reader's Digest,* and *The Saturday Evening Post* all did articles on her phenomenal rise. A person could go up to just about any little ten-year-old girl on the street, and she could probably tell everything there was to know about Barbie: her clothes, accessories, boyfriends, etc. In middle-class neighborhoods across the country, Barbie was in approximately seventy-five percent of the homes; and in upper-class neighborhoods, she reached a ninety percent level of acceptance. Mattel even organized an American fan club, which eventually was second only to the Girl Scouts in membership. There was also a European fan club, which wrote to children in twelve different languages and generated some 10,000 letters a week. The advertising agency handling Barbie could not even get a fan mail service to cope with all the flow, and they had to arrange their own mail services in Europe.

The ultimate goal had been reached: almost complete market saturation. And TV had done it.

AMERICAN KIDVID: THE CURRENT OUTLOOK

All this seems like ancient history now, but many of the patterns and attitudes which were set during the fifties and sixties continue with us today. It must be remembered that the very concept of advertising on TV directly to children was considered a new step; but once businessmen discovered it to be so profitable, children's commercials were pursued with even greater zeal. Today about twenty-five percent of the TV industry's profits comes from seven percent of its programming, directed toward young people.[7] It may be ironic to think that the Code of Hammurabi, almost four thousand years ago, made selling something to a child or buying something from a child without power of attorney a crime punishable by death! In the 1980s, however, American kids remain open game.

If we were to construct an imaginary child with average TV viewing habits, our unsuspecting boy or girl would see about 20,000 commercials on United States television every year, totaling some 350,000 ads by the time he or she reached age eighteen.[8] The majority of the sales pitches our imaginary friend might see would probably be aimed at the stomach, perhaps reaching as high as 14,000 ads for foods and drinks per year. Depending upon when the child watched, our friend could be exposed to many adult products as well. The following chart gives some idea how important the battle for the TV youth market has become.

Advertising on Children's Television: Recent Activity

1968: an estimated seventy percent of all children watching TV asked their parents for products advertised; eighty-nine percent of the parents purchased said products.

1970: $70 million spent by advertisers on network weekend children's programming.

1971: over $75 million in advertising revenue for commercial networks from children's television.

1975: $400 million spent on TV advertising to young people; fifty percent of commercials were for food products. Revenues from cereal commercials amounted to $24 million; candy and gum $11 million; toys, games, etc., slightly less than $22 million.

1978: television ads for children estimated at $600 million a year business.

9

Yet, while advertisers and networks make more money, the children get poorer- and poorer-quality shows, with more and more commercials. Here, for instance, is a typical Saturday morning offering:

- *9:00 a.m. Cartoon* about a talking dune buggy. Limited animation. All sorts of gimmicks, such as electro transformer tape and ray gun. Jerack is Metamorpho Man. Mark and Debby are the good guys.

- *Commercials*:
    sugar cereal
    candy
    sugar cereal (different from above)
- *Cartoon*: Secret ray tape is hidden in buggy. Metamorpho Man wants tape and gun. Chase scene. Lots of canned laughter. Updated the black-hat image by giving the bad guy dark glasses.
- *Commercials*:
    bubble gum
    chocolate drink
    PSA (Public Service Announcement)
- *Cartoon*: Good guys make ray gun and shrink buggy. Canned laughter. Another long chase scene. Good guys finally defeat Metamorpho Man by tying his shoelaces together so he trips. Show ends with more canned laughter.
- *More commercials*, etc.[10]

The rest of Saturday morning is not much different. In one cartoon, there will be two guys and one gal; in another, two gals and one guy. In one show, they are super heroes; in the next, super villains. On this particular Saturday, I watched six programs and over sixty commercials—twenty of which were for sugared products—and some shows had even more commercial interruptions than the example given above.

Broadcasters supposedly have a responsibility to the public, especially children, because they make such large sums of money for the use of the publicly-licensed airwaves. Yet, this public responsibility often gets pushed aside in the pursuit of heavy profits, particularly from children. As Peggy Charren, head of Action for Children's Television, says:

> The broadcasters are very concerned about the economic health of their stations, but nobody seems concerned about the economic health of parents of children (or the children themselves) who are subject to all this advertising.[11]

This is because the networks and stations, for the most part, do not *care* about high-quality programs or fewer commercials on children's television. Generally, they want ratings, leading to money, as the financial bottom line is their reason for existing. They are playing by the dictates of the marketplace, not necessarily by those of public welfare or service to the people. And businessmen can hardly be blamed for running it as a business when that is exactly how they perceive its function.

Not only do kids in this country see questionable cartoons laced with sugary foods, action, and adventure, but our attitude toward advertising to children is quite different from the rest of the world. American television definitely holds a unique position in this regard. A 1971 survey of sixteen countries, for example, revealed that the United States allowed more advertising on children's programs than any other country investigated and this by a considerable margin.[12] Only four of the countries surveyed allowed any advertising at all!

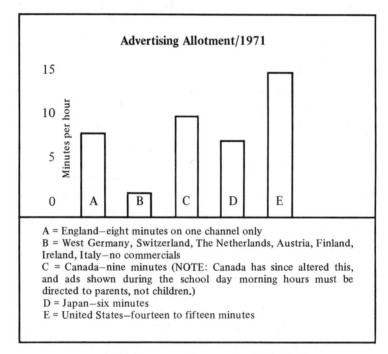

Advertising Allotment/1971

A = England—eight minutes on one channel only
B = West Germany, Switzerland, The Netherlands, Austria, Finland, Ireland, Italy—no commercials
C = Canada—nine minutes (NOTE: Canada has since altered this, and ads shown during the school day morning hours must be directed to parents, not children.)
D = Japan—six minutes
E = United States—fourteen to fifteen minutes

[13]

The National Association of Broadcasters (NAB) now calls for about nine minutes of advertising per hour on prime-time and weekend children's programs; twelve minutes per hour during weekday children's shows; and no more than sixteen minutes per hour at other times.[14] For children under twelve, however, afternoons and evenings account for more than fifty percent of their weekly viewing. So, in effect, young people generally are exposed to more commercials than if they watched on Saturday mornings only. Moreover, broadcasters frequently do not follow the ad time limits set for children in their own code. A recent study of sixty-one hours of children's television reveals that over half had nonprogram material (commercials, plugs, PSAs) *in excess* of NAB code standards.[15] So not only are children getting the commercial maximum from adult programming, they are also receiving excessive amounts on some of their own shows as well.

The foregoing facts and statistics give some indication how profitable children's television advertising truly is. The commercial warriors are entrenched and prepared for a long siege indeed. Children's TV in America is actually a perfect microcosm of what goes on during prime-time hours. The ad rates may be higher for the evening hours, but the same basic rules of the game apply: more eyeballs mean greater exposure means more potential profits. We certainly know that advertising on television is extremely effective, but those of us "on the outside" do not always know how or why commercials work so well.

Advertising agencies on Madison Avenue have compiled vast amounts of research on marketing techniques, but the general populace still knows little about their findings. Yet, it is part of our responsibility as educators working with children to become more aware of how commercials and TV advertising affect our students, since it comprises such a large segment of their world. Not only is their specific purchasing behavior influenced, but also beliefs and assumptions regarding products and consumption. As the following evidence suggests, much is taking place in the informal learning domain regarding attitudes toward *having* versus *not having* and how this in turn can affect self-concepts and interpersonal relationships.

REVIEW OF RESEARCH FINDINGS

Surprisingly enough, investigations into the impact of commercials on children outside studies conducted by Madison Avenue are a very recent event, especially when one considers how important merchandising is in our society. In fact, the National Science Foundation reports that three-fourths of all such studies have been conducted only since 1974.[16] Those of us in the classroom who are behind the ad agencies in our knowledge of advertising techniques might do well to give the matter additional thought, because the strength of television's advertising arm is formidable. What follows, therefore, is a brief survey of some of the information which has been accumulated over recent years regarding commercials, the way they work, and how children in particular respond to them.

One of the more interesting studies available involves the relationship between commercials and incidental learning. It seems that people of all ages can retain in memory a large number of TV ad campaigns; yet, whether they are conscious of this retention is another matter. Again, constant exposure is the key; and with children in this country seeing some 20,000 commercials a year, one can safely say that is fairly constant. Apparently, much advertising content is learned and meant to be learned as nonsense material based predominantly upon sound and repetition. Playing upon this child-like sense of rhythm and rhyme becomes an important technique in grabbing attention and getting advertising messages across. Such incidental or trivial learning, however, can be very effective. Indeed, one of the main reasons television commercials have such a remarkable impact is precisely because they require little involvement or concentration. Messages can be easily digested passively, without consciously seeking anything. As mentioned before, in cases of low involvement, an individual's defense systems are absent. He is relaxing and wants to be entertained. He certainly does not watch television with the intention of thinking too strenuously. So advertisers have him while his guard is down, and he is most susceptible during this type of learning mood.

Consequently, as trivia messages are repeated and learned and then forgotten, then learned a little more, one of two things can happen:

(1) over-learning may move some information about products and services from an individual's short-term memory into his long-term memory; or

(2) the individual may experience a change in the way he perceives a product.[17]

This, of course, involves the whole realm of incidental learning. The viewer may not think he has changed his mind about a certain item, but sometime later he may go out and buy it without much thought. As one investigator writes:

> ... the public lets down its guard to the repetitive commercial use of the television medium ... It easily changes its way of perceiving products and brands and its purchasing behavior without thinking very much about it at the time of TV exposure or at any time prior to purchase ... This success [of television advertising] seems to be based upon a left-handed kind of public trust that sees no great importance in the matter.[18]

Many people may believe they successfully ignore most of the commercials on TV. But, then again, they may be unaware how *deeply* some of these messages are going. This is particularly true of young children, for they are ignorant of the sophisticated, persuasive techniques employed to get them to want products. Moreover, since the very act of watching TV increases the relaxation factor in the brain, there is an even stronger possibility of manipulation and influence.

This change in the mood and reception conditions, accompanied by an increase in Alpha waves, is due in part to the fact that fixing one's eye on a moving object inhibits motor activity. The individual's mind is put into a yielding frame of reference, and when this relaxation is achieved, he is more apt to respond on a subconscious level to advertising (or program) content. This kind of mental relaxation is the very basis of hypnotic suggestion. In fact, a doctor teaching hypnosis to medical students at the University of Alabama has expressed concern over the way low involvement viewing is used to promote products and change buying patterns. He comments:

> Television programmers and advertisers have the TV viewer when

he is relaxed, his conscious mind distracted, his emotions aroused,
and they can implant repeated messages into his mind. These are
all conditions necessary for an effective hypnotic session. Once
hypnotized by TV, people are influenced to a degree they would
hardly believe possible . . .[19]

Marshall McLuhan offers a similar view. He believes that ads are
not meant for conscious consumption but rather are intended as
potent subliminal "pills" to create an effective hypnotic spell.

Ads seem to work on the very advanced principle that a small
pellet or pattern in a noisy, redundant barrage of repetition will
gradually assert itself. Ads push the principle of noise all the way
to the plateau of persuasion. They are quite in accord with the
procedures of brainwashing.[20]

In effect, we are doubly vulnerable: not only is there constant
repetition to remind us of products and brand names, but these
messages and repetitions are going deeper into our minds than we
suspect. A child may not pay much attention to the commercials
when he sees them on the screen, but when he is in a store later
on, he may see a product and recall is triggered. This is a basic
stimulus-response pattern.

Along with the appeal to sound and rhythm and the different
reception/mood conditions brought about by TV, commercials
also have their greatest impact on areas where people have. little
opinion or no previous knowledge about a given product or
service. This certainly applies to young children, because at five or
six they have not been around long enough to properly judge
commercial input. To them, what they see being presented is just
another show or something to want, or both. As the two charts
on the following page reveal, the younger the child, the better he
is for the advertiser's purposes.

When one begins to analyze other effects that commercials have
on a child's learning and behavior, the evidence is striking indeed.
Youngsters often declare that one of the things they like the most
about TV is the commercials—a good indication of their teaching
power. In one study, for example, children who were interviewed
remembered three times as many ads they enjoyed and which
made an impression as those which did not.[21] In another survey,
several hundred elementary school children were asked to list as

Degree of Understanding of Commercials by Age Groups

	LOW	*MEDIUM*	*HIGH*
	Confused, unaware of selling motive; may say commercials are for entertainment.	Recognition of selling motive; some awareness of profit-seeking; commercials are to "make you buy things."	Clear recognition of selling and profit-seeking motives; "commercials get people to buy and they pay for the shows."
AGE			
5 to 7	55%	35%	10%
8 to 10	38%	50%	12%
11 to 12	15%	60%	25%

22

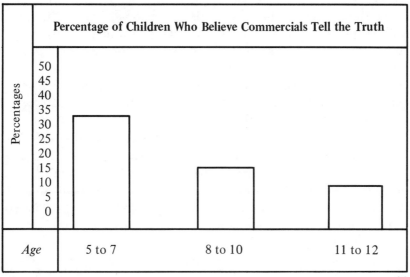

23

many TV advertised products as they could in only fifteen minutes. Surprisingly, even the youngest wrote down an average of twenty items each, and the eleven-year-olds named fifty![24] Moreover, almost all brand names were written correctly, even though many were much harder than words on school spelling lists. The mothers of these children also were questioned, and about seventy-five percent said not only did their children sing commercials by heart, but that nearly two-thirds did so by the time they were two. Yet, how many of these same two-year-olds knew any children's nursery rhymes, folk tales, or stories from memory? Numerous other studies, especially those performed as part of the *Surgeon General's Report*, reveal comparable findings. Children who watched TV regularly requested foods, toys, games, and many adult items advertised over the screen.

Not only do commercials affect behavior by stimulating the desire for specific items and services, but many are also filled with stereotypes which can influence a child's attitudes toward products and their consumption. Surveys have been conducted which show that in ads for candy, cereal, and drinks, boys outnumber girls by more than three to one.[25] The main reason for this, however, is purely economic: advertisers have discovered that young boys do not respond well to commercials with girls promoting products, but little girls will respond to ads with boys. Consequently, young females do not appear in promotions for action toys such as planes, cars, and so on, nor do they appear in cereal ads which offer such toys as premiums. Most toy and game ads aimed at girls generally emphasize beauty and popularity, whereas those for boys focus on size, power, noise, and speed— themes which again reemphasize male/female stereotypes. An overall view of commercials on Saturday morning American kidvid can be seen in the chart on the following page.

Nowhere does one find any advertisements for children's books, magazines, or more healthful food products. It is possible that ads promoting only a limited range of items and presenting stereo-typed characters may influence young children to form certain attitudes about people and life.

We teachers must remember that this type of instruction may be very covert and subtle. A child may respond openly and

> **Breakdown of 400 Commercials Monitored in Boston/1971**
> *Racial Types*
> 73% white actors only
> 24% mixed
> 3% minority groups only
> *Sex*
> 49% male
> 16% female
> 35% mixed
> *Products*
> 24% for cereals
> 22% for toys
> 22% for foods and snacks
> 20% for candy and sweets

26

noticeably to a specific article, but what kinds of ideas is he forming about the use of products and the act of consumption in general? Perhaps we should initiate widescale learning units describing how products are presented on TV in order to help our students better understand what they are being exposed to in the outside world. This might help counterbalance some of their informal learning from television about purchasing, or what to look for in advertising messages. This is one reason why consumer education is so important in our schools and society today.

THE COUNCIL ON CHILDREN, MEDIA, AND MERCHANDISING AND THE NATIONAL SCIENCE FOUNDATION

General Findings

The Council on Children, Media, and Merchandising (CCMM) and the National Science Foundation (NSF) represent two major nonindustry sources regarding the influence of advertising on young people. Both groups offer in-depth data on the impact of commercials and provide the most substantial body of information on children's advertising outside Madison Avenue. They cover numerous topics, such as attitudes toward family life, food and drug use, general health, etc.; and since they draw upon a wide range of professional expertise, their findings merit close attention.

The Council on Children, Media, and Merchandising is a Washington, D.C.-based consumer action group which has published various documents on children and advertising. One of the Council's more significant ideas involves what they called the status referral function of television. This means that by virtue of being on the TV screen, some sort of aura of acceptance and importance is given to the advertised products—whether they deserve it or not. Children see an item promoted on the screen and think it *must* be good, otherwise it would not be on the tube in the first place. A number of children who were questioned in one of the Council's surveys actually responded "yes" when asked whether products shown on television were "better" than those found elsewhere. In fact, a 60 to 40 ratio voted in favor of TV product acceptance.[27]

Another interesting point the Council provides about advertisements and their influence ties in with the idea of trivia, over-learning, and the sleeper effect. So much commercial information is crammed onto the screen that its influence often lasts much longer than one might expect. The Council comments:

> Recall of information of pre-test and post-test studies is *higher* for the commercials in a program than for the content of the program itself ... Children responded to the content of the ad much more consistently and accurately by a factor of two to one over the content of the program. The program deteriorated rapidly in its recall potential, whereas the ad remained stable.[28]

In this sense, commercials are even better than program content in their ability to influence attitudes and behavior. As one person declares:

> [Ads are] ... the most parsimonious method of establishing a single-dimensional attitude, belief, or concept yet developed. There is ample evidence that commercial type messages, once learned, are highly resistant to erosion through memory loss and are amenable to many repetitions without loss of impact or acceptability. When the commercial is linked conceptually and/or affectively with the program it carries, or with the known or

assumed qualities of its actors or theme, its potential for teaching and retention increases. *In effect, the TV commercial is the single best method of mass implementation of an idea, belief, or short, sequenced behavior pattern yet devised.*[29] [italics added]

The Council has found that young children need only twenty to thirty exposures of any given commercial before information is acquired. But this figure becomes meaningless when one considers that most advertising messages on U.S. TV have 500 to 1,000 exposures. With THAT much input, it would be hard for even the dull child not to get the point. In addition, CCMM has discovered that children from low-socioeconomic families accept advertisements twenty percent to thirty percent more readily than youngsters from a more affluent environment. This fact alone might affect curriculum planning in under-privileged schools. Affective lessons, for example, could be developed around how to handle feelings of frustration when certain products are unattainable or how to cope in a materialistic world.

The Council also expresses particular concern over the preliterate child, who responds first to sounds and images rather than written words, for he is especially vulnerable to commercial influence. In effect, TV can "get at" these children more easily and sooner than schools, because it depends primarily upon low involvement, unsupervised learning, and attacks both auditory and visual senses at the same time. Because most adults have grown so accustomed to the drone of promotions via the TV, they often fail to remember what a strong effect ads can have on children and adolescents. But this should not obscure the fact that commercials are extremely potent behavioral modifiers in the realm of informal learning, particularly among the young.

Next to the work provided by the Council on Children, Media, and Merchandising, the National Science Foundation has performed an extensive investigation on the impact of TV commercials. In many respects, their study is to television advertising what the *Surgeon General's Report* is to violence, and their findings present cause for concern, both in the classroom and out.

The NSF Report indicates that two- to eleven-year-olds represent almost twenty percent of the U.S. population, and some thirty-five million children are exposed to commercials for products not actually intended for them. The Foundation confirms the finding that there is a distinct difference in the way young people up to the age of seven or eight (Piaget's pre-operational stage) and older children perceive commercials. They write:

> A substantial proportion of children, particularly below eight years, expresses little or no comprehension of the persuasive intent of commercials. Younger children who are unaware of the selling motives of television advertising tend to express greater belief in commercials and a higher frequency of purchase requests for certain advertised products than do older children who display an understanding of the intent of commercials.[30]

Some fifty-three percent of the first-graders in one NSF survey wanted every toy and game they saw promoted on TV, whereas only six percent of the fifth-graders did so. Yet, this decline in credibility does not necessarily mean a corresponding loss of commercial effectiveness. Older children may possess more "cognitive defenses" against advertisements, but as the Report aptly comments:

> The economic realities of commercial broadcasting offer clear evidence that commercials sell products to viewers even when their sales intent is clearly understood.[31]

The Foundation also points out how production techniques and certain styles of presentation are manipulated in commercials for maximum influence. Animated characters, for instance, are used in over forty percent of all advertisements directed toward children. (It is important to recall Bandura's research in which he found that young people often respond better to animated subjects than to live ones. By using animated figures, therefore, children attend even more closely to the commercial message.) Humans, both adults and children, were used in only thirty-two percent of the ads surveyed, and men appeared in more commercials for children than women, because they supposedly represent greater authority. (Women, on the other hand, were looked upon as passive product users.)

The Report also states that personal enhancement appeals are used in about one out of every four advertisements for children. They fall roughly into the following categories:

(1) fun/happiness ("fun to eat or play");
(2) health/nutrition ("eat a balanced breakfast with our cereal");
(3) action/strength ("look at it go!"); and
(4) adventure ("excitement in every bite!").

Though superiority and uniqueness claims are prohibited by the NAB code, they still were found in a number of commercials directed toward children. Even the names of certain products emphasized this power/superiority motif.

Another interesting point discussed by the Foundation is how tone and approach in commercials can affect subsequent behavior and attitudes among children. In one study, for example, preschool and elementary school youngsters were exposed to two different versions of a commercial for the same product, and their actions were then observed. In one presentation, the children in the ad were shown constructing an elaborate building with blocks; the other commercial was more modest in nature. The accompanying sound tracks also were different. In the dramatic version, the viewers were encouraged to build "a sky-high tower so you can be the champion!" The other commercial merely said, "It's fun . . . anyone can play Blockhead."

Based upon observations of the children's behavior after the commercials, the investigator reported that those who were exposed to the extravagant claim displayed more hostile behavior, anger, and verbal/physical aggression (twenty-eight percent versus eighteen percent of the controls).[32] Also, the children who saw the more elaborate claim said they could build higher towers than the children in the commercial, and this was especially true of younger viewers. This brings into question the long-range effects of commercials based upon action, speed, competition, and power, and how commercials themselves might initiate potentially anti-social behavior. How might such orientations change a child's attitudes or affect his play with others over an extended period of time? The results in this study indicate a negative impact; and the more children see such ads and competitive claims, the more they might come to accept them as a basis for personal behavior in real life.

The Report also includes two other studies on the effect of commercials toward acquisition and interpersonal relationships which are significant. In one experiment, researchers took four- and five-year-olds and randomly assigned them to different test situations. One set saw a "Ruckus Raisers Barn" commercial during a film, while the others did not. The children then were shown separate pictures of two boys. One boy was empty-handed, but the other had the special toy. As the experimenter showed the two pictures, he said:

> I can bring one of these two boys to play with you. I can bring this boy who is not so nice and you can play with him and his Ruckus Raisers Barn, or I can bring this boy who is nice. Would you like to play with the nice boy, or would you like to play with the boy who is not so nice and his Ruckus Raisers Barn?[33]

A total of seventy percent of the control group (those children who had not seen the commercial) chose the nice boy, but only thirty-five percent of those who had seen the commercial did so. The difference was still significant, though smaller, when the children were retested twenty-four hours later. The point is this: if commercials can encourage children to disregard social values in the short term, they can do so in the long term as well. As a matter of fact, the long-term influence from such exposure might be the most profound because it works at the level of values and personal expectations.

A second NSF study worth noting involves TV ad exposure and how it affects a child's attitude toward adults who deny product requests. Four- and five-year-olds again were selected, and the experimental group saw a ten-minute film with the Ruckus Raisers Barn commercial, while the control group saw just the film. Afterwards, the children were shown a picture of a boy either embracing an adult or walking away from him. The experimenter asked:

> I know a boy whose daddy didn't get him the Ruckus Raisers Barn. When his daddy didn't give him the barn, do you think the boy wanted to play with his daddy like this (shows picture) . . . or do you think he wanted to go away from his daddy like this (shows another picture)?[34]

Three out of five from the control group chose to play with

daddy; only two out of five from the experimental group did so—a change of twenty percent. The commercial followed by the denial tended to bring out *less* desirable human characteristics, and the evidence suggests that exposure to the ad contributed to the negative feelings from the experimental group. The investigator then asked whether the boy who did not get the toy would be sad or still happy to watch TV. Two out of three controls thought he would still be happy; yet only one out of three from the experimental group gave the same response. The Report comments:

> It thus appears that direct exposure to a TV commercial for a toy increased the likelihood that children would consider failure to receive a toy as inducing sadness . . . Disappointment, conflict, and even anger are found when parents deny requests. Television exposure seems linked to these outcomes.[35]

Something is not right when a child is made to feel that he must have a special toy to achieve happiness. Not only does this kind of materialism distort values, but it may also make parents who cannot afford such merchandise feel guilty or inadequate because they cannot give their children what the TV world dictates. Moreover, such ads can disrupt attempts to teach youngsters personal responsibility, for it is not easy to say "no" to a pleading child. These experiments indicate that advertisements directed toward children can seriously interfere with social growth and family activity by creating conflict and friction. The way these problems are handled may have long-range effects on both family life and the child's development, which in turn could be reflected in his performance in school.

IMPACT OF FOOD COMMERCIALS

Both the Council on Children, Media, and Merchandising and the National Science Foundation express particular concern over children's food commercials and the way they can affect attitudes regarding eating habits and nutrition in general. This area of informal learning is an extremely important issue because food and drink advertisements represent the largest force today in promotions directed toward children. The Council believes that

TV advertising over the past twenty-five years has actually done more to change the eating habits of American youth than any other single factor. Presweetened cereals, for instance, were introduced prior to World War II, but most women rejected them for their children. With the advent of TV, however, advertisers could go directly to the kids, thus changing the consumer triangle and circumventing disapproving Moms. They discovered TV could easily influence a child's informal learning about food, so his stomach and eating became ready targets for ads and big business. Their tastes, desires, and food expectations already would have been patterned informally. Eating itself would be "fun" and "appealing," not simply a way of replenishing the body's fuel.

The Council points out other problems as well. Not only are questionable eating habits encouraged, but many youngsters pick up only fragmentary information about food, which in turn can give them unrealistic attitudes in general. They hear that a product may look and taste good, but they do not necessarily learn what it is made of. We Americans actually have more nutritional data on packages of dog food than in TV ads for humans. What does this say about us as a society that would be more concerned about the diets of our canines than our own children? If commercials can teach youngsters to consume products and remember toys, games, and food, they have the capacity to teach something about sound eating habits as well. It all depends upon focus and degree.

Yet the food industry works hard to block such actions because advertising usually emphasizes everything but nutrition. Nutrition is not the main point; buying the product is. Industry lawyers declare it would be "counterproductive" to consider nutritional commercials for children or to warn against sugar. Counterproductive by whose standards? Quite understandably, they are trying to protect the interests of their clients, but who is going to protect the interests of children? When it comes to food, what most children in America are seeing on TV as a matter of course is shown in the first chart on the following page. Clearly, the healthier items rank last. An even closer look (see the second chart) at Saturday/Sunday daytime advertising (so-called kidvid haven) again reveals that sweetened foods predominate, and sugared breakfast cereals lead the field two to one.

Total Network Advertising/First Nine Months, 1975

Product	The Networks' Commercial Totals
Cereals	8166
Candy and gum	4083
Shortening and oils	3208
Cookies and crackers	2129
Non-carbonated soft drinks	1637
Carbonated soft drinks	1387
Meats and poultry	1328
Macaroni and spaghetti	1031
Vegetables	571
Cheese	320
Citrus	311

36

Saturday and Sunday Daytime Advertising in USA

Products	Frequency
Cereals	3832
Candy and gum	1627
Cookies and crackers	841
Fruit drinks	582
Macaroni and spaghetti	208
Cakes, pies, pastry	104
Desserts	80
Citrus	78
Carbonated soft drinks	63
Ice cream	53
Soups	43
Meats and poultry	2
Vegetables	1
Cheese	1
Milk, butter, eggs	0
Vegetable juices	0

37

Once more, industry apologists argue that sweetened cereals, candy, and gum are advertised the most because they are what children *want*. Yes, kids *do* love sweets, but this does not mean they do not like other items as well. It is not an acceptable reason for pushing so many products made with high amounts of processed sugar. Most children very definitely can and do like healthful foods *if* they are invited to do so. It is simply a matter of attitude and training.

The National Science Foundation Report also seriously questions the role food commercials play in a young child's growth and development. The Foundation agrees with CCMM that most attitudes toward food are established by the age of. six when the child has already formed his or her feelings about what is supposedly "good" to eat. But what most commercials say is good is not necessarily based upon health and nutritional values but upon content, appearance, flavor, or texture. A 1975 NSF survey shows that when youngsters were questioned about general information regarding food commercials (i.e., "What kinds of things do you call 'snacks'?"), seventy-eight percent cited sweets. The Report comments:

> These responses indicate that the children's concept of what constitutes an acceptable snack usually includes those products heavily advertised to them on TV.[38]

The products which are heavily advertised generally are those high in sugar content. Advertisements for fruits and vegetables, unsweetened dairy products, or health foods are noticeably rare.

Yet, large cereal corporations argue that breakfast commercials encourage children to eat breakfast, which many of them do not like to do; and the snack and candy people say that taste and flavor *are* the primary qualities of their products, so that is what needs emphasizing in their commercials. When asked why ads for better eating cannot be provided as well, the following reply is common:

> It is our judgment . . . that the [30-second] television commercial does not lend itself to a constructive learning process. So it is not in itself an efficient means of instructing viewers in a complex and extensive subject such as nutrition.[39]

But if commercials can push cakes and candy, why not fruit and cottage cheese? If they "do not lend themselves to a constructive learning process," why advertise to kids on TV anyway? Why not just stop? All this is very contradictory, and I wonder how much *doubletalk* the public is willing to take.

The very obvious, straightforward answer is that such companies do not wish to educate young viewers about good nutritional habits because their sales might drop. Some argue that eating messages are better directed at parents than children. Why? Five-year-olds who can barely hold a pencil can still learn the basics of a balanced meal. Children are smart enough to handle a little information about food, especially since it is a subject near and dear to their hearts. All that other smacks of condescension toward children. They are capable of a lot more than many people give them credit for, and establishing proper attitudes toward food is critical in a child's early development.

Yet another argument offered by the food industry in support of their actions is that newborn babies respond to sugars and taste stimuli. They call this a sucrose drive for sweet stimulation and say this is why sweetness must be emphasized in their ads. But again: is this necessarily good for a child if carried to an extreme? A child can be attracted to any number of things, some of which may be harmful. This does not mean, however, that we should abdicate our responsibility to teach that child some sort of balance between desire and gratification. We need to teach them that the American Anthem of MORE is not necessarily BETTER.

Not only are certain food products heavily advertised on children's television, but the way to eat as well. A meal of an hour or more is almost unheard of in this country, unless one is willing to pay a lot of money for it at some exclusive restaurant. But who has that much time to eat? Consequently, fast-food chains are a rapidly expanding concern. A recent *Newsweek* article notes that one in every three American food dollars goes to eating out, which represents an $87 billion a year industry.[40] Nearly fifty percent of all women in this country now hold jobs, so Mom is not the only one fixing dinner. On any given day, 132 million Americans eat out, and fifty million families do so three or more times a week. Fast-food chains represent $16 billion in sales each year, and guess who rules the french fries with nearly twenty percent of the market? McDonald's. Is it coincidental that Ronald does his heaviest advertising on TV programs directed specifically toward children?

OVER-THE-COUNTER (OTC) DRUG ADVERTISING

Another area which has received considerable attention from both CCMM and the NSF and which more school curriculums should address is over-the-counter TV drug advertising and its influence on children.

The Council has estimated that some seventeen tons of aspirin are consumed each year in the United States—not to mention many heavier drugs—and they question how much of this is the result of informal television input. We Americans listen to commercials which tell us we suffer from headaches, pains, coughs, chest colds, stomach upsets, eye strain due to smog, smoke, cigarettes, tension, nerves, and so on. The general consensus is that we need to take drugs of every ilk to help us survive the stress of each day. And not only do adults hear these exhortations, but children and adolescents as well. To give some idea how frequently these messages are reinforced, here is a look at OTC drug commercials as they appear on American TV:

OTC: First Nine Months/1976 (networks only, no spot announcements)		
Product	*Number of Ads*	*$$ Spent*
Head remedies, sedatives, and sleeping products	5361	65.4 million
****		
Cough, cold, and sinus medicines	3839	45.9 million
****		
Digestive aids, antacids	1667	27.3 million
****		
Vitamins and tonics	1438	18.2 million
****		
Laxatives	876	5.9 million

41

According to the above figures, we Americans need the most help to sleep and relax. Our natural rhythms apparently are not good enough, and we must have outside aid. The NAB television code *does* prohibit OTC during advertisements on children's programs, but this makes no real difference, because children do not watch exclusively on Saturday and Sunday mornings. Their favorite shows usually are from adult prime-time hours. In 1975, for example, CCMM reported to the Federal Trade Commission that over seventy-six OTC drugs were advertised on many of the top forty TV programs watched by children. Consequently, many youngsters under the age of twelve could be exposed to some one thousand OTC drug commercials in the course of a year's viewing.[42] Moreover, many of these ads have no audio drug warning and frequently written warnings are white on a light background, which makes reading difficult. Even though warnings may be clearly indicated, there is still a learning process called selective obliteration, which means that after many repetitions of the same warning (i.e., "use only as directed," "caution," etc.), these tend to be ignored. The basic thrust of the commercial, naturally, is to use the product. In addition, children see actors using an item and getting better, so there is that positive reinforcement as well. Here is a typical example:

> Close-up of a little boy about four years old with his mother holding a handkerchief to his nose: Kid looking at mother. Move into extreme close-up of kid. He breathes in, instead of blowing out. Kid looks up at Mom again. She continues to hold handkerchief at his nose. Handkerchief flutters as kid blows out through mouth. Kid looks up at Mom again. Kid looks sad. Cut to the product. Cut to the woman's hand with tablets. Woman's hand puts tablets in kid's hand. Dissolve to kid, who's licking ice cream cone. Kid looks up with ice cream on tip of his nose. Cut to the product again.[43]

The implication here is that if the little boy uses the medicine, he will be rewarded with an ice cream cone or something else that is pleasurable. In conjunction with this, the National Science Foundation states:

> Children who are repeatedly exposed to OTC drug advertising— where adult or child role models are "rewarded" for taking medicine—are likely to learn a behavioral response from such ads and to act on that learned behavior at some future time—perhaps to their own detriment.[44]

Again, this is a classic example of deferred learning and the sleeper effect. No immediate change is evident, but attitudinal seeds are being planted for potential growth later on. The trouble with all this is how it affects a child's perception of medication and health in general. Drugs advertised on TV make physical comfort appear readily attainable, but how does this influence a youngster's conception of drug use now and in the future? If he repeatedly receives the message that he needs a pill or that something once taken will cure things quickly, how will the child learn to tolerate even moderate discomfort and to not rely heavily on drugs later in life? Just because children do not go out and buy the drugs themselves does not mean that significant changes in their attitudes toward such items have not occurred. Studies provided by both the NSF and CCMM indicate children do respond to OTC drug commercials by forming certain opinions toward the use of medicine. For example, one NSF investigation reveals that:

(1) Children with heavy exposure to medical advertising perceived people as being sick more frequently and taking drugs more often.

(2) High exposure to medical ads was associated with the child's belief in the quickness of relief after taking some medicine.

(3) High-exposure children worried more about getting sick themselves.

(4) High-exposure children were more likely to 'feel better' after taking medication.[4][5]

Perhaps we should ask ourselves whether some sort of electronically induced drug/hypochondria is on its way or has arrived already. This informal learning about medicine has important, long-term implications because it can affect an individual's behavior throughout life. It should also be of grave concern to those of us involved with young people because of the rampant use of drugs in school. How much of this is related to drug advertising on TV, and to what extent is this shaping attitudes and behavior among our students?

ADVERTISING CODES: WORD VS. DEED

There are, of course, a number of codes regulating children's programming and the commercials that appear on them. The National Association of Broadcasters (NAB) and the National Advertising Division (NAD), two major groups involved, both have guidelines to govern advertising directed toward young people. But the word guideline must be emphasized because these codes are not hard and fast rules which must be scrupulously followed. Quite the contrary: what some of the guidelines say and what happens in reality offers eloquent testimony to how ineffectual they truly are. It also points to some counterstrategic measures we might engage in to provide our students with more information regarding fairness in advertising.

The 1975 NAB code, for example, provides this general statement regarding the technique and format that commercials *should* follow:

> In order to reduce the possibility of misimpressions being created, all information on the characteristics and functional aspects of a product or service shall be presented in a straightforward manner devoid of language and production techniques which may exaggerate the characteristics or functions of a product.[46]

I wonder how long it has been since the writers of the above guideline have watched Saturday morning children's television and all the ads that go with it? How about the commercial for a candy that has people blasting off amid a shower of fruit flavors? Or the Wizard of O singing about wonderful, rounderful noodle-o's? Or Ronald McDonald traipsing around a multiflavored ice cream mountain with his companion, Grimace? Are these straightforward and devoid of methods which may exaggerate or distort the product? Furthermore, special visual techniques such as camera close-ups and animation are frequently used, which can also contribute to the aggrandizement of a product in a child's eyes.

Yet, the NAB code goes on:

> In order to help assure that advertising is nonexploitative in matter, style, and tone, such advertising shall avoid using exhortative language. It shall also avoid employing irritating, obtrusive, or strident audio-techniques or video devices, such as cuts of less than one second in length, a series of fast cuts, and

special effects of a psychedelic nature or other effects which
could over-glamorize or mislead.[47]

That most advertising on children's television is nonexploitative is
hard to accept. Its very nature and purpose is to get children to
want products. Several studies have been provided here which
reveal how vulnerable many children truly are to commercial manipulation. Moreover, loud rock music and other harsh,
rhythmic sounds which children readily respond to are also
frequently employed. One need only watch a few Saturday
morning commercials to know that the intent of most ads aimed
at kids definitely is to glamorize products and their use.

The NAB code also states:

> ... appeals shall not be used which directly or by implication
> contend that if children have a product, they are better than their
> peers or lacking it will not be accepted.[48]

Yet these kinds of results happen, nevertheless. Children often
achieve special distinction simply because they *have* a TV-advertised product, and a large number of other children may then want
it, too. This type of reaction ties in with the status referral
function of TV, and it is a very effective way of influencing
children. It also brings into question problems which may arise
from feelings of lack and deprivation because a child "can't have
what he sees on TV," say, for example, the latest pair of
"designer" jeans. How many teachers, especially in elementary
grades, have watched students look on wistfully at a TV-advertised
product or toy brought to school by a classmate? This sort of
thing *does* affect our job, because we have to combat feelings of
denial and frustration which can occur among the other children.
We need to learn more about these psychological and emotional
effects to become more efficient classroom communicators, and to
help our students deal with their world.

The NAD code echoes the NAB by saying that commercials
directed toward children should be "truthful, accurate, and fair to
children's perceptions."[49] But such criteria are so vague as to lose
all practical meaning. What, indeed, are children's perceptions?
Many people who have worked with kids for years are still trying
to puzzle that one out. Young people are constantly full of
surprises. The NAB code specifically prohibits *direct* advertising-

induced pressure, but how are most children to get the items they see on TV unless they go through Mom and Dad? If a child is old enough, he may have a job or an allowance or some other source of income. But, for many children, they must rely on their parents. The commercials may not say "Needle your folks to death" for some toy, or game, or item of clothing, yet the use of such phrasing as "Wouldn't you like to have this, too?" gets the same basic message across.

The NAD code also states that ads cannot tell children directly to coerce their parents; yet, again, is not this clearly the *indirect* purpose? If children were not supposed to coerce their folks for products, the logical conclusion would be to have no advertising on TV directed toward them at all. The NAD code *does* say that "advertisers are free to encourage children to request products from parents by means other than direct exhortation."[50] But, there is often a very thin line between the two. "Asking" and "begging" are frequently the same to the child who *wants*. Youngsters can and do exert a great deal of pressure on their parents for things they see promoted on the screen.

Moving on to food commercials and the guidelines governing them, the NAB code declares:

> Given the importance of sound health and nutritional practices, advertisements for edibles shall be in accord with the commonly accepted principles of good eating and seek to establish the proper role of the advertised product within the framework of a balanced regimen.[51]

Similarly, the NAD code states:

> Particular control should be exercised to assure that representations of food products are made so as to encourage sound usage of the product, with a view toward healthy development of the child and the development of good nutritional practices.[52]

Again, we must ask: if these people were genuinely sincere, why advertise candy, sugar-coated cereals, and sweetened soft drinks the majority of the time? How can encouraging the use of such products possibly be considered sound nutritional habits? Advertisers talk about representing a balanced diet, but in reality they plug almost pure sugar. It is absolute doublespeak. The average commercial for such items is supposed to occur only once every ten days, but these figures hardly coincide with viewing reality. Many repetitions of the same commercial can often be seen within only a few hours. Just sit down and watch the set some Saturday or Sunday morning.

Yet, the NAB code affirms:

> Commercials for products, such as snacks, candies, gum, and soft drinks, should not suggest or recommend indiscriminate or immoderate use of the product.[53]

Again, this is hard to accept. Many manufacturers of candy bars and cereals would probably be quite happy if lots of children ate nothing else. The frequency and sophistication of their ads demand this conclusion.

How is the public to react to such discrepancy between word of code and deed of advertiser? Both the NAB and NAD talk about the ethical responsibility posed by TV and children's viewing, yet Saturday and Sunday mornings are not exactly a stellar example of being concerned about "kids." There are a few PSAs encouraging good eating habits, but they are very brief, jazzy tunes lost amidst the general thrust of "eat candy, chew gum, and BLAST OFF!" Many people may not realize that an individual can become as addicted to processed sugar as to some drugs and can go through very definite withdrawal symptoms. These commercials for sugary products may be building damaging eating habits which are not healthy for youngsters and which may be very difficult to break later in life. Moreover, a child who eats large amounts of sugar and carbohydrates will not work as efficiently in school as the child who follows a balanced eating regime. The informal teaching young people receive about food from television prior to entering school can have a real impact on their classroom performance.

MARKETING RESEARCH TECHNIQUES: HOW THE PROS DO IT

Yet while the politicking and hyperbole continue, the tactical warfare conducted on children's marketing research continues to grow more and more intense. The preceding pages provide some background information on what nonindustry sources have discovered regarding the impact of children's advertising, but this pales in comparison to the research conducted by Madison Avenue and other key advertising centers. There is now a tremendous interest in children's advertising and the profits to be made from this sector of the general public—and not just in America, but around the world as well. Specialized marketing agencies are currently probing the various youth markets in their efforts to develop successful advertising strategies; there are numerous such agencies in New York City alone.

But the way many of these companies formulate their battle plans is questionable at best. Robert Choate, former CCMM chairman, has testified before U.S. Senate Committees how children are often used as "guinea pigs" in ad research. He states:

> Today, in motivational research houses across the country, children are being used in laboratory situations to formulate, analyze, polish, compare, and act in advertisements designed to make other children salesmen within the home. Armed with one-way mirrors, hidden tape recorders, and unobtrusive video recorders, professionally trained psychologists and experts in child behavior note every motion, phrase, and other indication of the children's responses.[54]

The comments below further reveal how many advertisers perceive young people in their attempt to capture attention and purchasing power:

> (1) When you sell a woman on a product and she goes into the store and finds your brand isn't in stock, she'll probably forget about it. But when you sell a kid on your product, if he can't get it, he will throw himself on the floor, stamp his feet, and cry. You can't get a reaction like that out of an adult.

> (2) A recent report on "How Race Affects Children's TV Commercials" indicates that black children respond better to advertising directed specifically toward them. The authors of this study conclude, "The investigation hopefully will generate increasing interest in the opportunities posed by the existence of a black children's market which eagerly awaits efforts specifically designed for it." (In other words, market exploitation.)

> (3) If you expect to be in business for any length of time, *think of what it can mean to your firm in profits if you can condition a million or ten million children who will grow up as adults trained to buy your product as soldiers trained to advance when they hear the trigger.*[55] [italics added]

In this respect, television acts as the Great Equalizer. It does not matter whether children are black or white, rich or poor, as long as they (or their parents) have money and are capable of being influenced. The youth audience is looked upon as so many buying soliders; not individuals, not developing minds, just a *market to be tapped*.

Some advertisers talk about the herd instinct of young children and how they do not have separate opinions but tend to group themselves around a leader (a phenomenon referred to as behavioral contagion). It is rather ironic that sociologists and other researchers will spend years testing for what appears to be the obvious—violence and its effects; commercials and their impact— while advertisers often base their hunches and plans on a sample of only a few dozen children. They have learned to generalize from the particular. Ad men reason that two or three groups of youngsters will probably tell them whatever they need to know about a given product. A person could test and retest and only learn what was found out the first time. In this way, advertisers move swiftly, whereas psychologists and behaviorists often get bogged down in their own methodology. Ironically, it is the advertisers who often possess a greater *intuitive* feeling for human behavior than many specialists in the fields of psychology, sociology, and education!

Another research technique employed by advertisers involves using children in movie theaters where a sample of several hundred youngsters is available. Cards with pictures of toys, games, and so on with no words are distributed to the children, and they are asked to mark what item they would like to win as a prize. The children see a film or presentation regarding certain products and are asked to mark again the item they would most like to have. If the choice is the same the second time, the advertisers know they have a product with good sales potential. This test is effective for filtering out those items with poor marketability and those which are particularly good.

These concentrated efforts to find out what kids think and how they respond are then translated into specific merchandising offensives called promotions. With Barbie, the promotion was to sell her not as an ordinary doll, but as a fashion model, an imaginary personality with whom a little girl could identify. So the way a product is promoted becomes as important, if not more so, than the product itself. Children may not even care to have a specific toy; but, if it is promoted well, they can be persuaded to change their initial opinion regarding the product. Here, for example, is a typical scheme used for launching a new cereal:

"Moonstones" is built around moon-based characters called "Moonbeams"—the good guys who work on the light side of the moon—and the "Moonbums"—the bad guys living on the dark side of the moon and who are continually trying to "get their dirty hands on" the secret cereal formula . . . (NOTE: The in-pack premium is a moonbuggy, and the package contains a T-shirt offer.)[56]

In this gimmick, as with many advertising campaigns, a complete, little story unfolds. It plays upon dramatic, emotional effects (good vs. bad) and also encourages children to want the product because of the premiums offered. Such offers are a frequent ploy to entice kids to want a specific product; quite often they go for the prize rather than the product itself.

Yet, this is only the beginning when it comes to getting at young people. The following article describes another method American advertisers and merchandisers use to push their profits, and it further accentuates how central products are becoming in our culture.

Toymakers Hitch Hopes to the Ratings . . .

As this season's television programs skyrocket to popularity or plunge to oblivion, so will the hopes of toy manufacturers. Toys of every description tied to network television programs crowded shelves at the Dallas Spring Toy Show . . . There were Fonzie coloring books, Starsky and Hutch pistols, Kojak cars, and Bionic Woman secret code puzzles.

"Toy companies are capitalizing on television exposure to sell their products," says Dick McGrail of H-G Toys, Inc. His products included puzzles, bulletin boards, poster kits, and police items based on seven current TV shows . . .

Says McGrail, "We've been lucky because we have a man in Los Angeles who does nothing but keep tabs on new and proposed shows . . ."

The article continues:

Gene Churchill, president of Southwest Toy and Hobby Assn., admits he has had some losers but the "successes have been terrific. We have a plastic model of Fonzie and his motorcycle which we have sold out through next February . . ."

Toy manufacturers buy rights from the programs' producers, allowing them to market an item based on the show's name and its stars. Jeff Lewis, Southwest representative of LJN Toys, Ltd., said many companies are buying licenses with money that once went into TV advertising. "It's a whole new way of using the TV medium. The show becomes your advertising . . ."[57]

In effect, there is double reinforcement of the commercial pitch because both show and actor do the selling, *not just the commercials*. The children get twice the advertising input, and their TV heroes become just another batch of salesmen in the home.

Then, only a few weeks later, came this:

Harvard Panel Hits Children's TV Ads

Young television watchers are being used as advertising bait to bolster toy and junk food sales at the expense of their minds and bodies, a panel of experts charged this week. Doctors, government officials, and private citizens said that tighter regulations were needed to safeguard children against false or deceptive TV commercials and potentially hazardous products . . .

Others criticized the advertising industry for taking trivial objects, like action dolls or breakfast cereals, and making them seem important in children's eyes . . .

The article then turns to industry representatives and their defense:

Broadcasters, toy manufacturers, and advertising agencies did not go unrepresented at the symposium. Squire Rushnell, vice president of children's programming at ABC, said, "I have never seen a commercial on my network that I would object to as a parent." Melvin Helitzer, president of a New York advertising firm, warned that too much regulation "strikes at the heart of our constitutional heritage."[58]

And so it goes. Mr. Rushnell's attitude is similar to the local booster in "Jaws" who led his own family out into the water to *prove* there was no shark. And it is interesting to compare Mr. Helitzer's call for "protection of our constitutional heritage" with some of the things he has written in his book, *The Youth Market: Its Dimensions, Influence, and Opportunities for You*[59] (co-author, Carl Heyel). The battleground between children, products, and parents is clearly drawn:

> Children, just like their parents, are highly status conscious. Commercials that appeal to the desire for stature in the child world are highly effective. Children respond to appeals that carry the promise of making them a better person, or smarter, or stronger, or someone that is growing up faster than other kids ... the idea [of being the first kid on the block to own such and such] is a tested and proven persuader. Every child strives to get an edge ... one-upmanship is far from being an exclusively adult phenomenon.

Regarding how to select the "right" character for a product promotion, Helitzer and Heyel comment:

> In our opinion, if you want to create your own hardhitting spokesman to children, the most effective route is the superhero/miracle worker. He certainly can demonstrate food products, drug items, many kinds of toys, and innumerable household items ...

And how is this superhero defined?

> *The character should be adventurous, and he should be on the right side of the law. A child must be able to mimic his hero—James Bond, Superman, or Dick Tracy—to be able to fight and shoot and kill without punishment or guilt feelings.* [italics added]

To be able to fight, shoot, and kill without punishment or guilt feelings? An interesting instructional goal, to say the least, and one which sounds curiously foreign to the glowing rhetoric of the NAD and NAB codes to protect children against exploitation, superiority claims, and violent, unsafe acts.

As for interfamily relationships, Helitzer and Heyel write:

> Children can be very successful naggers. By and large, parents quite readily purchase products urged upon them by their youngsters. In *Helitzer Advertising Research*, it was found that a parent will pay 20 percent MORE for an advertised product with child appeal—even when a less expensive, nonadvertised product is no different.

They continue:

> Mothers surveyed indicate that because their children ask for specific products and brands, they spend an average of $1.66 more per household weekly. Thus, "child-power" adds at least $30 million a week, or $1.5 billion annually to grocery retail sales—just to make Junior happy.

Is it possible that Junior could be as happy with a little less? Finally, Helitzer and Heyel predict:

> With the direct visual medium provided by television, manufacturers of such products as food, drugs, toiletry items, and clothing can advertise and sell as effectively to these youngsters as can the makers of candy, gum, toys, and games . . .

Their suggestion to win more shares of the market:

> . . . *The biggest mistake being made in basic advertising strategy today is aiming exclusively at the parents of this market segment, with adult appeals that sail completely over the youngsters' heads.* [italics added]

So much for the constitutional heritage of children. Apparently, they are now considered the most important group in the whole advertising/merchandising chain. The rationale seems to be this: Forget about Mom and Dad and go for the kids! Yet, as one critic warns:

> Current practices in advertising and in motivational research . . . indicate the industry's concept of children is shifting yet again. Preparation is being made for the final step in the process of changing the focus of commercial television from adults to children. *The idea is developing that children may be the best targets of advertising for adult products.*[60] [italics added]

It appears that children in this country will no longer be children. They will simply be small adults, exposed to adult products in an adult world. Their age will not matter, only their ability to influence purchase behavior. What does this say about the structure of our society, and how we teachers are to cope in a product-oriented world? Are kids now the main target for consumption under such a regime? Are parents that much out of control over what goes on with TV in the home, and have material objects truly gained such supremacy in our lives?

PUBLIC REACTION AND POSSIBLE CHANGE

Though the above examples of industry attitudes appear grim, the struggle between children and advertising is not completely lost. There are those concerned about the welfare of young people, and the public's attitude toward children's television commercials seems to be changing. Consumer action groups, such as CCMM, Action for Children's Television, the National Association for Better Broadcasting, Coalition for Children and Television, certain sponsors, and the Federal Trade Commission, among others, have spoken out against child exploitation via the TV screen. The battle over consumer rights will undoubtedly be a long and hard one in this country, for the economic interests are great and deeply entrenched. But at least people are beginning to work for some sort of policy change in an area which has been virtually untouched since television began.

Action for Children's Television

Some of the most consistent efforts made on behalf of better children's programming and advertising have been led by Action for Children's Television. ACT was formed in 1968 to try to improve the content of children's shows and to reduce the amount of commercials in their programs. In 1970, ACT submitted a petition to the Federal Communications Commission (FCC) requesting rulemaking regarding television for young people in the hope of bringing about some change. ACT wanted the FCC to require stations to air at least fourteen hours of children's programming each week and to bar all advertising on such shows. One year later the FCC issued a Notice of Inquiry and Proposed Rulemaking to investigate the claim of exploitative advertising practices. The options available to the Commission at that time included:

> (1) Imposing rules to curtail certain children's advertising and programming practices, such as host selling, using violence to advertise products, and/or establishing standards for commercials (i.e., the amount of advertising, hours of children's programming, and so forth).
>
> (2) Eliminating advertising from children's shows and developing more programming requirements for young people as part of the public service obligations of commercial broadcasters.
>
> (3) Initiating no policy changes based upon the assumption that the problems could be worked out through industry self-regulation.[61]

While all this went on, ACT submitted a revised version of its petition. Yet, the most important clause—the one stating that there should be no advertising on children's television—was omitted. Since the original FCC Notice of Intent and Inquiry in 1971, the NAB code has been amended *six* times but not in the direction of the ACT petition. As one person writes:

> Since the publication of the ACT petition, the broadcasting and advertising industries have responded with a continuing series of self-regulatory programs in an attempt to divert, delay, or dilute possible public policy action . . . proposals for self-regulation often function as a substitute for more restrictive externally imposed standards or policies.[62]

It is ironic indeed that the result of the ACT petition ended years later in a statement by the FTC "discouraging" the use of promotional devices in ads directed at children. Former FCC Commissioner, Nicholas Johnson, who anticipated this outcome, commented:

> . . . This is simply another case of due-processing [ACT] to death. It is Kafkaesque that after twelve months, after fifteen volumes of comments, all this commission has to tell concerned parents is that "we have reached no conclusions, tentative or final, on the desirability of a rule."[63]

Federal Trade Commission

Though the 1970 ACT petition did not bring about any significant policy changes regarding children's advertising, the problem of fairness in advertising directed toward youngsters was at least made more public, and the cause ACT started has not abated. If anything, it has grown even more visible with lawsuits and allegations flying back and forth between the public and business. FTC member Michael Pertschuk has been particularly vocal about children's advertising and other vulnerable audiences, such as the deaf, elderly, and non-English speaking people. Says Pertschuk, "We have a concern for ads directed at children, particularly when they deal with food, because of the health implications involved . . ." He also adds, "Centuries of common and statutory law give evidence that commercial exploitation of children is repugnant to a civilized society."[64]

But Pertschuk has received much criticism from advertisers and Congressmen alike. A House Appropriations Subcommittee actually voted to stop the FTC's inquiry into sugar advertisements directed at children. Eventually, the investigation was allowed to continue, but only after Pertschuk had been removed as the Committee's head. Months later, however, after a court reversal, he was reinstated on the probe. The whole situation appeared to be not so much aimed at fact-gathering and policy statement as fact-stalling and committee sabotage. Finally, the FTC investigation was scuttled altogether in another victory for the pro-business, pro-broadcasting camp.

Sugared Breakfast Cereals

One of the biggest areas of contention in this public warfare revolves around sugared breakfast cereals. ACT has filed against Ralston Purina for one of its commercials because they feel the spots use a variety of sophisticated photographic techniques to emphasize the sweet, snack-food characteristics of the product. ACT argues that the implicit message of the TV ad is that it is nutritionally all right to eat cookies for breakfast. They believe such techniques are unfair and deceptive because they are designed to confuse the child as to the nature of the product. Another suit involving questionable children's advertising cites General Mills and the 1976 Olympic Decathlon champion, Bruce Jenner. The White Collar Crime unit of San Francisco's district attorney's office accused the company of false statements. The unit was skeptical that Jenner has been eating Wheaties as his Olympic training food since childhood. (Jenner, however, has since appeared on television confirming his use of Wheaties.)

Naturally, the cereal companies have not taken all this lightly and are fully prepared to defend their market interests. General Mills has declared the FTC's posture on kidvid sweet ads "a backward step in the cause of good nutrition" and claims that its advertising to children "has been and is truthful."[6][5] General Mills has also charged the FTC with "disregarding completely the persuasive and factual data presented to the commission by child advertisers." The cereal corporation asserts its commercials help parents learn about the needs, wants, likes, and dislikes of their children, and Kellogg Company has already taken out newspaper ads to rebut the growing attacks.

But the cereal companies have other battles to wage because the American Dental Association has also joined the fight. They have accused Kellogg of misleading the public in a national advertising campaign that "tends to obscure the essential truth that children consume far too much sugar."[66] Kellogg has responded by saying they may sue the ADA for false statements about the company and its products, but the dentists' group believes that advertising for presweetened cereals *does* mislead children. To suggest that "sugary foods don't contribute substantially to tooth decay" is, in their minds, patently false. Kellogg, however, cites studies which indicate sugar breakfast cereals are highly nutritious and do not increase dental decay in children. So the skirmish grows more heated daily, and the war zone between consumer and advertiser rights appears substantial. Millions of dollars are at stake, to say nothing about some health factors of this country's children.

IN CONCLUSION

Obviously, the question of advertising to young people—as most issues in broadcasting—is fraught with diverse opinions and is extremely volatile. While the moneyed interests and citizens' groups engage in open contest, the FCC is mired in the middle, trying to weed out some sort of path between industry economics, consumer welfare, and the "public interest." Yet, the fight appears very lopsided. Broadcasters and advertisers have vast sums of money and manpower behind them ready to fight public attacks, and one wonders how some loosely affiliated consumer action groups could possibly hope to command enough funds to wage war against the momentum of networks and ad agencies.

It must be noted that being able to present products and ideas to the public for their selection or rejection is good. Consumption is a legitimate activity for children, *if* they are educated enough to understand the nature of advertising techniques and possible pitfalls involved. There *is* value in children being exposed to commercials and knowing what to expect from the world they are growing into, which is more and more a consumer's market. As one programming director states:

I am dead set against taking children's advertising out of television and NOT because of the economic reasons. Television survived taking cigarette commercials off and it would survive taking children's advertising off. But I think it is the worst thing you could do for children . . . You create one more little euphoric world where the big, bad guy does not exist. The biggest problem a lot of kids have today is adjusting to reality, surviving in that big, mean world in which we all live.[67]

In our efforts to protect children from unfair exploitation—as with the issue of TV violence—we must be wary not to protect them too much. Very young children certainly are quite vulnerable, but after the age of about eight, they begin to clarify their own ideas and impressions. They are going to see a lot of commercials, and they should learn how to judge them critically. And this cannot be accomplished by pretending advertisements do not exist or wanting them to go away.

What kind of negotiations or compromises can we hope for to counter the tremendous pull of informal television instruction? It is a question of education: how we go about exposing children to the world in which they will soon be adults. Not all advertisers are ogres out to entice unsuspecting children, just as all teachers are not bumbling incompetents, nor all politicians corrupt self-seekers. We must be cautious that public concern does not go too far the other way, condemning the good with the bad. The fact that material objects are assuming greater significance in a person's life than feelings and thought processes may upset me as an individual and utterly dismay me as a teacher; but, in the long run, my personal opinion does not matter. What *does* matter is that we equip our young people with the tools necessary to make varied choices and to carry on their side of the battle in an intelligent manner. The need for more consumer education at home and in school is as important, if not more so, than any single suit against exploitative advertising or the FTC's investigation into Saturday/ Sunday morning kidvid. This would not be retreating from the problems and issues described here, but rather challenging them head-on. Perhaps the best way we can prepare young people to judge and evaluate for themselves is by explaining to them the techniques of persuasion; different ways of influencing consumer behavior; how people react; subliminal suggestion; and so on. At least this way, we could help them make more meaningful and studied choices. Using such learning tools in the classroom could help counterbalance some of the informal advertising curriculum offered by TV.

Certainly, it would be naive to discount the immense forces and drives which motivate the broadcasting and advertising industries or their intense desire to guard television as a so-called "free" medium. Since commercials in this country are here to stay, the problem becomes one of how we can work toward a balance between seeing what is available and being unduly manipulated and inundated. To watch commercials presenting new home computers, complete with keyboard printouts, or a special video recorder capable of taping almost anything is an amazing thing. But to see talking shirts, dancing detergent bottles, hopping doughboys, and tires affectionately known as "foxy slippers" over and over again is something else entirely. Is there no room for fair and intelligent agreement somewhere?

To begin negotiations between the consuming public and the world of TV, one executive producer has suggested:

> I think what we have to do is aim for better sponsors. I think commercials have their place; and listen, they pay the bills. As far as I am concerned, this [commercial television] IS public broadcasting . . .[68]

There is a good chance that different sponsors could have an impact on the face of children's television. As indicated in Chapter Two, some companies are withdrawing advertising money from violent programs, and this is bringing about change. But why don't the producers and distributors of more nutritious foods, special books for children, or places to go and see new things advertise more on the tube? Are network time prices too expensive for these people? Are they being discriminated against because they cannot afford the TV price tag? Or, are special "deals" set up between the networks and *existing* advertisers which preclude others from breaking into and using the medium?

Another compromise would be to put commercials on more of a rotational basis. This way advertisers would not be competing so much for certain shows and times with high ratings; they simply would purchase a specific amount of time for product promotion. Commercials for all age groups could then be moved around the weekly schedule. A company might have ads appear on Tuesday night; then Thursday afternoon; then again on Sunday; and so on. This would also be one way of lessening the dictatorship of the ratings. But it is highly unlikely that this type of change will happen without outside pressure.

In all this controversy about advertising and children, the center of debate generally revolves around the problem of unfair practices, abusive techniques, and potential health and safety factors. Certainly, these are important issues, and dialogue here is vital. Yet, there is another area which is even more crucial, particularly from an educational point of view, and this is the way ads are placed during the programs themselves. It is quite possible that the constant commercial interruption is wreaking havoc to an entire nation's attention span—young and old alike. I have worked in elementary schools, in junior high schools, and in high schools; and at every level I have been impressed at how difficult it is for the majority of students *to attend, to listen, and to concentrate.* This is not solely TV's fault. There are many things in today's society which distract and demand attention besides the tube. But I do believe that television may be playing a large part in this trend. The present set-up of eight to ten minutes of programming followed by numerous disjointed commercials, then more programs, then commercials, could be conditioning people to have shorter and shorter periods of thought. This is diametrically opposed to what teachers—and education as a whole—should try to encourage in students: to expand and extend thought; to sustain questioning and reasoning over greater and greater lengths of time.

When I asked one advertiser how he felt about the shortened attention spans in this country, he remarked:

> Yes, absolutely, I think we have a whole society of people with shorter attention spans. With fifty hours of viewing per week and 97 percent of the houses in this country having televisions and some 75 percent having multiple sets—literally our society has

changed its focus, and I think absolutely the attention span has
been altered.[69]

The disruptive nature of commercial television may be having a
profound impact on the mental/emotional structure of both
children and grown-ups. Such constant interruption of thought
cuts down on the mind's ability to attend to cognitive tasks.
Rather than working toward cohesion, advertisements work in the
opposite direction: show/action/commercial/commercial/com-
mercial/split/action/show/commercials *ad infinitum*. It is a ten-
minute world, always leading up to a product merry-go-round.
Every few moments we are talked at, pleased with, cajoled, and
encouraged to go out and BUY! How does this affect our nervous
system or anxiety and frustration levels? Is our ability to focus
becoming impaired because we are losing the capacity to listen, to
be patient, and to wait? Imagine reading a novel and having
someone call on the phone or knock on the door every five pages
trying to sell you something! It truly is enough to push an
individual's tolerance to its breaking point. How does this affect
an individual's learning ability or his behavior in general? How
might this, in turn, alter our job as teachers and the instructional
techniques we employ in school? We expect children to sit and
listen, but perhaps this is becoming harder and harder for many
young people, due to the informal psychic agitation offered in
plenty by their television screens. Are the falling literacy scores we
hear so much about in America due in part to this strange
oscillation between action-drama, situation comedy, and commercials, commercials, commercials?

These are the subtler areas of television's influence that must be
considered: the breaking up of reality into so many disparate
items and messages that perceiving unity becomes harder and
harder. In a way, commercials represent violence to the mind, as
much as aggressive heroes and TV crime shows do to feelings and
social behavior. We may be altering our ability to listen and think
clearly. We must ask ourselves—as psychologists, school administrators, and teachers—whether people are being channeled informally from seeing wholeness and investigating complexity. Such
programming may be very beneficial for a commercially-oriented

society which promotes things over thoughts and ideas, but it is disastrous for democracy, which stands or falls according to the ability of its citizens to think and to have informed opinions.

How can we in education work toward something more helpful to the collective intelligence and imagination of the American public? What classroom/TV detente might we employ? One way of lessening the disruptive influence of television commercials would be to encourage cluster rather than pod advertising. Clustering ads would group sales pitches at the beginning and/or end of a show but not interrupt the program while in progress unless it were a very long one. The viewer might have more commercial minutes at one time but then would be done with them for twenty or thirty minutes. This is the pattern used by the Independent Television Network in Great Britain and is very successful. It is a technique that could be applied to children's special programming and weekend kidvid in America.

Most advertisers, however, would consider such a suggestion as folly at best and sheer heresy at worst. They undoubtedly would fiercely guard pod advertising because they can interrupt our involvement while it is building. Advertisers *want* to get us at precisely that moment when we are involuntarily absorbed, for we are more vulnerable to commercial suggestion *at that time*. We are frustrated, then offered material objects to assuage that frustration. This constant start/stop is nothing more than influence through irritation, and we must consider what this continual *lack* of fulfillment is doing to us on a subconscious level.

It has been said that skepticism and distrust are the results of a society run amuck with salesmanship, and this certainly puts America in an equivocal light. What other country in the world has managed to SELL the way America can sell or refined the art of psychic pressure into such neat TV spots? This emphasis on things and the desire to own objects may be one of the contributing factors to some of the social malaise which we see in the classroom and which many generally attribute to aggressive television programs. By constantly harping on our emotions and what we do not have, a state of perpetual dissatisfaction is set in motion. Young people see so much, so frequently that they cannot have or cannot be that it is possible they will reach a point where defeated longings break out for all they are unable to possess. Could it be that TV commercials produce expectations and aspirations that can never be fulfilled? Just the desire itself being forever tantalized?

We must also consider what impact the repeated negative reinforcement implied by commercials has on us and our students, for we constantly are being told that we need something or lack something, and so on. This could result in a desire for approval and acceptance which can never be met, because the marketplace says there is always something else to need or somewhere left to go. Aggression and emotional upset may stem from this aspect of television and the pattern of interruption and irritation which advertising employs. In this respect, the commercial curriculum on TV may be as antisocial a force as a preoccupation with violence.

In the final analysis, however, these thoughts and suggestions should not obscure the fact that lobbyists in this country for powerful vested interests are in control, regardless of what effect this commercialism and psychic disruption may be having on the general public. Witness, for example, the demise of the FTC investigation. Even the writers of the *National Science Foundation Report*, though their study presents some damaging evidence regarding commercial influence, state they are "loathe to say anything bad" about children's advertising in general without extensive empirical proof.[70] They furthermore state that "no policy-relevant conclusions" can be made at this time. *Why not?* Are such statements merely more red herrings to throw us off the track, similar to the coverage of the *Surgeon General's Report* on violence? How much justification is needed to prove what is really intuitively *obvious* anyway? Are we *that* out of touch with human behavior and reactions? Or do we simply not care enough about what all the commercial input may be doing? How are we to react to the fact that on at least one documented occasion in 1963, when the FCC attempted to control excessive commercialism on television, the NAB actually opposed the plan and organized committees in each state to lobby against its own code![71]

As always, there are more questions and problems than answers, but it is important to explore the questions. The push toward materialism and consumption begins at a very early age in this country and should be a hotly debated issue in our schools. In comparison to the interest in the impact of television violence, the field of consumer education via the TV screen has received scant notice, though there is some indication this now is changing. In a country as commercially oriented as America, however, the influence of advertising merits much greater attention, particularly in the classroom among students, as *they are now the prime targets for TV ad manipulation*.

I suppose, ultimately, it is a matter of values, which not many people may wish to confront. Perhaps we might find that America does not have too many—except for amassing money and having "fun." But if a property owner can be held liable for an "attractive nuisance," perhaps we could apply the same criterion to TV advertising. Perhaps we *are* being unfairly tempted—especially the children. Perhaps there *is* more subliminal impact from commercials than many of us realize. As indicated earlier, there is a growing movement within the American advertising industry to concentrate exclusively on the child audience as a terrific dollar source. The children of this country may be the last rich source open to full commercial exploitation. The recent advertising blitz on TV for "designer" jeans—directed largely at children—is a harbinger of more to come. How should we educators react to this? What should we tell parents who complain about all the things their children want? Maybe we could offer them special counseling programs regarding TV commercials, and the way they work, or encourage parents to consider monitoring the advertising input their children are subjected to as well as the programs. In the long run, such activities might do a lot of good for both the adults and their children.

Finally, Marshall McLuhan writes that historians and archaeologists will someday uncover the ads of our time and find they are the most faithful source of information about our society. If I were currently teaching English or Contemporary Studies in high school, I would ask my students to write an essay according to the instructions below; it is one combative technique for classroom use in fighting our war against television—between the classroom curriculum and what appears on TV.

> Evaluate McLuhan's statement against the reality of these examples from American television. Why are such fantasy presentations used, and what do they reflect about us and our society?
>
> (1) A man rolling down the highway in his easy chair, praising the comforts of four-wheel drive.
>
> (2) A man masquerading as a glue bottle, coming to rescue a distraught *housefrau* from broken dishes.
>
> (3) A man dressed up in a dog suit, talking to a lady in a supermarket.

Finally, I must ask the reader: Are the above examples of TV advertising *really* as innocuous as they seem? Or, are they, in fact, rather ominous in their ultimate implications?

IV

What's Left After
Violence and Advertising?

AREAS OF GREY

American TV offers such a multitude of disparate images that a wide spectrum of learning experiences is readily available merely by switching on the set. As a source of informal teaching, youngsters can pick up just about anything from the screen: from soap opera to news; from sports to drama; from trivia to national and world events. How many of these themes and images are being informally recorded and absorbed? It is when we enter the region of television's impact on opinions, feelings, and general behavior that it becomes much more difficult to assess precisely how much power the medium truly has. TV may be as forceful a teaching agent in these other learning domains as it is in the realms of violence and advertising.

When analyzing this aspect of the television curriculum, it is again important to bear in mind the concept of incidental/low involvement learning and how it relates to learning from TV. As mentioned earlier, the informal television curriculum has an important advantage over formal classroom presentations because it quite literally can go "straight down the hatch." The student/ viewer is not called upon to perform or give back new material, but *merely to take in what he sees and hears*. That leaves a wide margin indeed for the passive acquisition of TV-promoted information.

For example: in an experiment conducted during the 1960s, a group of school children was asked to pick out enemies of the United States from a list of countries. Oddly enough, Japan and Germany were selected with far greater frequency than one would expect. When these children were questioned later, it was

135

discovered they got their information from TV programs, primarily old war movies. It did not matter to them that the historic portrayals they saw centered around events which occurred two decades earlier. The youngsters merely assimilated the data. They accepted what they had seen on TV as *true*, and it showed up later in their work at school.[1]

How many teachers and parents in America today are having to combat misinformation acquired incidentally from TV? What implications does this type of informal TV curriculum have for our formal classroom procedures? We must remember that this type of television influence can affect a child's development and educational progress as much as excessive violence can alter his social behavior or advertisements can affect him as a consumer. Will a child's view of life be distorted, prejudiced, or just plain wrong because of television's frequent misrepresentations of reality? If he learns something incidentally which is incorrect, will it be easy to unlearn the false information in school? How does the very act of watching TV affect the Piagetian developmental sequence discussed in Chapter One? These points deserve thoughtful consideration from those of us in education because they affect the whole tone and tenor of an individual's life and his later learning career. Alfred Whitehead once wrote, "As we think, so we live," and indeed our attitudes toward life and people in general are the most crucial factors in determining our behavior.

The question is: What has our informal television curriculum contributed to these areas of grey?

AMERICAN TV ENTERTAINMENT: A BRIEF OVERVIEW

Before going into some of the research exploring television's influence on children outside violence and advertising, some words are called for regarding "entertainment" itself and what this means in terms of our TV/classroom battleground.

Attitudes Toward Entertainment

If the average person on the street were stopped and asked what the three most frequent offerings on American television are (excluding commercials), he would probably answer action/adventure, situation comedy, and musical/variety talk shows. This same person then most likely would turn around and classify these all under the rubric "entertainment."

But Shakespearean plays and grand opera are also "entertainment," yet they are hardly the same kind as is usually offered on our TV screens. This is a problem we Americans face when discussing television programming and its instructional implications, because we have grown so accustomed to think of TV material as general entertainment when it is, in fact, light fare of a very specific kind. The vast majority of TV offerings in this country have been and continue to be fantasy/escapist entertainment, *not* the entertainment we get from Othello or Beethoven. Some entertainment, to be sure, can be very engaging and very moving without being escapist, but those who organize TV material in America usually give the broad name "entertainment" to what is only a narrow section of the whole. This is not *always* the case, but generally it is.

Consequently, over the past thirty years, viewers have been exposed with great consistency to fantasy/escapist entertainment and a narrowing of tastes to fit "the average," not entertainment of a more serious, thought-provoking kind or one based predominantly on real life. So when we discuss the impact of television on young people, we are talking about the impact of three decades of fantasy/escapist fare. Even during the mid-fifties, light entertainment constituted approximately seventy-five percent of total TV time, and a brief glance at *TV Guide* today hardly reveals much of a change. Escapist entertainment still dominates the screen. In this sense, TV material has become what one broadcast historian calls a strategy word, for it minimizes the importance of what is presented.[2] Rather, entertainment is there to lull our critical faculties by sending us into the domain of low-involvement learning. It has no meaning, essentially, other than diverting and filling time between commercials.

This brings to mind several questions. With such a heavy diet of fantasy material, where are viewers, especially children and adolescents, to receive a comparable amount of reality presentations? Is it better to get a solid footing in reality or fantasy? Or at least an equal grounding in both? These questions are particularly relevant to preliterate youngsters who cannot read to counterbalance what they see and hear, for they are even more susceptible to informal television influence.

The effect of this fantasy/escapist entertainment has to be different in character and kind than if we had had three decades of plays and dramas from renowned writers; a spectrum of musical offerings; fewer commercials; or more quality programming geared specifically toward children. This is self-evident. TV has been promoted as a window to the world, and in many cases, this has been true. But, in many other ways, it most certainly has not been so, due to the fantasy material which has dominated the screen. One need only look at American TV entertainment over the past three decades to see what a distorted view has been presented as life.

The Sexes and Racial Groups

As far as men, women, and various racial groups are concerned, television in this country has generally shown the following picture:

(1) The most powerful group is the white American male. He usually is young, middle class, and unmarried—and is likely to be involved in violence.

(2) Women make up a smaller proportion of all TV characters, regardless of ethnic background. They usually appear in a sexual context or in romantic roles. Two out of three are married or engaged, though this is now changing.

(3) Women participate less in violence but are victimized more, and if a woman engages in aggression, she is not as likely to succeed as a man.

(4) Women are also cast more frequently in domestic/comedic roles.

(5) Married women are less likely to be victims of aggression. Housewives are not portrayed as villains as much as single women or those who are employed.[3]

It was not until 1968 that the first black series was offered over the TV airwaves. A young child growing up with TV during the fifties might have thought that blacks and other minorities did not exist. Not only were many people and races virtually ignored at TV's inception, but when they did appear, they often were presented as unfavorable stereotypes (i.e., Indians as bloodthirsty drunks or Chinese as cooks, servants, and laundry owners). For nearly three decades, television has concentrated on showing the twenty- to fifty-year-olds, thereby ignoring the very young and the elderly. There has been a constant push in the informal learning domain to telescope all age groups into a young adult market, focusing intently on the NOW.

Themes and Format of Programs

Not only has our escapist TV entertainment centered on specific races and ages, implicitly denying the existence of many other people and life styles, but recurring themes and ideas emerge as well. As indicated previously, violence has been a staple on the American TV screen, but even though it has occurred with mind-boggling regularity as "true-to-life action drama," it still follows the same pattern of unreality. Street crime, for example, has not been as important in the world of TV as it is in real life. Murder and assault have accounted for about fifty percent of all TV crime, yet this is not true of life on the outside. As one can see below, almost a complete inversion has taken place.

Comparison of Television Crimes and Real-Life Crimes

Frequency Ranking of FBI Crime Index from 1970	Frequency Ranking of TV Crimes from 1972
1. Burglary	1. Murder
2. Larceny	2. Assault
3. Auto Theft	3. Robbery
4. Robbery	4. Auto Theft
5. Assault	5. Burglary
6. Rape	6. Larceny
7. Murder	7. Rape

[4]

Generally, crime on American TV has:

(1) overrepresented violent crimes directed against individuals; real-life crime is usually nonviolent and directed at property;

(2) underrepresented blacks, young people, and lower-class individuals involved in crime;

(3) reinforced the moral that crime does not pay; the main intent is to reassure society that right will prevail; in the real world, however, this obviously is not so, for crime often pays quite well;

(4) concentrated on "the hunt" as being all-important rather than the legal processes involved after apprehension;

(5) underrepresented nonwhites as murder victims;

(6) underrepresented violent crimes between family members; and

(7) made crime movies appear simple and easily understood; in real life, this often is not the case at all.[5]

Quite clearly, this picture has little to do with reality, even though it has been presented as "true" life. Yet, how much misinformation is being assimilated incidentally by children who watch a moderate to heavy amount? How much do they accept at face value? A very false image of the world could be in the making, which might be difficult to untangle later on.

TV Employment

Aside from these misrepresentations of various groups and crime in our society, another important aspect of television distortion concerns employment. Not surprisingly, the most frequent form of TV work is law enforcement. Nearly one-third of the American TV labor force at one time or another has been concerned with the pursuit of law and order. In reality, however, only about one percent of the population is so involved; and it is quite possible that this imbalance may be contributing to Gerbner's fear syndrome mentioned in Chapter Two. Jobs associated with entertainment rank second in the world of TV, which is hardly true to life either. Professional workers have been overrepresented, and there has always been that push for a higher socioeconomic status—informal messages consistent with the consuming world of TV. A corresponding underrepresentation of worker roles has been evident, though this is changing. As a source of incidental learning for young people about jobs and work, television provides a very slanted view of what is considered important, which could have serious ramifications in children's attitudes regarding employment later on.

A case in point: when a group of children was questioned about work, they overwhelmingly chose *power* as the most important factor to consider when thinking about employment. Money, prestige, and travel came next; helping others was last. The interesting point here is that these results held for both rich and poor children; urban and rural; male and female; dull and bright.[6] Television's influence was pervasive in all areas of society. The fantasy/escapist material had been successful in changing their attitudes and aspirations toward a career.

Is this a form of programmed discontent? Does television teach unhappiness about work in general by presenting a false picture of the way life really *is*? If a child consistently sees powerful or dangerous jobs cast in glamorous settings, what kinds of ideas will he form about what he wants to be? His informal learning from television may be a source of disappointment and conflict when he finally starts to work, for it is not easy to become rich and powerful. In effect, such portrayals take the child away from the ordinary, which is a very real part of living, a part which needs to be met and dealt with often. How might all this influence his evaluation of work or his choice of job opportunities after leaving high school or college?

These instances of misrepresentation are but a few examples of how television escapist fare has twisted and turned images of life. All this may be obvious to the adult viewer, but how the past thirty years have affected children growing up under TV's powerful, informal gaze is another matter entirely. We are talking about analyzing human reactions and emotions in the area of incidental, deferred learning, which certainly is not an easy task. Yet, the impact of all this may be profound and go much deeper than many of us suspect. Will youngsters who watch a fair amount of television experience some sort of emotional conflict between what their TV twin has learned incidentally over years of living with TV and what they experience in their own lives? Remember: the informal nature of TV learning makes this likely, because information is imprinted so easily on the subconscious. Once the aggression and advertising are removed, there is still a vast array of human experience which has been affected by years of living with TV, one which represents a crucial area of investigation for professional educators today.

THE BRITISH STUDY: MID-1950s

One of the earliest and most comprehensive studies regarding television's influence on children was conducted in England during the mid-fifties by Himmelweit, Oppenheim, and Vince. Even though the medium had been broadcasting only a short time when these people began their research, they rightly assessed its power as an important, informal learning source, especially for children. Among other things, they discovered:

(1) Children liked television and were therefore favorable to what was shown.

(2) They spent a lot of time viewing, and since the values and themes presented were fairly consistent, youngsters received messages which directed their thought in the same general way.

(3) Since television affected two senses at once, it provided more than the same material would if heard on the radio or read in a book.

(4) Dramatizations also helped promote longer-lasting effects because they elicited predominantly emotional rather than intellectual responses.[7]

In addition, Himmelweit, Oppenheim, and Vince noted considerable differences between regular viewers and those who did not watch. They found TV material had a consistent impact on the way children felt about jobs, values, success, and social surroundings. The investigators had not, in fact, expected to find so many differences between viewers and nonviewers, but even they were surprised. The ambitions of TV users and the importance they attached to certain values all were affected in ways which could be traced to TV content.[8] And *this* was in Britain, twenty-five years ago; the exposure of American children to TV today is much *greater*, and the content of programming generally much more escapist!

The British cite a 1955/56 Norwich study to support some of their findings. They discovered that viewers were more eager for ready-made entertainment and had narrower, less mature tastes. A greater number of TV users thought about leaving school at an early age, and few were interested in attending a university. Compared with nonviewers, the TV children had greater need for external stimulation, and their general outlook showed them to be less alert or concerned about social problems. Because of this, Himmelweit, Oppenheim, and Vince felt that viewers would steadily lag behind nonviewers as far as general knowledge was concerned. They also found that viewers were not as interested in creative activities, which tended to be solitary and more demanding in nature, and that they showed aspects of spectatorism—just watching life go by.[9]

In general, it appeared that television profited only the younger, duller child. Other youngsters did not gain much; in fact, they proved a little *less* knowledgeable than those without TV. Himmelweit, Oppenheim, and Vince conclude:

> A new generation is now growing up who will never have known a home without TV . . . such children will grow up in a society in which television and *the conveying of information through television will have become thoroughly accepted and respectable and to that degree possibly more influential.*[10] [italics added]

Twenty-five years later, how much less knowledgeable are today's viewers, young and old alike? How much more do they accept from TV whether it is true or not? Are teachers having to communicate through entertainment simply to enliven their student audiences conditioned by years of TV? These long-range effects from continual exposure should be carefully considered because our young people consume so much TV. They pose a real challenge in terms of teaching techniques, curriculum planning, and general instruction.

THE AMERICAN STUDY: EARLY 1960s

A second major survey regarding TV's impact on youngsters was conducted in America during the early sixties by Schramm, Lyle, and Parker; and, though separated in time and location from the British study, one finds similar evidence.

The Americans thought the sheer amount of time devoted to viewing was impressive. In only a few short years, TV already had come to dominate young people's leisure time. Peak use occurred during childhood, when a youngster "normally" would be out playing, learning communication and physical skills, and how to get along with his peers. A definite shift in the activities associated with growing up was beginning to emerge; even during the late fifties and early sixties, children were consuming television with relentless consistency.

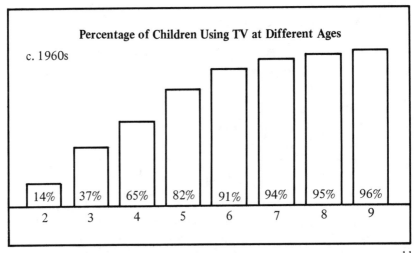

Schramm, Lyle, and Parker discovered other influences as well. Children came to school with larger vocabularies, but this gain diminished through the grades. They knew more about adult life, crime, and violence; and heavy viewers also had more knowledge about things directly related to fantasy/escapist content.

Pursuing this last point in greater detail, the researchers conducted a survey in which they compared heavy and light viewers. They found that the former group knew much less about real events and personalities. The light viewers, however, were able to name more political figures and people in the news. They could also identify more faraway places and important individuals in public affairs. The following chart gives some indication of the disparity between the two groups and what they knew about life.

Heavy vs. Light Viewing Results

Test	Results
Ability to name writers	In favor of light viewers 11/12
Ability to name statesmen	In favor of light viewers 10/12
Ability to name singers	In favor of heavy viewers 11/12
Ability to name band leaders	In favor of heavy viewers 8/11

12

As with the British study, Schramm, Lyle, and Parker found that television mainly benefited the duller child. They provide these conclusions regarding its overall impact on the young:

Amount of Viewing Time	Above Average	Below Average
High IQ	Probably less well-informed than comparable children	Probably better informed if child selects reality shows
Medium IQ	Probably not much difference	Probably not much difference
Low IQ	Perhaps slightly better informed	Probably not much difference

13

Their general opinion: the more time spent with TV, the less well-informed and aware the majority of the viewing public.

TELEVISION'S IMPACT ON A CHILD'S PLAY

One of the most significant areas to consider in relationship to television's impact on behavior is its effect on the play of young children. This area is of particular importance in the field of early childhood education because play is so vital during this developmental stage. It must be emphasized that the word "play" represents more than leisure activity, fun, and games, or something opposed to work; rather, here it connotes *learning through imitative behavior*. As a child watches others, he translates much of what he sees and hears from informal observation into his own actions. In this respect, play is the main job of childhood. It is far more than mere amusement or a time-filler; it is the primary vehicle for learning and development during youth. Play becomes a means of assimilating and testing reality, exercising the imagination, and rehearsing past experiences. In this context, it forms the foundation for deduction and the construction of thought. In discussing television's impact on play, it is important to keep this differentiation in mind, for TV's effect on altering a child's play—making it more violent or otherwise—is one of the most crucial areas to consider in the battle between television and teaching.

Indeed, the evidence compiled regarding TV and children's play reveals some disturbing trends. In one Surgeon General's survey, for example, nearly 300 first-graders were questioned about the medium and how it influenced their thoughts and actions when away from the screen. Some fifty percent said they used things seen on TV as models for play, and solitary play based upon television content was reported by thirty percent of those interviewed.

First-Graders' Use of TV as Models for Play Behavior
"Do you remember if you ever play either by yourself or with friends about things you've seen on TV?"

	By Self	*With Friends*
Often	5%	7%
Sometimes	25%	42%
Not very often	16%	14%
Never	54%	37%

14

In a second Surgeon General's study, over sixty percent of the mothers questioned responded that their youngsters' play was influenced by TV. In a third, slightly more than half of those children interviewed believed the young people shown on TV were like themselves or friends; and nearly sixty percent felt TV personalities were like people they had met.[15] The majority in both age groups thought TV programs generally presented life "as it really is" and accepted what they saw as a basis for their own social interaction.

In conjunction with this, another researcher asked several hundred elementary school students how they would respond in certain play situations. Their choices included:

(1) what they themselves would do;
(2) what was the "right" thing to do;
(3) what their parents would want them to do;
(4) what a best friend would do; and
(5) what their favorite television character would do.

It was found that TV characters were influential models for a sizeable number of boys, particularly in the area of aggressive play behavior. There was also a strong relationship between what a child said he would do in both play and problem situations and what his favorite television character would do. In fact, some of the very strongest similarities were between what the child would do and his favorite TV character.[16] In some cases, television characters actually were more important models for play behavior than parents! The investigator writes:

> The one general conclusion which seems warranted is that favorite characters are seen as behaving quite consistently with the child's description of his own behavior, his judgments of what is right or appropriate, and his perceptions of a friend's behavior. *While evidence of parental influence is apparent, it does not seem as strong as the influence of peers and favorite television characters.*[17] [italics added]

More recently, the National Institute of Mental Health discusses similar findings. Their 1982 report provides one study, for example, which investigates the relationship between children's television viewing and their play behavior. In this particular survey, youngsters who preferred specific television shows, such as cartoons, superheroes, and action-detective programs, used these TV characters as models for play, especially in aggressive and antisocial play. Furthermore, the Report also states that by the age of three, many youngsters demonstrate a great deal of consistency between their play behavior and their television viewing styles and preferences.[18] Apparently, more than a few young people today place a great deal of importance on television and TV characters as models for imitative play.

What kind of impact is this having on a child's play activity or family and school life in general? Are many parents experiencing trouble with their children and wondering why their kids prefer to listen to TV rather than a member of their own family? Are teachers and school supervisors seeing more and more play behavior, both in the classroom and out, based upon TV characters and personalities? The fact that children may be learning more from television people than individuals in real life is a matter of great concern, because the child copies but gets no feedback from his model; there is no dialogue involved. Moreover, ideally in terms of learning theory, children should be out making up their own games and play strategies, not using prefabricated themes or characters from TV. This change in the pattern of imitative play may be hindering the full and rich development of a child's personality and creativity. It represents a profound shift in the way youngsters approach and assimilate reality. As one person comments:

> Television has changed play patterns, and they in turn have altered relationships between friends. In the past, you would wait for a small neighbor to drop by on rainy days, and the two of you would launch some project. Now television has become a kind of playmate substitute and kids are apt to content themselves with watching the tube rather than wandering out in the rain in search of companionship . . .[19]

By using TV as an intermediary for friendship and play, children are not learning how to interact, communicate, or create for themselves; and this can only be detrimental to their growth. All the imagination and talk which comprise a child's play that are neglected because of TV or influenced by TV subtract from the child's own arena of thought, action, and choice. Again, this shift away from personally-inspired play or having play indirectly influenced by TV may have deep-seated effects on an individual's creative imagination, his education, and the process of human communication as a whole.

TELEVISION AND FORMAL EDUCATION

Earlier in this book, I cited some statistics about dropping literacy scores and a decline in general student achievement. Naturally, television is by no means the only culprit in this trend, but many teachers and educators in America today should be more concerned about the medium's role in a child's formal educational career. Indeed, the comments below illustrate how effectively television has penetrated the lives and thoughts of many students and further delineate the nature of the classroom combat zone regarding TV.

(1) Since 1927 I have maintained a private school for children of three to six years. About the middle of November, 1950, my assistants began to observe a change. The children "got" television. Any toy that had any possible resemblance to a gun became one in the free play time; a group barricaded itself in the doll house; another group, armed to the teeth, galloped up and attacked them. For several days I found drawings, all done by the same artist, and complementing some conversation which we had heard about "The Clutching Claw." The children are tired nervously, physically, emotionally, and mentally; they show effects of eye strain; they have acquired erroneous ideas; and their minds are so completely engrossed by television that they have no capacity for learning. They have no sense of values, no feeling of wonder, no sustained interest. Their shallowness of thought and feeling is markedly apparent, and they display a lack of cooperation and inability to finish a task.

(2) Parents seem to welcome [TV] as an easy way of keeping their children entertained. It's no wonder they are bored by school. How can I compete? I have the feeling my pupils expect me to go into a song and dance act.

(3) The programs most appreciated [by the students] seem to be those of substandard quality. As a result, children today are not amused or entertained by anything offered in a classroom unless it parallels this low standard.

(4) To the second-generation TV viewer, interest is something external. It lies outside the mind of the individual. It is a commodity to be acquired rather than nurtured. Boredom is inexcusable, for television teaches that a minimum level of pleasure is always possible and that the viewer need only remain a stationary target to receive it.

(5) I find there is a decrease in imaginative play and an increase in aimless running around ... low frustration tolerance, poor persistence, and confusion of reality and fantasy.[20]

The above are but a few examples of how television has permeated our classroom lives and why its impact on formal education and student/teacher relationships is so crucial a topic in our society.

Reading

One of the most significant areas of television's influence on formal education is its effect on reading. The importance of reading in an individual's education—both in school and after formal instruction ends—cannot be overemphasized. People talk about television being a window to the world, but what TV offers pales in comparison to all that is available through books and the written word.

Yet, it is becoming increasingly difficult to stimulate young people to read today or to convince them of the vital importance reading holds throughout a lifetime for both fact-gathering and entertainment. Their interest in the printed word simply appears to be dying. When teaching in high school, I learned very quickly not to accept any reports on books which were also currently-running movies, either on TV or in the theater. More often than not, students "watch" the book rather than read it. When I spoke with one educator regarding this problem, he declared:

> Think of what fine literature is going by these children! It's really like *Fahrenheit 451*. What these kids are missing today! Let me give you an example: I had a sixth-grade class, and I read them out loud from Howard Pile's *Book of Pirates*, and they absolutely loved it. I had a very old book, and I read it just the way Pile wrote it, which is not in modern English. And these kids would ask me every day to read them that book. Now my eighth-graders write book reports, and guess what some of them were on? "Roots," the television series, *not* the book, and they just put

down that it was a book report. I just wonder what America would be like today and what her students would be like if we didn't have television. Would that put us behind the rest of the world? I don't think so . . .[21]

Teachers and educators are not alone in this assessment. Even an executive producer of children's programs admitted to me that the first thing parents should do today is teach their children where the library is and how to get there on their own steam.

I think children should not be allowed to watch as much television as they watch. It's wrong. It's just wrong . . . I think one of the biggest holes in our lives today is the fact that the library isn't the center of activity anymore.[22]

When I asked another broadcaster about his feelings regarding television's impact on reading, he commented:

Sure I think TV has affected reading. It certainly has. There's no getting around it. I don't know how to stop it from happening. All I can do is handle it in my own household . . . I've made a deal with my nine-year-old daughter that if she wants to see a movie on TV or in the theater, she has to read the book first.[23]

Yet, how many parents and teachers set the same standards for their children at home or in school?

The following charts give some idea how much TV has affected reading among students. To pick up a book—even twenty years ago—was by far the most infrequent choice made by children.

Statistics on Reading and Television/Circa 1958-60			
	Grade 2	*Grade 6*	*Grade 12*
Hours of TV watched per day on average	2.2	2.6	2.3
Number of books read (not completely)	1.1	2.1	1.0

24

c.1960s	Percentage of Media Use		
Medium	*Grade 2*	*Grade 6*	*Grade 12*
TV	62%	60%	46%
Radio	27%	20%	37%
Books	6%	8%	4%

25

In a more recent survey, similar results were obtained: the majority of children did no reading whatsoever. Without a doubt, this is affecting their performance in school and their educational progress. There simply is no way around it.

Number of Books Read	Paperback		Hardcover	
Last Month c. 1970s	*Grade 6*	*Grade 10*	*Grade 6*	*Grade 10*
None	30%	49%	25%	66%
1	17%	22%	17%	16%
2	14%	15%	13%	9%
3	10%	7%	9%	4%
4	8%	3%	10%	2%
5	6%	2%	6%	1%
6 or more	14%	2%	20%	1%

26

The National Institute of Mental Health provides two studies in particular which illustrate a strong negative association between watching TV and reading achievement in school. One investigation, for example, compares sixth graders in homes with constant television exposure (set on all afternoon and evening) to sixth graders from so-called non-constant homes. Results indicate that two-thirds of the youngsters from the constant homes read *below* a fifth-grade level, whereas in the non-constant homes two-thirds read *above* a fifth-grade level. In a second study, young people showed a large negative correlation between the amount of viewing they engaged in before they entered school and their scores on reading as well as arithmetic and language tests in the first grade.[27] The NIMH reports that where extent of viewing is considered, almost all the research has confirmed that children beyond the fourth grade who watch a great deal of television tend to have lower school achievement, especially in the area of reading.[28]

The fact that children are reading less since the advent of television is not all that surprising; on the average, grown-ups are reading less, too. Adult Americans, for example, spend approximately forty percent of their leisure time (based upon 1,200 hours per year) watching TV and less than one percent reading books, and more money is spent annually on thirty-second spot commercials than on the entire book publishing industry.[29] It seems that reading itself is becoming a marginal activity, and it is quite possible that parents who watch a fair amount of TV and do not read may be passing on nonreading habits to their children.

There are other points to consider as well. Not only are young people reading less, but also their ability to comprehend what they read also seems to be diminishing. There appears to be a growing gap between reading words on a page and translating them into understanding; parroting words means nothing unless the individual can assimilate what he reads. Moreover, many TV children want to see the pictures in a book rather than allow their own imaginations to paint a scene. They want to be told or shown rather than explore and create for themselves. As one teacher comments:

> When I read them a story without showing the pictures, the children always complain, "I can't see!" Their attention flags. They'll begin to talk and wander off. I have to really work to develop their visualizing skills . . . Children never needed to learn how to visualize [i.e., how to imagine] before television . . .[30]

Also, many young people today—if they *must* read—prefer books that have pictures and unusual facts, such as *Ripley's Believe It or Not* or *The Guinness Book of World Records*. This kind of book does not require the same mental or emotional response as *Moby Dick*, *Pride and Prejudice*, or more traditional novels and stories. With the former type of book, the reader is not asked to sustain intellect or feeling over long periods of time. He can pick and choose bits and pieces without maintaining intense involvement—

just like switching the channels on a set. No real personal depth or resonance is achieved, which is one of the most valuable by-products of reading in general.

Listening Skills

Not only has television influenced reading, but also it appears to have affected the ability to *listen*, surprising as that might appear at first thought. Today's students often walk into class talking with their friends, and their conversations do not necessarily end at the door or with the bell. They frequently shout out answers without raising their hands, and they interrupt not only the teacher but each other as well. When corrected or admonished for talking too much, many students look up from their desks with bewilderment on their faces, because they are not even aware they have been disrupting the class or speaking out of turn. They simply seem to be accustomed to having TV as background sound, then talking over it, and competing with its incessant noise. They may be so used to speaking above the drone of the set and the constant commercial interruptions that they carry this behavior over into the classroom. Yet, next to reading, listening attentively is crucial to the learning process. Even listening to silence can be productive, but students today find this extremely difficult. It may be unrealistic to think that students will always listen to their teachers, but it is disturbing that they are inattentive to their own peers and treat fellow classmates with such lack of concern. The chances of them learning from each other may be even greater than learning from the teacher. But, in many cases, it is a struggle to get pupils to pay attention to what their contemporaries have to say.

Homework

Homework has also suffered, as all parents know. Again, this is not solely television's fault, yet I believe there is a correlation between watching too much TV and not doing assignments. Prior to television's entrance onto the American scene, most parents expected a certain amount of homework to be completed during a quiet time, either before or after dinner. TV has altered this to some degree. Even in the early sixties, when Schramm, Lyle, and Parker did their study, they found that children who had television in their homes did more poorly in school. The chart below gives some indication why:

Homework and TV	With TV	Without TV
No Homework Done:		
Weekdays	54%	43%
Sundays	92%	69%

31

Today many students go home and make a halfhearted attempt to study or do homework while watching the box. Rather than directing and concentrating their attention on one task, they constantly are tempted to *look at the screen*, watch a few minutes, return to their work, watch again, and so on. Again, this is not television's fault by any means. Parents should be more concerned about allowing their children to do school work in front of the tube. But parental concern on a wide scale does not appear to be evident. For instance, a recent news broadcast discussed a new studying contract developed by a local school between pupils and their parents. One of the most important clauses in the contract involved the parents' promise to demand at least two hours of quiet study time from their children—study time *sans* radio, records, and especially TV. This gives some idea how difficult it is for many teachers today, because thirty years ago such a contract would not have been needed. Now, however, we literally have to compete for a student's attention and get parents to *promise* to keep their kids away from the box.

At the farthest end of the scale are those TV children who do no homework at all. They simply do not seem to care. One teacher, writing in *Today's Education*, discusses a sample survey she made of her junior high school students which illustrates this change. Nearly fifty percent of her second-generation TV learners consistently did not do their homework. Some sixty percent watched television before school, and seventy-five percent watched even *during* the dinner hour. And what was the response to her assessment? Teachers' letters in the next issue agreed four to one with the above description of the "typical" American classroom.[32]

Writing

Heavy television consumption may also be affecting the way students think and approach other learning activities, and this is nowhere more evident than in their writing. When a pupil has to compose an essay, for example, he or she is expected to follow a point-by-point exegesis building to a final conclusion. Today this appears most difficult for many young people. When forced to produce something in writing, it is truly amazing what more than a few come up with. A single paragraph about nothing in particular with no topic sentence or supporting information is supposed to pass for an essay. Their writing jumps around, skips, backtracks, and presents ideas at random with no thought toward order and structure. Yet, these are the same habits of mind that television cultivates: swift cuts to nonrelated material, all chopped up. The constant change of focus demands that the viewer's reference point shift every few seconds. This technique literally programs a short attention span, which in turn affects an individual's ability to concentrate and follow a specific trend of thought. The disjointed essays that many high school teachers receive today may stem in part from this pattern of TV presentation.*

*It should be noted that Marie Winn, author of *The Plug-In Drug*, puts forth an interesting argument about television's impact on writing. Winn believes that TV affects the right hemisphere of the brain, which has to do with spatial and visual concepts, more than it does the left hemisphere, which deals with language and logical thought. Consequently, words themselves may be losing their importance and power to evoke feelings, images, and impressions. Winn feels writing is becoming harder for us because the right side of our brain is getting more input than the left. Hence, the latter may be losing its facility with words and linear thought progression due to lack of stimulation and use.

Play and Formal Education

Discussing TV's impact on reading, listening skills, writing, and doing homework is only the beginning when analyzing its effect on formal education. Some of the findings regarding the medium's influence on a child's imitative play have already been mentioned earlier in this chapter, but its relationship to formal learning must be stressed again here. Play is *so* vital to a child's educational development! This point simply *cannot* be overemphasized, so I hope the reader will forgive the heavy stress placed on this point. Play—and the talk that goes along with it—are the most important avenues of learning during childhood. Through play, a child acquires social skills, develops his imagination, and learns how to manipulate the environment. All these activities in turn affect his formal educational career. When a child watches too much television, his time for play—both group and solitary—diminishes proportionally, and this may hamper learning progress later on.

As indicated previously, many teachers have complained how too much TV has adversely affected the quality of children's play and their creativity, both of which serve important roles in their education. There is one study, for example, which illustrates how heavy television consumption affected several hundred mentally-gifted school children. These youngsters were exposed to three weeks of intensive TV viewing, and tests conducted before and after the experiment reveal a marked drop in all forms of creative play ability.[33]

In conjunction with this, the National Institute of Mental Health reports comparable findings. They cite several studies reviewing television's impact on creativity and the imagination which provide some disturbing results. In one study, children's comprehension of a story was compared when either read to them or seen on TV. The children (ages seven to 12) who saw the TV version remembered more of the story action but relied more on actual visual presentation for information and thought. They did not formulate new ideas or material for themselves. The children who listened to the story, however, recalled more of the vocabulary and drew more inferences based not only upon the content of the story but their own general knowledge and personal experience as well. They also asked more questions and made more comments about the story than the TV group.[34]

In another NIMH study comparing print, audiotape, and videotape presentations, there was a distinct difference in the capability of each medium to stimulate or inhibit creative, imaginative thinking. Children who watched the videotape solved problems only on the basis of facts and concepts that were presented to them. They did not infer or create new patterns of thought. Those who listened to the audiotape or read the material, on the other hand, gave more "stimulus-free and transformational ideas."[35] In other words, they thought and imagined more of their own making. Indeed, the National Institute of Mental Health reports that the majority of evidence suggests heavy TV consumption is associated with lower imagination and creativity, especially under unsupervised viewing conditions.[36]

It seems that what a child misses out on when he is watching TV may be even more significant than what he sees and learns incidentally from the screen. He may spend less time on play and interpersonal conversation through which he can practice sensory discrimination, motor coordination, and social skills—activities which form the basis of early education and which will affect performance in later school years. A child cannot overlearn these skills, but a reduction in the amount of time he spends practicing them may interfere with their internalization.

There have been other studies using monkeys to monitor the relationship of play to learning and social behavior. Those animals who were play-deprived were more hostile and aggressive and consequently less "teachable" than the ones who were allowed to interact.[37] The monkeys who did not play had not learned the "rules and regulations" by which their society functioned and therefore did not know how to respond when on their own. They simply were at a loss how to behave and interact constructively. The results of these tests with monkeys can be related to children and TV. The fact that television cuts down on the amount of time a child spends doing such things as playing with toys and talking with friends and family or riding a bike may bring about very serious educational as well as social and physical problems.

Eleanor Maccoby, whom I mentioned earlier, estimated that as much as one and one-half hours a day had been shifted away from creative play and conversation to watching TV even during the early and mid-fifties. Just imagine the tremendous time realloca-tion today when children watch up to six hours daily or the cumulative effect of this time redistribution! As Maccoby asks:

> Are children substituting TV for other fantasy activities which are essentially similar in their function, or does TV watching represent a major shift in the nature of children's activ-ities? ... Reading books or comics, listening to radio stories, watching movies, and watching television have in common the fact that the fantasy experiences the child has while engaging in these activities are almost entirely externally controlled ... In contrast to externally controlled fantasies are such activities as coloring, playing, working on hobbies ... all of which are in some sense creative.[38]

Instructors and administrators must ask what kind of long-range educational ramifications this time/activity shift may have. Twenty-five years later, how much more energy is taken away from talking and playing; studying and listening; school and books, in favor of the box? It is hard to believe that many children in America now spend five to six hours a day *watching*, but it is happening nevertheless. Yet, this means thirty-five to forty-two hours a week spent *not* running, *not* playing, *not* interacting, *not* day-dreaming, and most importantly, *not* thinking. If these habits of *not doing* are formed early enough—even before a child enters kindergarten—how hard will it be for us to break them in favor of action in school and later on in life? The time spent with TV today in comparison to Maccoby's time is staggering indeed, and the areas of play and education, imitation and imagination represent a critical area in our fight with TV to reclaim America's children.

TELEVISION'S EFFECT ON GENERAL HEALTH AND EMOTIONAL GROWTH

In addition to those battle zones already discussed, there is yet another arena of television influence which merits close attention and that is its effect on a child's bodily development. There is growing evidence that apart from the medium's misrepresentations of reality and its influence on play and formal education, excessive viewing can also negatively affect a youngster's physiological and psychological health and growth. Again: this has grave implications for student and teacher performance in school.

Sleeping and Eating Patterns

Two areas which reveal the most obvious change from television exposure are sleeping patterns and eating habits. There is one study, for example, which indicates that seeing certain types of movies, either on TV or in the theater, can be more disruptive to a good night's sleep than staying up past midnight. Some TV programs may actually affect children as badly as drinking two cups of coffee before going to bed, and these effects can extend far beyond twenty-four hours, depending upon the age, sex, and mental level of the child.[39] Another survey of some 7,000 children between the ages of six and eleven shows that the sleep problems of more than twenty-five percent were considered by parents to be directly related to TV. These adults reported that many children suffered nightmares based upon what they had watched on their television screens.[40]

Though literature throughout the ages bears witness to the importance of dreams, it has only been during the last century or so that the careful analysis of dreams and their significance has begun. From Freud and Jung, among others, we know how vital dreams are in human activity and mental health. But if TV causes more nightmares than usual, or disrupts normal dreaming patterns, how might this change some interior psychic balance or the mind's playfulness in dreams and fantasizing? By altering our dreams, does TV affect our performance during the day as well? One TV critic suggests that television functions as a *dream substitute*, for both TV and dreams:

    (1) are highly visual and symbolic;

    (2) involve wish fulfillment;

    (3) contain much that appears disjointed and/or trivial;

    (4) provide powerful content which is easily absorbed; and

    (5) make consistent use of materials drawn from experience.[41]

By watching more TV, are we dreaming less content of our *own* making? Instead, our subconscious may be relying on artificially implanted material, and this in turn could be altering some inner mechanism for psychic and physical well-being.

In conjunction with this, there are others who believe our dream pool itself has been contaminated by television's brash sounds, violent images, and myriad scene changes. As one author writes:

> While these [violent] actions may be condemned by the total context of the film, direct representations of violence *improve* every viewer's capacity for imagining brutality. Since they never can be erased from the mind, they increase the chances of violence being programmed into our [dream] future.[42]

Empirically testing for this is very difficult, yet the question in relationship to an individual's health and growth is vastly important. Perhaps the images which are being imprinted passively and incidentally on our minds may affect our dreams in ways more profound than we think. Does the fact that television alters brain waves, as noted in Chapter One, add to this change as well? All this is speculation, to be sure, but these differences within an individual's mind could bring about some alteration in day-to-day behavior or dreaming or in the imagination itself which could subtly influence behavior in school.

Television's impact on eating habits has already been touched upon in Chapter Three, but it must be mentioned again here because sound nutritional practices and a balanced diet are vital to good health and growth. Any teacher knows that a child who does not eat properly is not going to perform efficiently in school.

What is television contributing to this area of a child's development? A great deal, it appears.

The National Institute of Mental Health, for instance, declares that television has been ranked by many as second only to physicians and dentists as a source of health information.[43] But *what kind* of information is being presented? A 1970s study, covering one week of commercial TV, rated only 30 percent of the health information presented as useful. A full 70 percent was considered inaccurate, misleading, or both.[44] The NIMH also found that 17 percent of prime time has mental illness as a theme, and drinking is a regular and popular TV pastime, carrying few negative consequences.[45] Yet, how accurately does this reflect real life?

As far as eating goes, the Institute declares that children who view a lot of TV have less knowledge about proper nutrition and that their diets actually vary inversely with the amount of TV they watch. As with the studies cited earlier, in Chapter Three, the NIMH reports that TV-promoted foods for children fall into four basic categories: snacks, fats, cholesterol, and sugar—certainly not a balanced regime. The general consensus of the NIMH is that television is falling far short of its positive health potential.

The Council on Children, Media, and Merchandising reports similarly depressing findings. For example, obesity among children is now a prevalent public health problem in the United States today. Among children in particular being overweight is far more common than undernutrition in both low- and high-SES families. As the Council states:

> ... this epidemic of obesity in childhood, a totally new historic
> phenomenon and still confined to our country, is a societal
> phenomenon...[46]

The fact that children in this country are eating more and more TV-advertised foods high in sugar and carbohydrate content or fried, fast-food take-aways is probably contributing to this change. Yet, these kinds of foods provide little real nutritional value. If anything, they tend to make the body and mind sluggish and less alert than a diet of protein, vegetables, and fruit.

There are related diseases as well. It has been discovered that cholesterol levels of young people in America are higher than those in non-Western countries. Dental decay, diabetes, hypertension, cardiovascular troubles, and saturated fats associated with improper eating habits are also more pronounced in this country than elsewhere. The chart on the following page gives some idea how serious these dietary problems truly are.

Without doubt, television is partially responsible for these sobering statistics because it continually encourages us to consume food which we do not always need and much of which is downright unhealthy.

Health/Nutritional Problems in the United States
(1) 40 million Americans (approximately 20 percent of population) are overweight.
(2) 50 percent of the 700,000 annual heart disease deaths are diet related.
(3) 50 percent of all cancers in women and 33 percent in men have dietary origins.
(4) Americans spend some $10 billion a year fighting fat.
(5) Weight control is a factor in diabetes, hypertension, and arteriosclerosis.
(6) Diabetes has gone from 27th most common cause of death in 1900s to 5th in 1970s. There is a 6 percent annual rise in diabetes.
(7) High cholesterol diet causes coronary heart disease, which accounts for one out of three deaths in U.S.
(8) Cancer doctors call for reduced intake of saturated fats and cholesterol and moderation in meats, dairy products, and fried foods. They advise more fresh fruits and vegetables.

47

Yet, proper food and sleep are two of the most important aspects for personal growth and are absolutely essential for optimum performance in school. Television may be affecting these areas of childhood development in ways which have many harmful consequences for our students.

Other Physical and Behavioral Influences

Sleeping and eating habits, however, are only the *start* in describing the various aspects of our TV/learning combat. Additional evidence has been accumulated which shows that other, more subtle health and emotional factors are affected by the medium as well.

In 1964, for instance, two United States Air Force physicians noticed that thirty youngsters on their base, dependants of military personnel, were suffering from the same disorders. They were nervous, fatigued, had headaches, were not sleeping well, and had chronically upset stomachs. Tests for typical childhood diseases were run, but nothing turned up. Food and water supplies were also checked; but again, nothing. The doctors then discovered that these thirty boys and girls were heavy TV consumers, so they suggested a reduction in the amount of viewing. Twelve of the thirty youngsters stopped watching completely, and within two to three weeks, their symptoms disappeared. Others reduced their TV intake to two hours or less a day and were well after five to six weeks. But those children who did nothing about their viewing habits remained ill.[48]

More recently, an article appeared in a popular women's magazine discussing a similar incident. A school administrator noticed children behaving rather strangely and not feeling well. With the cooperation of their parents, a number of these youngsters were put on "TV diets" of no more than one hour a day for one month. When the children were asked to give up television, some were cranky, fidgety, and nervous—almost as if they were experiencing drug withdrawal symptoms. Those parents who cooperated with this experiment saw noticeable changes in only a few weeks:

(1) One little girl began playing more with others.

(2) Another boy stopped blowing things up. He also teased and poked the family pets less than when he was watching a lot of TV.

(3) A girl who had been scoring D's and F's on school spelling tests started receiving B+'s.[49]

Another administrator had similar problems in her school and also asked parents to monitor the programs their children watched. Most of the parents went along with the plan by limiting viewing to one hour a day, and within weeks, some remarkable results were reported. Many children seemed calmer and more relaxed at school, and they began to play out their own dramas and running games rather than those inspired by TV. In addition, they were less easily distracted and could work creatively either alone or in a group—something which only a few had been able to do previously.

Some parents are even beginning to notice TV's effects on very young infants. One mother actually reports how television made her sixteen-month-old baby more restless and crankier than usual. She was in the habit of keeping the set on most of the day "for company," and though there seemed no obvious connection between the TV and her child's behavior, she decided to turn the set off. She then watched her baby change: he slept better, was less distracted, and developed a new ability to concentrate on his own play. The mother believed doing away with TV was directly responsible for this improvement in her son. In conjunction with this, one child psychologist writes:

> Most of television is too much noise, too much stimulation, too much syncopation, for a young child. If it can have so dramatic an effect on an infant who is not even watching, what does it do to an actual viewer![50]

It should also be noted that the very young child is attracted to color earlier than he is to form. Color TV, therefore, which most people have in America today, is likely to gain a baby's attention months before he can understand what is happening on the screen. This neurophysiological makeup of humans, plus the fact that more than a few parents put their infants in highchairs and then turn on the TV, makes it easy for young babies to become addicted to watching color television before they have any notion of *what* is going on.[51] They become captive prisoners in their chairs or cribs for absorbing informal messages from TV. The infant may not understand the program, but that does not mean he remains untouched by the harsh sounds, colors, and rapid shifts of focus parading across the screen. In many cases, this sort of image/sound jumble is the first "language" learned by many children. Imagine what all this may be doing to confuse and distort the infant's perceptions of people and life!

There are other noted professionals who are becoming vocal about television's role in capturing and captivating the young. Dr. William Glasser, who has spent much time with children and who has written numerous books on education, is deeply concerned about television's influence on youngsters' emotional and physical growth. He considers TV a very real danger to any child between the ages of two and five, because during this time the child needs many social experiences to gain confidence in his ability to *do* and become involved. Glasser feels that one of the greatest obstacles to a child's socialization is excessive viewing of television, and he suggests that parents carefully restrict their children's use of the medium during these early years.[52]

Glasser has his reasons for this harsh view. He believes television stimulates a child's nervous system enough to feel comfortable but not enough to satisfy his need for real involvement with other people and physical activity for sound bodily growth. He feels when this same "TV child" is then put in a school situation, he may react with erratic movement, confusion, or hostility, because he has not learned how to cope either by himself or in a group. As Glasser explains, this youngster then becomes the so-called hyperactive child:

> Because I work extensively in elementary school, I am often asked to suggest ways to cope with five- to ten-year-old children who seem to have no social responsibility. They cannot cooperate in the necessary give and take of the classroom. Often disrupting the class because they cannot settle down or listen, they sometimes overwhelm the teacher with their senseless, erratic activity. When asked to become actively involved in learning, they are passive. Used to receiving, they do not know how to put forth effort. *I believe there is a cause and effect relationship between excessive viewing of television at a young age and this recent hyperactivity syndrome in children.*[53] [italics added]

Yet, this hyperactivity problem was virtually unknown thirty-five years ago; now it has reached epidemic proportions. *Why?* Is too much television partly to blame? Perhaps some of today's students would not have to take Ridilin, a drug used to calm children down, if they simply watched less TV. Rather than sitting passively at home and then having their unused energy explode later in the classroom, these youngsters could be outside exercising and literally blowing off steam. The rapid shifts in focus between programs and commercials may be another factor contributing to this new wave of restlessness in children. Are today's youngsters simply being programmed informally to bounce back and forth between different points of view without having any real focus? The large amount of refined sugar and carbohydrates children are encouraged to eat by the tube may also be contributing to this hyperkinetic syndrome.

These random comments made by parents also support Glasser's conclusions that too much TV can frustrate energy and cause nervousness in children:

> (1) The children come away from the set and try to assuage some sort of inner dissatisfaction in some way—by drinking a lot, eating, or jumping . . .
>
> (2) The main thing about television is the fact that there's a lot of energy there coming out at you, and you sit there passively, and it's going into you. When you turn off the set, it has to come out again. What I notice in my children is that it comes out in a very mindless way—mindless, spasmodic energy . . . pushing, shoving, being dissatisfied.[54]

How many parents, teachers, and other people who work closely with youngsters have experienced similar problems?

PERSONAL ISOLATION AND TELEVISION

Another important aspect in the conflict of television and children is the personal and emotional isolation fostered by TV. How does this affect individual growth and development? It must be remembered that when a child accepts the box as a form of leisure activity or comfort, he turns away from *people* and all the direct stimulation they provide. His learning becomes vicarious rather than first-hand; he substitutes something inanimate for live, direct interaction. TV allows him to escape from personal involvement by substituting something that *seems* like close contact but which in fact is not. Some people believe television is the perfect refuge for those who are unable to cope with life because it acts as solace to the individual who cannot deal with the outside world. Rather than encouraging him to face his problems and learn from other people, TV offers him a place to hide or becomes a way to kill time so he will not have to cope with reality.

The following case study is a good example of this type of influence and how it can directly alter a child's behavior in school. A little girl named "Susie" exhibited marked antisocial tendencies in class. She would not participate in group activities and refused to become involved with other children. When her teacher discovered that Susie was a heavy TV viewer, she suggested to the mother that she put her daughter on a TV diet.

During the first week without TV, Susie was very upset over not being allowed to watch. Her teacher reported that she was moodier than usual and would sit and stare at the ground. After only one week, however, changes began to appear. Susie started to ask her mother to invite playmates over to the house after school. This was something she had never wanted before, and her teacher also noticed her playing more with the other children during classtime. By the end of the four weeks, the youngster no longer was just an outsider but a participant. She played by herself and with other children, and both mother and teacher thought her a much happier child. Several weeks later, however, when the girl's mother allowed her to resume watching television, Susie's previous symptoms returned. She simply refused to interact with other people. There appeared to be a direct relationship between the little girl's social maladjustment and her TV-watching behavior.[55] (This example also ties in with the experiments mentioned earlier involving school children, TV diets, and the positive results obtained from decreased consumption.)

There is also the possibility that those who consume large amounts of television may possess certain introverted personality traits which are only reinforced by the medium's tendency to isolate and remove. As one can see below, there is evidence to support this claim.

Amount of Viewing and Personality Characteristics			
Characteristic	*Watch a Great Deal of TV*	*Watch TV Frequently*	*Watch TV Seldom*
Lonely	95%	5%	0%
Shy	70%	22%	7%
Listless	51%	22%	27%
Pampered	49%	25%	28%
Emotional	39%	39%	22%
Obedient	4%	79%	17%
Has Friends	4%	29%	68%
Active	1%	34%	65%

[56]

Though television by no means warrants universally adverse effects, among heavy viewers certain patterns do begin to emerge. Like the little girl just mentioned, the heavy user is lonelier, more listless, and shy. On the other hand, children who watch little TV, according to the above figures, are almost the opposite. Nor is it merely the only child or the child whose parents work who is the heavy viewer, but more importantly, the insecure child who has trouble making friends or who feels safer alone than in a group.

Whether television stimulates these personality/emotional tendencies or draws individuals to it who are already predisposed to such traits does not really matter, because the net result is a negative influence on personal development. TV can prevent a child from being lonely, but this is not necessarily good, especially if that child is inclined to shyness in the first place. He should, on the contrary, be encouraged to participate with those around him. In other cases, television may keep children from learning how to be alone and cope with aloneness, both of which represent vital aspects of growth. As psychologist Bruno Bettelheim suggests:

> Children who have been taught, or conditioned, to listen passively most of the day to the warm verbal communication coming from the TV screen . . . are often unable to respond to real persons because they arouse so much *less* feeling than the skilled actor. Worse, they lose the ability to learn from reality because life experiences are more complicated than the ones they see on the screen, and there is no one who comes in at the end to explain it all . . . If this block of solid inertia is not removed, the emotional isolation from others that starts in front of the TV may continue. This . . . is one of the real dangers of TV.[57]

This isolation and lack of personal involvement may lead to an increase in all dependent behaviors and may hamper the development of individuals into people capable of forming their own decisions. This type of subtle influence from TV exposure may in turn affect classroom activities and student interaction.

It must be remembered, too, that television's isolating effect has been going on for several decades now. It is not a question of a few random individuals like little Susie holing up with the box, but if the Nielsens are correct, almost an entire nation! This fourteen-year-old's comment states the case well:

Television is perfect to tune out to the rest of the world. But I don't relate with my family much because we're all too busy watching TV.[58]

NARCOTIC DYSFUNCTION OF TELEVISION

This tendency of television to isolate individuals may have further educational and social ramifications. As people substitute watching TV for *doing,* and as they interact less with one another, they cease in a sense being social creatures. They decrease their actual involvement and learning from others and the world around them, though they may vicariously see a great deal. In this way, television acts as a narcotic or drug, as some people have claimed, for it removes people from people by taking real life away. At the flick of the switch, seas of fantasy/escapist material are readily available to pass the time of day.

But by providing the individual, especially the growing child, with so many escape valves from outside pressures, television may simultaneously stunt the growth of personal and group responsibility. It may provide steady relief from daily life and all the tensions that go along with it; but if used to hide from anxiety or duties, it can also reduce the likelihood of involvement and genuine concern. Using the medium to run away from problems or to put them off indefinitely makes the viewer less aware of troubles that do in fact exist. Continually accepting a dream world or confusing reality with fantasy is not conducive to the development of social consciousness. It is quite possible that gradual changes could result in attitudes and behavior, *away* from individual awareness and public commitment.

The term narcotisizing dysfunction has been coined by psychologists to describe this particular effect of television.[59] Even though the medium exposes us to vast amounts of information, it still may evoke only minimal interest in real social problems, and this could develop into mass apathy. Excessive TV exposure may actually deaden rather than enliven the emotions of the average viewer, because the more time he spends with television, the less time he has for action and work. Similar to the case of excessive violence viewing, a general habituation or desensitization to life's problems may take place. A person might have enormous amounts of material available to him but still fail to make any decisions regarding that information or to act upon his own feelings and instincts.

TV will not necessarily reinforce apathy among those already committed, but it will tend to do so with those who are poor self-starters in the first place. The problem here is that the apathetic generally make up a far larger number of the whole. There are always more people who do not wish to act or who have trouble overcoming their own inertia. Teachers and educators have always been confronted with the problem of student motivation. Yet, however difficult genuine social concern may be to achieve, it does not change the fact that we need a critical, perceptive, and caring citizenry, particularly among the young growing to adulthood. In an age of global politics, social awareness and responsibility toward the whole are crucial to all.

Television certainly has great capacity to foster the development of such attitudes, but something seems to have gone amiss along the way. There can be no doubt, for example, that TV helped to encourage some of the awareness and concern which manifested themselves during the sixties. Some very real and disturbing events found their way onto the screen, events which have left a deep impression on an entire generation. But perhaps the habit of escaping into fantasy and materialism—also promoted by television—was stronger in the long run than the effort required for continual commitment to social activism. In the short term, TV can inspire concern among people because immediate events are exciting or disturbing. But over longer periods of time, a different pattern may emerge. The preponderance of escapist fare, which allows the viewer to avoid real life or which places material above ideological concerns, may contravene both social and political action. And, if we are in school to try to impart some sort of social/political awareness among our students, we should take the potential narcotisizing effect of television exposure into serious account.

AMERICAN SCHIZOPHRENIA

There are other points to consider in relationship to this narcotisizing aspect of the medium's power. In conjunction with TV's tendency to isolate and its potential for, in effect, drugging people not to care, there is also the real danger of much personal, internal conflict resulting from heavy exposure. Constantly shifting between what is and what is not; between shows, ideas, images, and channels literally is enough to push some people over the "deep end" or to make them nervous temperamentally. So much TV is based upon illusion and fantasy that it becomes very difficult at times to know what is truth and what is not. This is especially true of young children, who have not yet accumulated a vast catalogue of personal experiences against which to evaluate TV content.

One wonders: is there something inherently jarring and debilitating about the American television experience? The National Institute of Mental Health Report actually cites a study comparing American and foreign TV which suggests this may be so. Foreigners who are accustomed to a much slower pace of television say they find American TV unnerving and experience a kind of physical pain when they first see commercial television in this country. The Report declares:

> The rapid form of presentation characterizing American television in which novelty piles upon novelty in short sequences may well be counterproductive for organized and effective learning sequences. The young child who has not yet developed strategies for tuning out irrelevancies may be especially vulnerable in this respect; even programs that seek to be informative as well as entertaining may miss the mark because they allow too little time for reflection ... Extremely rapid-pace material, presenting novelty along with high levels of sound and fast movement, may generate surprise and confusion in a viewer whose anticipatory strategies ... are not yet prepared for coping with this material.[60]

All this points to the fact that a very disturbing element of schizophrenia lies at the very heart of American television. On the one hand is a vast display of random bits of life; on the other is the constant psychic irritation of rampant consumerism. If mental breakdown is the common result of endless new patterns of information, then TV in this country certainly provides agitation in abundance. All the contradictory input could very well create a widespread state of subconscious confusion. This is most true for the young, because they generally need reassurance, structure, and freedom within reason in order to grow and learn at their best.

Yet, how can youngsters possibly analyze and catalogue all that they view on television—especially if their parents do not take the time to discuss with them what they see? Is television somehow grooming us for mass nervous disorder and resentment? A pervasive malaise existing just below the surface of our lives? There is evidence that this is indeed likely. A survey of fifth- and sixth-grade students, for example, reveals that many emotional and personal problems suffered by these children, such as worries about looks, being fat, having bad complexions, and being accepted by others, all related to the kinds of television they watched.[61] Moreover, this country's mental hospitals are now overloaded with young patients, and many children today currently undergo some form of counseling or private therapy because they seem so unable to cope with life. There is also growing evidence that many children in the United States suffer from clinical depression and suicidal tendencies even though very young.[62]

Can television be held at least partially accountable for all this because of its tendency to isolate individuals and promote personal dissatisfaction? Perhaps this one fact—that TV disrupts a natural rhythm of accommodation and assimilation among people—is the saddest statement to be made about its potential impact on human well-being and an individual's educational growth.

IN CLOSING

What are we to conclude about these grey areas of our teaching combat zone? If we were to construct a picture of the average TV consumer based upon the data presented thus far, the image we come up with is rather disheartening. The moderate to heavy viewer is somewhat duller, more materialistic, and less knowledge-able about life. He reads less and may lack a certain amount of spontaneity and creativity. He is less interested in the real world and people than in an edited, fantasy version of life. He may be somewhat shy and introverted; and though he may crave human contact, he has not had the practice to know how to go about being a friend. He may even be a personality type bordering at times on the mildly neurotic and mentally unstable. Or, he simply may be an inert mass which does not care and is willing to watch life go by.

Naturally, just because a young person watches a fair amount of television does not mean he will fit the above general description. Much depends upon his family environment, intelligence level, formal education, and what other activities he engages in when not watching TV. If, for example, he reads a great deal and talks with people, much of what he sees on the screen will be counterbalanced by what he reviews in print or hears from others. The imaginary portrait given above provides only a broad picture of tendencies within the individual who consumes more than a few hours of TV each day.

It must also be stressed that the studies and information presented in this chapter may only represent the tip of a far larger iceberg of television influence. When one is working in the domain of deferred imitation, sleeper effect, and involuntary/incidental learning, it is very difficult to assess the whole range of television's impact on behavior and thought. The material provided here may only be a fraction of what still needs to be unearthed and discovered regarding the medium's effect on our lives and how it is altering the process of human communication as a whole. There are now several generations of TV twins available for questioning, and these areas of attitude and behavior change certainly need to be more fully explored. There may be literally volumes of data yet to be uncovered and brought into the classroom to help in our struggle with TV.

But perhaps it is best to end with the following, rather sad comments made by young people themselves about what television has done to them. As always, children—in their own special way—speak the truth.

(1) TV gives you stories like a book, pictures like movies,

voices like radio, and adventure like a comic. Television has action while you stay in one spot.

(2) I'd rather watch TV than play outside because it's boring outside. They always have the same rides, like swings and things.

(3) Sometimes when I watch an exciting show, I don't blink my eyes once. When I close them after the show, they hurt bad.

(4) When I see a beautiful girl using a shampoo or a cosmetic on TV, I buy them because I'll look like her. I have a ton of cosmetics. I play around with them and have them for when I'm older.

(5) If I didn't have television, do you think I could find something to do every night?

(6) It bugs me when someone is watching with me. If your friend is bored, you have to go out and make conversation . . . That's hard.[63]

V

A Look at the Television Industry

THE TABLES TURNED
The previous chapters have covered various aspects of television's impact on the growth and development of children, how their learning has been influenced by the medium, and what this means in terms of classroom activities and teaching as a whole. The information indicates a real conflict between the formal school curriculum and the informal curriculum of television and represents a challenge which must be confronted in a positive manner if we are to remain successful classroom leaders.

Yet, there is another perspective from which this ideological combat should also be analyzed, and that is from the viewpoint of the television industry itself. It is one thing to want to know more about our informal teaching rival, what it does to young people, and how we can manipulate its influence to our students' advantage. But what about all the people involved in making TV happen, their attitudes and aspirations, the business and economic strategies employed in their side of the struggle? After all, these people are responsible for creating the TV twin we have been studying, and we need to learn more about the makers themselves and their part in the battle for viewer attention.

In one of my first conversations with a broadcaster, however, he graphically outlined the dilemma we "outsiders" face in trying to appreciate the mechanisms of the television world:

> I would suggest this: Before you really attempt to go any further, you better do a little more homework and find out what television is about. Do not attempt to look at this business until you understand what the underpinning of the business is. Most people who write about television, who try to do things with television, fall on their faces because they don't understand the nature of the business . . . both publicly and commercially. You can't really do much. You can write all you want to. You can

write all about teachers and what they may do. You may write about what parents should do or how we can change it. But you really can't deal with how the broadcasters will relate until you do get to what the nature of the business is. And it's a business unlike anything else in this country. Unless you understand how it came about, why it is what it is, and the different forces that made it what it is, it is difficult. You're just like a voice in the wilderness. What you're doing and what you're asking now are all in a vacuum.[1]

After another year or so of reading about the history of radio and television, of talking with other people in the industry, perusing *The Wall Street Journal*, and learning the lingo of *Variety*, there are only three things I can conclude about this one-of-a-kind business: money, power, and—especially—*winning*. Our industry opponent is formidable indeed. Certainly, we must acknowledge the energy and resourcefulness which went into the early development of radio and then TV. Both truly are remarkable feats of creativity and imagination, and the men and women who pioneered these fields with their ideas and inventions deserve more credit than many presently get. It must also be appreciated, especially by "outsiders," that many of the policy decisions regarding radio and television were difficult to make and often came under great pressure and duress. We must ask ourselves whether we would have done any differently or any better if we had been there at the time. And, regardless of programming quality on American television or whether we actually "need" so much TV, the technical achievement of providing almost constant material, virtually twenty-four hours a day, seven days a week, fifty-two weeks a year is without doubt impressive. Across this country, we have wires, cables, lines, broadcasting stations, receivers, transmitters, technicians, engineers, producers, writers, actors, directors, and businessmen, all working to keep our airwaves open and to provide us with more auditory/visual stimulation than any other country in the world. Many people in various occupations make this possible, and their collective power and in many cases talent must be recognized. The fact that we do have so much material available in America—whether good or bad—is a tribute to technology and the industry's ability to sustain momentum and keep it all going. Imagine a single classroom capable of teaching a nation of over 230 million people, twenty-four hours a day, seven days a week!

I realize that the patterns and motifs which emerge from this one-of-a-kind business and the attitudes expressed by the industry as a whole toward its audience are narratives which merit far greater attention than I can possibly give in one chapter. The following pages provide only a brief sketch of the industry's past and present in an effort to bring a little air into that vacuum alluded to previously. The historical background, the excerpts from programs and advertisements, and the speeches of the people themselves paint an intriguing picture, one which is light-years away from a teacher's world and the information in the previous chapters. But a balanced view is important, especially for those of us in the field of learning who wish to better understand the creators of our informal TV rival in an effort to bring about meaningful dialogue and change. Though this chapter may seem to represent a shift in focus from teaching and education, it nevertheless is necessary to place the preceding research against the backdrop of the American broadcasting system. In attempting to provide a practical yet thorough survey of children and television, a look at the business behind the box is critical for gaining an understanding of the current battleground. And, truly, it is an astounding story.

EARLY BEGINNINGS

In order to appreciate many of the mechanisms which govern television in America today, it is necessary to dip back several decades and look at the beginning of radio, for much of what determines the TV business now stems from the structure of that medium during the twenties and thirties.[2] When television finally entered the American scene in the late 1940s, it was thought of as "radio with pictures," so the link between the two, both philosophically and pragmatically, is very close.

Marconi started the airwaves rolling when he learned how to send wireless transmissions in the late 1800s. This, however, was actually the culmination of numerous experiments and interest in sending messages by wire and electrical impulse which had intrigued scientists and inventors throughout the nineteenth century. By 1917, only a few decades after Marconi's initial discovery, there already were over 8,500 individuals in America offering radio broadcasting to the people. This was unique in the western world because the early development of the medium took place predominantly on a grassroots level outside the domain of government control. Radio brought with it—or should I say symbolized—a new era, a period of great expectations, because people recognized something new, a different sort of journey. Men and women could "talk" with others they previously had never seen, and physical distances were overcome. Not many knew where it was going, but there was tremendous energy and enthusiasm in the fledgling radio era.

Very quickly, however, the individual inventors and small broadcasting concerns which initially started radio were taken over by larger corporations, such as RCA, GE, AT&T, and Westinghouse. Here, sensed the business interests, was a vast area of influence and profit-making. When World War I broke out and attention was drawn to the fighting in Europe, these corporations consolidated their power by gathering together many of the major patents concerning radio parts, ideas, and improvements. Consequently, this put businessmen in the primary position to steer the future development of broadcasting in America.

By the early twenties, radio sales were skyrocketing, and people were thoroughly enthralled with this gadget. Activity was brisk, and things were moving so fast that it was difficult to keep pace with it all. Numerous legal suits were already plaguing the industry; and RCA, GE, AT&T, and Westinghouse were battling who had jurisdiction over what. Radio units were sending and receiving messages in greater number than there was physical capacity to deal with, and the confusion among radio signals was enormous. By 1923, Congress asked the Federal Trade Commission to conduct an investigation into radio, because they felt it was developing almost too quickly, and this has been one of the main problems in broadcast regulation ever since. The economic facts and the entrenchment of business incentives came prior to any in-depth questioning or philosophical analysis of how broadcasting should be handled for the public's benefit. The government's primary role, right from the start, was to act as a kind of traffic cop, keeping order among broadcasting signals (there are only so many radio frequencies available in the spectrum, and it is essential to devise means of keeping the signals of the various stations clearly separated from each other). Because of this, any regulations or rule-makings the government tried to enforce—even in the twenties—were looked upon as too late from the broadcaster/businessman's point of view.

So while Congress and the FTC waded through the mire, the big companies were prepared to preserve what they felt was their territory. Patents were fought over; copyright laws were violated; and inventors, song writers, and musicians whose ideas and talents were being exploited complained about the muddle. In the meantime, bits and pieces of advertising began to appear. AT&T suggested having people come into radio studios and pay a fee for broadcasting to the public. This system, called toll broadcasting, later developed into the commercial basis for radio advertising.[3] Though commercials were not regular, over-the-air advertising had at least gained a foothold in the broadcasting scene, and the 1927 Radio Act did little to alter this trend.

Here one sees many of the tendencies which characterized the industry during the next few years. Business was attracted to the medium and quickly gained the upper hand. Social and educational concerns were put in a secondary position to money-making incentives, and many people involved in radio lacked a comprehensive vision of how it should be used for the common good. Things were happening much too quickly, and the money being generated by the medium and the advertising which stimulated business at large became primary considerations.

DEPRESSION AND THE THIRTIES
When the stock market crashed and the Depression lowered on America, radio was affected as well. It was during this time that

commercials began to dominate the air. Broadcasters wanted to keep the industry growing despite the harsh times, and if advertisements would do the trick, then so be it. After this, commercial penetration came quickly. Everything was becoming economics and business, and agencies were channeling money into radio through ads and programs. Having this financial support is one of the main reasons why radio not only survived the Depression but actually expanded while other businesses failed.

Yet, after the initial flush of excitement over radio's birth, some began to wonder about all the advertising that had crept into the air. As one observer declared:

> The American apparatus of advertising is something unique in history and unique in the modern world ... It is like a ... gargoyle set at the very top of America's skyscraping adventure in acquisition ad infinitum ... The gargoyle's mouth is a loudspeaker, powered by the vested interest of business as a whole, of industry, of finance. It is never silent, it drowns out all other voices, and it suffers no rebuke, for is it not the Voice of America. . .?[4]

Needless to say, the general business philosophy at that time did not hold many kind feelings toward noncommercial interests. Those with influence continued to support the system as it was, much to the dismay of various educational and religious concerns. The governing rationale went something like this:

> Commercialism is the heart of broadcasting in the United States. What has education contributed to radio? Not a thing. What has commercialism contributed to radio? Everything—the lifeblood of the industry.[5]

Broadcasting, an industry trade magazine, stated that the disappearance of numerous educational stations from the air proved they were the "misfits" in American broadcasting and questioned how "misguided pedagogues" could possibly have the audacity to "oppose commercial broadcasting."[6] Thus, the pattern was set.

By the early thirties, the organizations which dominated radio and which would come to dominate TV had already flowered. An intricate chain of businesses, entertainment personalities, and promoters had developed, consisting of the following:

(1) advertising agencies,

(2) syndicates which marketed recorded series,

(3) recording companies,

(4) script syndicates,

(5) independent producers,

(6) station representatives,

(7) merchandising services,

(8) trade papers and magazines,

(9) press agents and public relations managers,

(10) trade associations, such as the National Association of Broadcasters (NAB),

(11) unions, and

(12) entrepreneurs (multiple-station owners).[7]

The so-called American system of broadcasting had been born, and it was a system which gave businessmen control. The main factor in deciding who would run a station did not depend upon the applicant's sense of ethics or social responsibility but upon whether he had the money to buy the equipment necessary to broadcast.

During the next few years, the broadcasting industry rose swiftly in prestige. Advertising agencies grew at a fantastic pace throughout the Depression, and the networks expanded their power. Time brokers and more ad writers and programmers came onto the scene; and along with them, a new business pattern began to emerge which would strengthen in time to affect television as well. The idea was taking hold that those paying the bills, i.e., the advertisers and sponsors, could participate in program content and decision-making. Dispiriting news, either about affairs in Europe with Hitler or the financial crisis in America, was felt to be too sobering for the audience and therefore not good for business. More than anything else, the economy depended upon the "up" trend of radio, and word of Hitler might not encourage people to spend money. The evolving mentality worked something like this:

(1) When one broadcaster denounced Hitler and the Third Reich, he was "told from above" to stop. When he did not, his show was cancelled.

(2) Another writer during the thirties was instructed that scripts about dictators and the fall of nations were "too mature" for the typical radio audience, and horror stories were wanted instead.[8]

So while the world was undergoing tremendous change, broad-casters in America thought listeners were incapable of handling adult topics and truth. The public simply was looked upon as being unprepared for too much reality, so "buy this" instead. As one man commented:

> American radio seemed a conspiracy of silence regarding all those aspects of the individual and social life that did not contribute to the objectives of the advertiser.[9]

The mid-thirties brought with them further attempts to regulate the fast-spreading industry from complete takeover by the commercial interests, but with little success. Schools, churches, and the print media all felt threatened by radio and the business motivations behind it. A number of people wanted to preserve twenty-five percent of the spectrum for educational, religious, and cultural programs; but *Broadcasting* magazine again chastised these "self-seeking reformers."[10] Congress passed the hot potato on to the Federal Radio Commission, thereby relinquishing responsibil-ity in the matter, and called for the Commission to decide.

All this sidestepping finally led to the 1934 Communications Act, *which we are still governed by today*. In reality, however, this piece of legislation was more a victory for the way things were, as it was basically a rehash of the 1927 Radio Act. The 1934 Act did call for the establishment of the Federal Communications Com-mission (FCC), a body to oversee broadcasting events, and because public concern was growing, one of the agency's first projects was an inquiry on the allocation of cultural and educational channels. Vast amounts of PR and propaganda were tossed back and forth between the opposing camps. A member of the National Associa-tion of Broadcasters actually described the commercial channels as being so good that any change in the existing system would be "disastrous for the vast majority of all religious, educational, charitable, civic, and similar organizations."[11] Yet to give some idea of the industry's point of view, the networks testified to the FCC that "Amos and Andy" was a prime example of their efforts on behalf of "educational programming." The cause for more educational channels died because the FCC reported back to Congress, which had passed the buck to the Radio Commission in the first place, that commercial broadcasters were providing ample time for educational and nonprofit needs. The *people*–to whom the airwaves belonged, according to the 1934 Act–were left to struggle for bits and pieces of air time, and local and regional interests were pushed aside as the industry and business grew.

By the mid-thirties–about two decades after the first radio transmission–commercial broadcasting was firmly entrenched. But the fear that business was making too much money, too quickly, led to another FCC investigation. It would be into the next decade, however, before the Commission finished its probe.

THE FORTIES AND WAR

During the early 1940s, the broadcasting industry was plagued with struggles for control and power. Work also continued on the development of television. CBS and the now defunct Dumont network began some telecasting in the United States, and the latter already had sets on the market. In May, 1940, there were twenty-three stations broadcasting pictures in America, and over 10,000 sets had been sold. But technical problems, the FCC, and World War II entered the scene, and television was put on *hold*.

Aside from these difficulties, another disturbing trend began to manifest itself at this time. A tremendous fear arose that Communists and "pinks" might invade the American broadcasting system. This fear was to have its full impact during the McCarthy Era of the fifties–a subject which I shall come to again later–but the seeds of this malaise began prior to World War II.

Apart from the uneasiness over Communism, the forties also witnessed continuing conflicts between the networks and government. The FCC investigation which was begun in the previous decade ended in 1941, and this time the regulatory agency actually voted against the business interests. The FCC stated that no licenses would be issued to a broadcast station affiliated with a network which held more than one set of business concerns. So in order to keep half of its affiliates, NBC had to relinquish all others. After much protesting and legal maneuvering, NBC gave in and put its Blue Network up for sale. This eventually became ABC.

The forties also brought with them an era where stations were bought and sold for considerable amounts of money. This again put the FCC in an equivocal position because such transactions, strictly speaking, were prohibited under the letter of the 1934 law. Stations and the federal licenses which authorized them were not to be viewed as private property for sale. Another practice, known as trafficking in licenses, also came into being, which meant that many station owners received licenses through purchase, *not* application to the FCC. The buyer was thus able to circumvent agency investigation and approval. Each station sale involved more and more money; and with such substantial outlays, purchasers wanted to make the most of their investments. One result of all this is that multiple-station owners or entrepreneurs began to emerge, and these people were able to accumulate great power and wealth with vast broadcast holdings. One man owned stations in Detroit, Cleveland, and Hollywood—three very profitable and influential areas—yet such entrepreneurs often received little public notice because of their strictly behind-the-scenes positions.

Yet, even though all this was going on and program quality declined, especially after the war (commercialism during the war itself declined amidst the generally shared national patriotism— shared even by the broadcasters), the FCC approved license renewals *en masse.* As long as there were no blatant violations in engineering reports, which involved only the *technical* side of broadcasting (signal problems and interference), a license renewal was given. The result of all this is that programming suffered terribly because it never was closely checked as part of license renewal procedures.*

Many people became so upset by such discrepancies that the FCC was eventually forced to make another inquiry. The outcome

---

*Since, as noted above, the airwaves are strictly limited in regard to availability of frequencies, the 1934 Act held that licenses to use the public airwaves should be given to those who were best qualified to serve the public interest—in theory, an admirable piece of legislation. In actuality, however, the "public interest" was never defined, and the FCC assumed a simple broadcasting signal traffic policeman role, just as its predecessor had done earlier.

of this investigation into broadcaster responsibility, led by Charles Siepmann, was outlined in the infamous (in broadcasting industry circles) *Blue Book*. Among other things, the *Blue Book* revealed that often the contrast between what a station *said* it would do, in its radio license application, and what it in fact *delivered* was staggering. In 1938, for instance, a Toledo station applied for a full-time operating license by arguing that it needed additional time to serve public needs. The application promised that some eighty-four percent of the evening hours would be devoted to local, live programming. But a sample week in 1944 showed that nearly ninety-two percent of the time on this station went to commercials! So obvious, in fact, was the misuse of this public property (the public airwaves) that during the dinner hour the station had commercial spots *only*, with no *interruptions* for programming![12]

In reality, the *Blue Book* did not point out anything new. People involved in the business already were aware of such violations. *Broadcasting* magazine considered the *Blue Book* "nothing to get alarmed about," and the President of the National Association of Broadcasters called the uproar over the FCC statement all "hooey and nonsense." But because the Commission had spoken out against broadcasting practices, attacks on the agency were waged with increased vigor. The NAB declared the Commission was "the type of government from which our forefathers struggled to escape," and *Broadcasting* reported, "There is more at stake than the ultimate pattern of American broadcasting. There is at stake the pattern of American life!"[13] FCC members were automatically dubbed "stooges for Communism," and one Commissioner was characterized by *Broadcasting* as a jousting knight who carried banners tinged with pink.

The industry carried on its side of the fight by declaring that a government organization had no right to any decisions regarding programming content, for such actions were tantamount to censorship and an abridgement of First Amendment rights. All this, however, was nothing more than broadcasting doublespeak, since program decisions were being made on a daily basis which censored many themes and ideas from the American public. The censors were businessmen, however, and not the government. In any case, the thrust of the *Blue Book* was *not* to censor content but to get the broadcasters themselves to try to live up to the very statements they had made in the first place (regarding plans to meet the public interest) when they applied for their licenses! While subjects of a more serious, thought-provoking nature were suppressed, the audience continued to be fed soap operas, horror stories, and commercials.

During this war waged by the business elements, the FCC's power to work in the public interest slipped further into the mire. The agency was put in the dubious position of being a regulatory body which could not regulate: a classic example of "Catch-22." But this nonaction proved a boon for industry members; while the FCC dawdled, broadcasters could consolidate their business concerns. By attacking the FCC's *Blue Book*, industry people hoped to stop further outbursts of public spiritedness; and to a large extent, they were successful in doing just that. The *Blue Book* was supposed to reaffirm the 1934 Act clause concerning licensing "in the public interest, convenience, and necessity," but the following example taken from a Chicago station before and after the FCC report indicates how ineffectual the findings were in bringing about any change.

BEFORE *Blue Book*	AFTER
phonograph record	commercial
commercial	commercial
phonograph record	commercial
commercial	phonograph record
phonograph record	phonograph record
commercial	phonograph record

14

All the accusations, attacks, and counterattacks between the broadcasting industry and the FCC amounted to nothing more than a demonstration of Bureaucratic Boogaloo. The following pattern began to emerge:

(1) moves by the FCC to function as a regulatory agency in the public's behalf produced:

(2) moves by Congress resulting in investigations and hearings which caused:

(3) industry protests and demands for further investigations before any decisions or rule-makings which brought about:

(4) more resolutions and proposed amendments to the 1934 Communications Act which caused:

(5) further industry outcries and stronger lobbying to protect their interests in Washington . . .[15]

And so on down the line. William Paley's comment to Norman Corwin, a renowned writer of radio drama, best exemplifies the change in tone and tenor between the industry's inception and the post-World War II market:

> Well, you've done epic things that are appreciated by us, and by a special audience, but couldn't you write for a broader public? That's what we're going to need more and more. We've simply got to face up to the fact that we're in a commercial business.[16]

Why a commercial audience still cannot be looked upon as a special one is hard to understand. But Paley's comment reveals a definite shift in the industry's attitude toward its listeners, and this alteration reflects philosophical as well as economic changes. The trend by the late forties was toward more advertising and making money, *not* an emphasis on reality, humanity, and public spiritedness which the war had demanded. Before the war, one-third of all radio time was commercially sponsored; afterwards, this figure doubled. Though some broadcasters were questioning their role and function in this new communications society, many more were turning their attention once again to the marketplace. The post-war years meant a return to business, *not* a period of self-analysis. Indeed, pangs of conscience and regret were not shared by many. By the end of the decade, more radios were selling; advertising increased; and people began preparing themselves for TV. Business boomed; engineers and salesmen came to the television medium with extraordinary speed; and a ruthlessness between broadcasting competitors was on the rise.

TELEVISION AND THE FIFTIES

It was during the early 1950s that television finally materialized onto the American scene and began to penetrate households throughout the land. As with the beginning of radio, activity was brisk and intense, the only real difference being that the businessmen and advertisers were fully prepared, right from Day One, to exploit the commercial/merchandising potential of this new medium.

Yet, along with the initial enthusiasm over TV, the strange undercurrent of worry about Communist take-over again emerged. FBI head J. Edgar Hoover began sending memos to the FCC, warning against issuing any licenses to those with "pink" leanings, and the FCC took heed. Who such people might *be* was difficult to determine; nevertheless, the squeeze was on.

The effect of this on broadcasting, and television in particular, was far-reaching. Between the late forties and early fifties, an era of witch-hunting, championed by Senator Joseph McCarthy, entered American life, and this wave hit broadcasting especially hard. Broadcasting meant power, and those in control were loathe to let this power slip away or fall into what they considered the "wrong" hands. Certain magazines began to emerge whose purpose was to "single out the guilty." Among those listed as "questionable" individuals were, ironically enough, some of the most gifted people in Hollywood.[17]

Besides books and pamphlets speaking out against the creative community, networks would not hire anyone until staff checks had been run on potential employees, and security chiefs began to police broadcast activities. As McCarthy began to dominate the scene, these special warnings were put away in desk drawers at ad agencies, networks, and with sponsors. Producers had to submit the names of writers, actors, and directors they wanted to use before they could do any work. Even plot and program themes were affected during this time. In history plays, the word "peace" was thought to make people uneasy because it "sounded Communist."[18] The McCarthy syndrome changed sponsor attitudes and their commercials as well; and, once pressure was applied, some rather devious methods were used to insure appropriate cooperation.[19]

What entered next from an artistic and humanitarian point of view was a bleak period in the history of American broadcasting. Though technical progress and money were being made daily and the general public was fascinated with TV, this obsession with Communists brought with it a stifling atmosphere. The average American had little idea of all the behind-the-scenes maneuvering and paranoia. A number of artists and creative people sensed a *difference*, but few could explain why. Many simply could not get work because they had been blacklisted. Other artists and actors fled to Europe as the only place where they could find employment and tolerance, and there were those who became so depressed and despondent over not being able to find work that they committed suicide.[20]

In the broadcasting field, responsibility and choice generally were abdicated in favor of repression and simply not thinking. All controversial types were to be avoided, and Paley's comment to Corwin became prophetic and indicative of the times. As the industry went after the mass market, tremendous conformity and uniformity of outlook began to emerge. One could not risk losing access to the enormous cash flow that was inherent in broadcasting. But by denying the public a diversity of opinions and presentations, broadcasters were violating the public's right to know and to be well informed. Artists and the creative people were the first to get the ax because it is their job to be free-thinking individuals. Given the tone and tenor of the times, however, this would not do.

Part of the problem is that rather than exerting effort to change this situation, most industry members remained silent and acquiescent. Nonaction was considered by most to be much safer, because business was good. Why rock the boat? The system of American broadcasting had developed into an intricate pattern of various entities, none of which really bothered with philosophical and ethical matters. Most local stations, which were supposed to be in control theoretically, since they held the broadcasting licenses, had abdicated their power in favor of the networks, which acted as time brokers. The networks in turn sold time to advertising agencies, and with this sale of air space went a great deal of decision-making power over program content. The ad agencies then dealt with the sponsors by finding out what the latter wanted. This pattern had grown during the radio era, although some outsiders believed (or hoped, at any rate) that TV would be different. But it was too late to change the structure of the business. The pattern of dispersed authority, coupled with the irrational fears of the McCarthy Era, did not promise an auspicious beginning for television, even though the medium itself gained rapid public acceptance and people were enthralled with the box.

When TV finally did get into full swing after the Korean War, some effects were readily apparent:

1. Movie going and taxi cab use declined.
2. People used jukeboxes less.
3. Public libraries reported drops in the circulation of books.
4. Book stores cited losses in sales.
5. Radio listening went down sharply in TV cities.
6. People eating out appeared to gulp down their food in order to return home for a night with TV.[21]

The early staples of television were game and quiz shows, which offered prizes galore.

In the meantime, the FCC continued in effect to become, more and more, a pawn of the broadcasting industry. Every time the Commission tried to go against the business interests in favor of the "public," broadcasting lobbyists checkmated their efforts. This resulted in the strengthening of the industry's position. In only a few short years, broadcasters managed to:

(1) make the *Blue Book* appear to be of no importance whatsoever;

(2) persuade the FCC to rescind its 1949 Mayflower Decision and to allow licensees to editorialize, which could have the effect of denying the public access to balanced presentations;

(3) convince the FCC to reverse another 1949 ruling, the Avco rule, which called for competitive bids in license transfer situations. This move gave the industry greater control over buying and selling; and

(4) get Congress to forbid the FCC from considering any applicants for licenses other than transferees proposed by the industry itself.[22]

When an FCC Commissioner tried to set aside channels for educational and cultural purposes, *Broadcasting* condemned the move as "illogical, if not illegal." There did not seem much the FCC could do.

By the fifties, broadcasting had successfully created a national audience. Chapter Three provides some indication of how TV affects the child market, but its impact on adult purchase behavior has been remarkable, to say the least. For example: in 1950, Hazel Bishop was a $50,000-a-year cosmetic and lipstick company when it started using TV to promote sales. By 1952, Bishop was taking in over $4,500,000, and figures were steadily rising.[23] Alberto Culver went from a $1.5 million concern in 1956 to $80 million by 1964, and Lestoil cleaning fluid climbed from 150,000 bottles sold annually to 100 million in only three years.[24] There was virtually *nothing* TV could not sell!

This great merchandising power was to have far-reaching consequences. Sponsors and advertisers began to exert even more pressure on TV from behind-the-scenes positions. The old rationale from radio days was growing stronger that those footing the bills should have the say over what should go on the air. In one program, for example, sponsored by Camel Cigarettes, the writers were instructed to:

> ...not have the heavy or any disreputable person smoking a cigarette. Do not associate the smoking of cigarettes with undesirable scenes or situations plot-wise.[25]

Word also was given that cigarettes should be smoked "gracefully" and should never be used "to calm nerves."

Not only were products to be presented in a certain light, but programs in general began changing to accommodate the business incentives. Offerings such as "Philco Theater" and "Playhouse 90" were quite popular; but, as TV grew, the ad men and sponsors became increasingly alarmed about these so-called "heavy" dramas, dealing with real life and real people. They argued that the economic problems such people represented were not pro-business, and these powerful groups consequently demanded script changes and different presentations. Again, no one really questioned whether this was an abridgement of the public's rights or the freedom of the creative people involved, for it was considered more important to keep those who supplied the money and products happy. According to broadcast historian Erik Barnouw, the prevailing industry attitude was this:

> Most advertisers were selling magic. Their commercials posed the same problems that . . . drama dealt with: people who feared failure in love and in business. But in the commercials there was always a solution . . . The problem could be solved by a new pill, deodorant, toothpaste, shampoo, shaving lotion, hair tonic, girdle, coffee, or floor wax. The solutions always had finality . . . [But] . . . writers took these same problems and made them complicated. They were forever suggesting that a problem might stem from childhood and be involved with feelings toward a mother or father. All this was often convincing [and] that was the trouble. It made the commercial seem fraudulant . . . The marvelous world of the ordinary seemed to challenge everything advertising stood for.[26]

Elmer Rice, a Pulitzer Prize-winning playwright of the time, actually received a letter from some business executives which clearly outlined the prevailing industry attitude:

> We know of no advertiser or advertising agency of any importance in this country who would knowingly allow the products which he is trying to advertise to the public to become associated with the squalor . . . and general 'down' character of *Street Scene* [Rice's play for TV] . . . On the contrary, it is the general policy of advertisers to glamorize their products, the people who buy them, and the whole American social and economic scene . . . The American consuming public as presented by the advertising industry today is middle class, not lower class, happy in general, not miserable and frustrated.[27]

Subsequent investigations later in the decade revealed other dubious practices used by advertising agencies and sponsors over decision-making and thematic material. When questioned before a governmental committee, one ad agency VP admitted:

> Actually, there have been very few cases where it has been necessary to exercise a veto [on programs and ideas] because the producers involved and the writers involved are normally pretty well aware of what might not be acceptable.
> Questioner: In other words, they know already before they start writing and producing what the limitations are, the subject

> matter limitations, what you will accept and your client will
> accept—is that correct?
> VP: That is correct. . .[28]

This was hardly encouraging. As Barnouw aptly points out:

> The vista of a generation of producers and writers so attuned to
> sponsor wishes that they automatically avoided 'areas' considered
> controversial was scarcely inspiring. The tamed artist was perhaps
> as ominous a phenomenon as the vetoing sponsor.[29]

Other programming and philosophical changes also began to
manifest themselves at this same time. Aside from reality and
anthology dramas being phased off the air, news programs and
specials, such as Edward R. Murrow and Fred Friendly productions, were gradually deleted and more quiz and game shows
appeared in their place. The latter were considered safer because
they had audience allure by offering the promise of material gain.
They also fit in neatly with the general "up" trend of industry and
business as a whole. Yet pushing products and merchandise over
feelings and ideas had the further effect of stifling the creative
energies of many people. Once more, the public was denied
diversity of opinion and presentation.

As anthology dramas and news specials were being deleted, a
new series concept began to fill the void. Such programs revolved
around the same major characters and accepted themes. Since
there would be little change in content from show to show, the
sponsors and ad men could breathe more easily, even if the public
were receiving recurrent themes and format. There would be an
answer (or product) for all problems presented because "solutions,
as in commercials, would be clear cut."[30] By the late fifties, this
attitude came to be reflected in westerns, the new staple of
network TV. In such programs, good always triumphed over evil: a
neat counterpoint to the housewife in distress being saved by some
new detergent or floor wax. A few years later this good/bad
dichotomy moved from westerns to the spy and intrigue programs
of the sixties. Such simplified themes also were considered
advantageous to toy manufacturers because they believed action/
adventure shows would be good sales vehicles for their products.
Even though spies and secret agents might lie, cheat, and kill in the

name of law and order, the programs they appeared in often were described by advertisers as "safe and satisfying for kids." During Christmas, 1966, for example, children were offered war games, tanks, guns, gas masks, and "everything real fighting men use" which would "add real dimensions to their play battles."[31]

By the end of the fifties, more than a billion dollars were being spent annually by sponsors, and many advertisers were becoming increasingly interested in subliminal merchandising techniques and other forms of behavioral manipulation. Frantic competition for station licenses continued, and many license holders became wealthy overnight.

But because the financial stakes were so high, it was almost impossible to avoid graft and payola, and during the next few years, some rather unusual business practices again came to light. Writers often received notification from a publicity agent that if they would arrange for certain products to be shown in a scene, and told the agent in advance, they could get money after the broadcast. In 1956-57, writers and directors were receiving whole lists of similar opportunities for such merchandising "pay-offs."[32] One agency was described by *Broadcasting* as soliciting clients at "$250 per insertion." Its promoters explained, "We work very closely with the writers, producers, and stars of top-ranking, coast-to-coast radio and television programs."[33]

A series of quiz show scandals also broke out during the late fifties, which received widespread public attention. Apparently, some of the people who had been winning large amounts of money and goods on TV were doing so in less than ethical ways. At subsequent investigations before governmental committees, one participant admitted:

> ... [the producer of the show] asked me if, as a favor to him, I would agree to make an arrangement whereby I would tie [the current champion] and thus increase the entertainment value of the program.

The same witness continued:

> I asked [the producer] to let me go on the program honestly without receiving help. He said that was impossible. He told me that I would not have a chance to defeat [the champion] because he was too knowledgeable. He also told me that the show was

merely entertainment and that giving help to quiz contestants was a common practice and merely part of 'show business.' This, of course, was not true, but perhaps I wanted to believe him. He also stressed the fact that by appearing on a nationally televised program I would be doing a great service to the intellectual life, to teachers, and to education in general by increasing public respect for the work of the mind through my performance. . .[34]

While this was going on, the FCC stood by and watched. Many of its own members were also engaged in questionable practices, such as accepting money from broadcasting sources, making speeches before broadcasting groups, and traveling on large expense accounts. So it did not behoove the agency to come down too harshly on broadcasting interests in spite of the unethical practices which the quiz show investigations revealed. Again, industry self-regulation was thought the best answer to stop further irregularities in the system.

In only a few years, television had become akin to Aristotle's Prime Mover: there seemed nothing this new medium could not sell or convince the public it needed. But because society as a whole was so captivated by goods and products, concern for the educational, humanistic uses of TV—similar to the situation with radio—was slim. Prime-time evening hours were sold out to commercial interests, and most items dealing with current events or cultural affairs were positioned during time periods which were not attractive to many sponsors. Some fine programs disappeared simply because they could not gather advertising support. The main excuse for dropping them was that they were unpopular, even though this often was not the case at all. As with anthology dramas, programs such as "See It Now" and "Omnibus" were considered either too controversial or too upsetting for TV and the mentality it promoted. As Barnouw comments:

> The hierarchy of restraints made it always easy for industry leaders to cite their liberality, while at the same time keeping the peak hours as a world of refuge. Those who dwelt in that world, either as programmers or audience, could—and apparently were— almost oblivious to problems of the fringe worlds. Accepting the magic hours of THE world, they could scarcely believe in the reality of problems rumbling in the distance: poverty, race unrest, and so on. *They could even be unaware of their unawareness.*[35] [italics added]

The invasion of Hungary, Martin Luther King's efforts for racial equality, and the Supreme Court's decision to desegregate schools, to name but a few, made little headway into the world of fifties TV. Blacklisting and fear of Communists continued, while programs and commercials remained white and reflected the best of all possible worlds. There was a close link between television, the economy, and big business, for TV played an important role in this chain of merchandising and power. It was able to sell so much with such ease—thereby stimulating the general economy—that keeping people mesmerized by escapist entertainment and products was deemed wiser than filling their eyes and ears with pictures of reality and doom. The general philosophy behind all this appeared to be: keep the public distracted and buying.

Yet while television profits escalated, certain programs continued to get the ax because they were declared too expensive to produce. CBS business affairs managers may have been upset over the cost of Murrow's "See It Now," but the network made a hefty profit the year this show was dropped. Murrow's program, however, did not cost as much to make as some of the other regularly scheduled entertainment offerings. It was Murrow's belief that integrity, not salesmanship, should be the heart of good broadcasting, but the times were against him. As he himself predicted:

> If there are any historians . . . a hundred years from now and if there should be preserved the kinescopes for one week of all three networks, they will find recorded, in black and white or color, evidence of decadence, escapism and insulation from the realities of the world in which we live . . . If we go on as we are, then history will take its revenge, and retribution will catch up with us.[36]

But few paid attention to Murrow's words. The television industry was making millions. The general public continued to lap up game shows, westerns, and spy programs. Who had time for Murrow and his predictions of doom?

THE SIXTIES: GROWTH AND EXPANSION
The sixties were a period of tremendous growth for the

television industry. Technical advancements were made in transmission; coast-to-coast broadcasting became commonplace; and toward the end of the decade, the industry was beaming back pictures from space. People were buying sets—black and white and later color—and being drawn to the medium in greater and greater numbers. Viewing hours between 1960 and 1970 escalated steadily, and programming became a frantic game of one-upmanship between networks. The business itself was looked upon as tough, fast-paced, and involving a special form of combat all its own.

During the sixties, the networks began to assume even greater control over broadcasting practices and content. This was partly due to the worry generated by the quiz scandals during the late fifties and partly due to the general trend of the business toward concentration of power. The networks called this step "a move toward greater corporate responsibility"; but, in effect, such alterations brought larger profits and more control than they did ethical concern. Sponsorship also changed at this time because new demographic information on audience sex, race, and socio-economic status was now available. This relieved the sponsor from personal reactions to his programs, since all he needed were charts, figures, and computers to tell him where to buy and position his advertising spots. As one person describes it:

> When the advertiser was sponsor, it behooved him to be sensitive to the frequency and length of his program interruptions. As a buyer of minute packages which disperse his message over an assortment of programs on various nights of the week, he is unburdened of that aesthetic decency as well as other responsibilities.[37]

Words and strategies such as counterprogramming and counterattack began to evolve in network vocabulary, and these concepts further accentuated the fierce competitive attitudes which were developing between NBC, ABC, and CBS.

The first President of the decade, John F. Kennedy, sensed the vast importance of broadcasting in society and had the unique opportunity of testing the medium's power in politics. He certainly used the television image to his advantage in the 1960 Presidential Campaign. Shortly after taking office, however, he

appointed Newton Minow as the new FCC Chairman; and it was
Minow who, speaking to broadcasters, later made this now classic
indictment of American TV and the informal TV twin which had
emerged:

> When television is bad, nothing is worse. I invite you to sit down
> in front of your television set when your station goes on the air
> and sit there without a book, magazine, newspaper, profit and
> loss sheet, or ratings book to distract you—and keep your eyes
> glued to that set until the station signs off. I can assure you that
> you will observe a vast wasteland . . .

He continued:

> You will see a procession of game shows, violence, audience
> participation shows, formula comedies about totally unbelievable
> families, blood and thunder, mayhem, violence, sadism, murder,
> western bad men and western good men, private eyes, gangsters,
> more violence, and cartoons. And endlessly commercials—many
> screaming, cajoling, and offending. And most of all boredom.
> True, you will see a few things you will enjoy. But they will be
> very, very few. . .[38]

Broadcasters could not have disagreed more with the above
assessment of American television—publicly, at least. But whether
they agreed or disagreed, it did not matter. They were businessmen; and since business was good, that is all that counted. If the
programs were not uplifting, *that* was not the point: sound
economic practices were. People *watched* the "vast wasteland"! In
the end, Minow came, and he went, and the industry remained
basically unchanged.

As in earlier decades, disenchantment regarding the overcom-
mercialization of the public's airwaves again welled, and once
more the FCC was put in a questionable position. A sample survey
of TV stations in the early sixties revealed that some forty percent
were going over code limits set for advertising, yet nothing was
done. In fact, when one FCC Commissioner remarked that the
agency should try to enforce the industry's own advertising code,
NAB members were so appalled that they lobbied to prevent the
FCC from making any statements regarding commercial limitation.
The NAB sent out this message to its members:

> Broadcasters should immediately urge their Congressman . . . to
> vote for HB8316 . . . A vote for this bill is a vote of confidence in

the broadcasters in his district. A vote against the bill would open
the door to unlimited government control of broadcasting . . .[39]

The bill passed, and all was preserved for the status quo.

It was also during this time that the Vietnam War raged, and the television industry responded to the conflict in curious ways. More and more spy/war programs, which tended to support the concept of fighting and aggression, began to fill the air. Moreover, not only were adults being fed secret-agent propaganda via their screens, but the same type of mentality was being promoted in children's shows and their playthings. Everything seemed to be joined together in a neat chain of approval. Of the one hundred largest governmental military suppliers, over fifty percent were heavily involved with broadcasting, either as licensees, manufacturers, or sponsors. As one writer states, "These incentives had the effect of making TV entertainment an integral part of the escalation machine."[40]

Yet even though television was supporting the concept of war via its programming, what the American public heard regarding Southeast Asia was often of an inconsequential nature, so-called TV filler. One Canadian critic commented:

> . . . anyone who relied on [U.S.] television would have been far less well-informed than his Canadian counterpart even though the total time devoted to Vietnam on American networks was undoubtedly greater.[41]

In place of the 1966 Vietnam hearings in Congress, for example, were the fifth rerun of "I Love Lucy" and the eighth rerun of "The Real McCoys." Apparently, great pressure was exerted by advertisers who were upset that their commercial messages might be preempted by hearings in Washington, and broadcasting executives were worried that such interruptions would cost them thousands of dollars in revenue. CBS Chairman William Paley declared, "We're still running a business," and he could not support any kind "of organization unless it was economically healthy."[42] And Frank Stanton, another long-time CBS executive, echoed the Chairman of the Board:

> The specific cost incurred by the CBS Television Network in covering the . . . Vietnam Hearings, for example, amounted to just over one million dollars. Obviously, since CBS News cannot

be self-supporting, we must pay some attention to the economics of broadcasting in making decisions involving such costs.[43]

Though Paley may have lamented that the TV machine ran away with itself instead of keeping pace with the needs of society, it already was too late. Some political discussion and dissent were allowed, to be sure, but basically it was the business mechanisms which won out. As Barnouw suggests:

> During peak hours almost everything implied a reassuring view of American society. The only exceptions were occasional documentaries which were often so at odds with the prime-time view of the world that they aroused indignation ... Some people invariably attacked them as propaganda ... Evening television confirmed the average man's view of the world. It presented the America he wanted and believed in and had labored to be a part of. It was alive with handsome men and women and symbols of the good life. It invited and drew him into its charmed circle. If the circle was threatened, it was surely not by flaws within itself but by outside evil doers.[44]

By the mid- and late sixties, the global market which many broadcasters and businessmen had envisioned in the fifties flowered. As one can see below, television penetrated the world with extraordinary speed.

Growth of TV Sets Abroad From 1955 to 1964	
Place	*Change in Number of Units*
(1) Western Europe	6,018,400 to 45,931,000
(2) Eastern Europe	1,063,200 to 19,704,000
(3) Near East and South Asia	200 to 938,800
(4) Far East	259,700 to 20,977,200
(5) Africa	5,000 to 227,100
(6) Latin America and the Caribbean	619,000 to 6,645,700

[45]

By 1968, there were approximately seventy million television sets in America and over 140 million abroad. Apart from the vast national market that broadcasters were reaching, more than one hundred foreign countries were purchasing American television productions, and this global marketplace had become lucrative indeed. In a very brief span of time, television had provided the impetus for a large international concern. In only one decade— from 1958 to 1968—the foreign sales jumped from $15 million to $80 million yearly; and now industry sources estimate that U.S. TV sales abroad are at the $400 million mark.[46] In the language of the broadcasting business, these figures reflect a market characterized by continual growth.

AMERICAN TELEVISION TODAY

By the seventies, the broadcasting industry in America had entered its maturity. Innumerable technical achievements had been made over the past twenty years, and global communication via TV was a reality. The broadcasting industry had a good national market, a steadily growing international trade, and strong profits. The world of contemporary television had become a sophisticated chess game of bottom lines, revenue margins, profit and loss sheets, stock dividends, Nielsens, HUTs (Homes Using Television), and a firmly entrenched philosophy of action and attitudes. What had started out as a rather ungainly piece of furniture only a few decades earlier had become a streamlined, compact unit with pushbutton remote-control panels, color tint adjustors, UHF, and VHF. What once was considered a novelty item had become a complete and total *way of life*.

Yet, not surprisingly, many of the themes and issues discussed thus far have continued into the present, for they are an extension of previous trends within the business as a whole. Though industry costs have soared in recent years, advertisers still clamor for air time. TV commercial prices now range from several thousand to over one hundred thousand dollars per minute, depending upon the time, location, and program involved.

These increased costs for shows, stars, and advertisements, however, have resulted in even more spot interruptions. The degree to which people in this country are now exposed to TV commercial messages is staggering indeed. In 1967, for example, viewers watched an estimated 100,000 commercial minutes (approximately 103,000 commercials) on the networks. But in 1974, there were 105,622 commercial minutes (approximately 170,400 commercials).[47] This represents a sixty-four percent increase in only seven years. As recently as 1978, *Variety* reported other violations by all three networks regarding advertising time and spot commercials, particularly on news programs. And a survey conducted by the Station Representatives Association (SRA) revealed that ABC, CBS, and NBC pocketed some $31 million in "found money" during the first three months of 1978 by slipping in extra prime-time commercials. According to the SRA, the networks ran 350 *more* ad minutes than if they had followed the NAB code of six minutes per prime-time hour. Even outside prime-time, which allows more commercial minutes, the networks still exceeded the standard by 193 minutes for the first quarter.[48] There are, of course, a number of evenings when the NAB code is followed by various stations, but there is no doubt that Americans today are being subjected to more product messages via their TV screens than ever before.

Not only have commercial abuses continued, thus carrying on a tradition of broadcasting's past, but internal shake-ups and external lawsuits have now become a network way of life. In the late seventies, both CBS and NBC realigned their broadcast teams in an attempt to catch then first-place ABC in the Ratings race, and NBC let three vice presidents and 300 employees go as part of its "staff reduction plan." In the meantime, Fred Silverman, broadcasting's Golden Boy, was enticed to leave ABC to head the floundering NBC team in the hope that he could perform the same miracles for the Peacock as he had done for the former Number Three. But several years later, when Freddie failed to raise the sinking ship, overboard he went and a new entertainment programming captain was hailed. There is no room for loyalty or sentiment in the TV world hotseat.

All this maneuvering, however, is described by network brass in glowing tones. CBS president and chief executive, John Backe, since dismissed himself, declared such reorganizations are not "quick, off-the-cuff changes to fix the problems of the ratings," but rather reflect "the growing complexities of the television business and recognition that the task of being network president has become an onerous assignment, too much for one man to handle."[49] This shuffling is due only to the desire on the part of broadcasters to "accelerate the generation of more innovative programming, more popular programming, and more quality programming." Yet, all these explanations and statements are really nothing more than euphemisms for getting ahead in a cutthroat business.

Legal suits regarding questionable business activities also continue to rattle the industry. In the early seventies, the Justice Department filed against all three networks for allegedly monopolizing prime-time entertainment and restricting competition from independent producers. The suit was dropped and then reopened in 1974, and NBC finally agreed to settle out of court. CBS and ABC, however, have not indicated any willingness to do the same. In addition, Grand Juries in New York and Washington have issued indictments to approximately twenty middle-level executives at NBC. These network employees apparently were found guilty of cashing in on unused plane tickets and then pocketing the money themselves. And CBS has had its problems, too. The FCC has been investigating questionable sports broadcasts and business practices. The network recently promoted a winner-take-all tennis match which was actually rigged, because even the losers got a slice of the money pie. The network also accepted "perks" from Caesar's Palace, where the match was staged, such as free hotel services for a one-time CBS sports executive. In return, the hotel received on-the-air plugs. Similar "plugola" violations also involved the Cerromar Beach Hotel in Puerto Rico.

Finally, the Federal Trade Commission (not the FCC!) has considered initiating a large-scale investigation into the entire industry, concentrating on media ownership and how this affects TV advertising in particular. The Commission believes there is evidence that restraints and barriers may be set up which hamper independent advertisers in the business, thereby affecting free trade. The governmental agency has already found examples of such debatable practices.

(1) If a soap maker wants to introduce a new product on TV,

access to the medium would be very important for merchandising. But if other soap makers were allowed to include in their
advertising contracts a restriction that the network could not
accept ads from competitors, access would be denied, thus
restraining trade.
    (2) A credit institution advertising on a TV network might
exert pressure to prevent a news special that included information
on credit rights from being aired.[50]

Advertiser and sponsor influence is nothing new in the broadcasting game, but the proposed FTC investigation would be one of the
most thorough examinations of the industry yet undertaken by
the agency.

Another trend which has been consistently apparent throughout
broadcasting history but which is even more acute today is the
diminishing of program diversity. When early radio advertisers
complained that certain themes and shows were too 'down' or too
controversial for them to sponsor, such programs were dropped.
When Joseph McCarthy entered the scene, his irrationality, leading
to wholesale blacklisting, certainly did not help foster creative
innovation or experimentation. During the sixties, further program
homogenization took place as networks and sponsors accepted the
series format and went after the great mass audience. Today we
see the cumulative results of this telescoping movement. Autono-
my and diversity—such as they were even at radio and television's
onset—have been traded in for market security.

Most of the programs currently appearing on American TV are
produced by a handful of companies, and these organizations
generally do not offer a wide range of material. Los Angeles has
been nicknamed Television City, and the Gospel of Hollywood as
one journalist calls it is faithfully espoused from this place, where
most major prime-time series are produced. Yet, as one reporter
asks:

> How healthy can it be that virtually everything on prime-time TV
> comes out of a creative community in which people leave work at
> 4pm in their Porsche 924s so they can get in a couple of hours at
> their backyard swimming pools before the sun folds for the
> day?[51]

A recent quantitative study of the three network schedules
indicates that the American television audience now has fewer

choices regarding shows from fewer distributors, though they technically have "more" TV. The figures below show a reduction of almost fifty percent in the number of series offered over the past twenty years.

Number of Network Series in Prime-Time Viewing	
1956	123 series
1966	97 series
1976	67 series

52

The author of this survey reports:

> With so few series in production, there is less opportunity for the training and testing of new talent, less opportunity for experimentation, less innovation. The loss of employment for actors, writers, directors, and other creative-technical people associated with a television series is a real and significant by-product of this decline. It means that not only do television viewers have fewer series to choose among, but the series they do watch rely upon tired faces in familiar situations, faced with duplicative problems. Cliché plots become the rule, with variety and quality programming the exception.[53]

Another method used to hamper competition and diversity is by buying an idea from a lesser known production house and awarding it to a larger company which provides prompt and efficient delivery. As one critic writes:

> The networks argue that they just cannot take the risk of dealing with an untested newcomer, unaccustomed to the networks' demand for prolific yet speedy production. The effect of this ... power in the programming market is that it denies imaginative and innovative efforts at programming and reasonable access to viable markets except at enormous risks to the producer. In most circumstances, the great majority of the market for his product is simply foreclosed to the innovative producer.[54]

Once again, this leaves the audience with less and less.

HOW THE TV GAME IS PLAYED

As one can see, many of the trends found in the broadcasting business today are merely an extension of what has come before. Yet, from another point of view, television in America is now quite unique and refined. The business itself has become an efficiently running machine, and the makers of our TV twin have solidified the rules of the game into a very fine art. The pattern has been set; the equipment and facilities are there; and the players know how to manipulate their battle strategies for maximum effect. Today most programs are taped, and mistakes can be cut and redone. A highly stylized method of writing and producing TV has evolved as well. While analysts plot curves and juggle figures and communication lawyers make a bundle, the broadcasting business focuses on salesmanship and PR. Pending strikes or other industry setbacks, the Network Rhythm goes something like this:

(1) Plot the season in January and February.

(2) Sell it in March.

(3) Pitch it to the affiliates in May.

(4) Promote it to the public after July 4th.

(5) Premiere it in September.

(6) WATCH THE RATINGS between October and December.

At present, the main thrust of the business is to keep the ledgers showing healthy profits and to keep the FCC, Congress, the FTC, and the public at large from legislating restrictions on the industry. To be sure: these activities and struggles have characterized the business throughout its history; only today keeping the ballgame going and the various parties at bay is a triple-time job.

Our contemporary broadcaster has been painted as a highly energetic, yet nervous, businessman who goes about contemplating the Nielsens, the chief instrument by which the broadcast game in America is played. Network men have been described as generally one part conscience and nine parts profit motive (even the better ones being only three parts conscience) and are caught in the precarious position of playing the Public Service Game and the Revenue Game both at the same time.[55] One TV critic and long-time associate of industry people writes:

The most fascinating species of broadcasting executive is the one who fails his way to the top, and it is interesting that the species is not rare. Some careers have been freaks of lucky timing, some have been built on personality, some on an exceptional golf game, and some on good connections. They refute everything American children learn at school about the virtue of diligence, education, and dedication. In the business world, ineptitude is often rewarded.[56]

Another network executive gives this appraisal:

It's a terrible thing [i.e., getting money and power]. You begin to love the prestige and the authority, and the first thing you think about is how to preserve that and how to keep the money from stopping. Suddenly every new idea becomes a threat to you. It means you have to act on it, one way or another. You can't afford to be reckless. So you try to push the ideas down, make them go away, or, if possible, make them someone else's responsibility. Listen, there is a technique, and I got wise to it right away. You learn to say "no" to everything. "No" doesn't get you involved. "Yes" does.[57]

One of the main causes for the pressure of the American broadcasting business today stems from such a heavy reliance on the Nielsens and the right to keep tabs on the largest possible audience. Winning Nielsen points means greater advertiser support, more money from time-selling, hence larger profits down the line. This rating system, which has "life and death" power on Broadcast Row, is based upon a nationwide sample comprised of 1,200 Nielsen audiometers and 2,000 personal diaries. It is upon this information, and data also supplied by Arbitron and Voxbox, that advertisers can determine which shows and what types of programs the majority of the audience is viewing and the number watching at any given time. To the industry scorekeepers, prime-time television is not three and a half hours every night but so many saleable *advertising minutes*. And though some broadcasters may try to deemphasize the strong hold the rating system has on today's broadcasting business, the realities of the marketplace revolve around just these figures.

To give some idea how fierce is this rivalry for viewer eyeballs, some examples of how the game/battle is viewed are indicated in the figure on the following page. Aggressive metaphors abound. Strategic plans of attack, counter-offensives, and similar descriptions are frequent because this is precisely how the industry perceives its struggle for capturing viewer attention.

(1) The 1978-9 CBS TV prime-time schedule was formulated as a continuation of last season's ploy of concentrating firepower on the heavy set-in-use nights of Sunday through Tuesday . . . Last year, CBS concentrated on establishing a beachhead on Sunday, the highest sets-in-use night, using "60 Minutes" and "All in the Family" to prime its thrust. The tactic worked and at mid-season the same theory worked again . . .

(2) WEBS TRICK OR TREAT AFTER HALLOWEEN: Stunts Supreme for November Sweeps . . . The three networks are stuffing their program arsenals as they prepare for all out war in the November sweeps.

(3) *Variety Weekly Rating Scorecard Wednesday April 12, 1978*: ABC TV won week 29 with a 20.3 taking three nights as NBC TV and CBS TV took two each. NBC was second with a 17.5 average and CBS had a 16.7.

Season-to-Date Averages: ABC 20.8; CBS 19.0; and NBC 17.3.

[58]

Yet this struggle for Nielsen supremacy begins well before the fall season actually goes on the air. The pre-season skirmish starts July 4th, for it is then that "Selling the Fall Season" goes into effect. Remember, these battles are thoroughly premeditated campaigns to capture viewers, advertisers, and TV critics alike. A good part of the broadcast season in America is spent not on creating new and diverse program material but on promoting certain images and styles to the public. On various channels at different times of the day, viewers can see flashes, zooming stars, and space odyssey visuals—all in an attempt to gather them into the network's respective September folds. One television critic calls this TV's Annual Rites of Promise, and declares:

We all know what the Fourth of July means. It's the first day of promotion for the fall TV season. NBC's fall ad campaign will feature the singing slogan "N-B-See Us." ABC will follow on Sunday with "We're the One," and CBS a few days later with "Turn Us On, We'll Turn You On."[59]

This battle to *get at you* in some form or another rages on apace and has become an integral part of the current broadcasting machine. Not only are viewers and advertisers hustled, but TV critics as well. On July 4th, the same day we can see all sorts of song-and-dance routines for the new fall season, ploys for winning over the critics and journalists are going into effect, too. Note this modest *soiree*:

> CBS and NBC put up the visitors [critics] at Los Angeles' posh Century Plaza Hotel, filling their leisure hours with free excursions to Dodger games and Disneyland. But it was ABC . . . that mounted the most lavish reception. The network flew the guests to the exclusive Kona Kai Club in San Diego Bay. A three-masted barkentine was on hand for harbor cruises; a sports fishing boat stood by for deepsea jaunts. And after treating its guests to an evening of jai alai in nearby Tijuana, ABC shipped them off to Los Angeles—aboard three private railroad cars.[60]

As well as being fun and entertaining, such activities are also good pre-season politicking. This exercise involved thirteen days to the West Coast, eighty-two writers, and cost nearly $250,000. Many of the reporters on this spree declared it is "all part of the job" and that "a lot of this beat (meaning TV and Hollywood) is social." Another admitted, however, that this really was nothing more than a bribe because no questioning or real discussion of controversial issues regarding TV programming was allowed.

So if television in America appears something like a highly stylized war complete with strategies, game plans, and offensives, it is with good reason: *that is the way it is perceived* by the insiders. After several decades of evolutionary development, it has reached a very refined stage of competitive art. However much those involved try to make this peculiar battle seem more respectable, there still remains the fact that winning—scoring the ratings lead and advertising sales—is the ultimate goal.

HOW TV SHOWS HAPPEN

Because of industry policies and politics such as those just described, an intricate pattern of making TV has emerged. Writers, producers, and directors must follow a broadcasting standards code, allow for commercials, not offend, conform to budgets and schedules, juggle plots, and satisfy everyone from tots to teetotalers. The description given by many people associated with television production today is disconcerting to say the least. For example, a member of the Canadian Broadcasting Corporation, while visiting a writer friend in Hollywood, actually witnessed the following scene take place:

> The phone rang. It was the story editor of "Mannix," and the dialogue with my writer friend went like this: "You need an episode of Mannix right away? What subject. A water subject? One on the surface then? Okay, to be shot in the marina at Marina del Rey. When do you want it?" This was on a Monday. "Wednesday? Okay, no sweat."
>
> He hung up and crossed to his filing cabinets . . . and pulled out the "Mannix" fact sheet. The fact sheet gives a breakdown of the character, explaining what is allowed and not allowed in terms of both the character and the star. Mannix will never be seen without a shirt or with his hair mussed. Mannix will never be seen drunk; Mannix is chivalrous with the ladies, austere with tarts and homosexuals. [The writer] pinned up the set of rules on a large bulletin board. He then went back to the filing cabinet headed A to Z containing different openings. He went through, rifled down the cards, down to W for water. (My mind boggled when I noticed that the card before water was wasps!) He had four different cards for water "hookers," as they are called—those thirty-second grabbers at the beginning of the show. Next came a three and a half minute segment called "the problem," in which the client meets Mannix and tells him she is in desperate trouble . . . Commercial break. Next comes a seven minute segment: Joe Mannix goes out [to solve the problem], finishing with suspense action leaving the hero in jeopardy. Next comes a four minute segment, then another seven minute segment, all with their appropriate names, and finally there was a seven minute homestretch with a two minute thing called a "diver," a twist that puts the hero in sudden trouble. The diver is necessary because it is feared that during the homestretch, which is usually conventional, the audience will switch channels. At the end of the homestretch, there was another commercial break, the one minute wrap up, another commercial break, and finally the thirty second "teaser" for the next week.
>
> My writer friend just kept pulling out filing cards appropriate for the various segments. He shuffled them about and pinned them up on the board. He finished an hour script in a day and a half and delivered it on Wednesday.[61]

Writers working for television today must conform to the realities of their business which is not so much *writing* as it is *making filler* to go in between the commercials. As one female writer declares:

> TV writers are the lowest . . . You can't even talk. I started out as Carl Reiner's secretary, and then I could say anything I wanted. But as soon as I became one of his writers, I couldn't say anything. Then, even if I told him one of my own scripts was bad, he'd say, "What do you know?"
>
> Interviewer: Didn't it bother you to be treated so shabbily?
>
> Writer: Naw. The money is too good to worry about minor details like integrity.
>
> Interviewer: Tell me, exactly how does a freelance writer like you . . . go about doing a half-hour script?
>
> Writer: It's easy. You go in with a bunch of story ideas, they pick one they like, turn on a tape recorder, and tell you exactly how to write it. Then you go home, listen to the tape, type it up, and fill in the spaces where the jokes go. When you're finished typing, you bring it back and they give you a lot of money.
>
> Interviewer: That's it? That's how TV comedy gets written?
>
> Writer: No, that's how TV writers get paid. Nobody knows how TV comedy gets written. After your script is accepted, you tune in to watch the show and all the lines are different.[62]

Television may actually have done more to stifle individual creative response than any other single force in America today. From the reports of insiders, it is a third-rate world for third-rate minds who are willing to crank out garbage for incredible amounts of money. It is ironic indeed that television seems to crave respect—the one thing it generally does not get. Is that why it must keep patting itself on the back? It is also quite possible that Hollywood never effectively recovered from the trauma of Joseph McCarthy and the blacklisting fear which permeated the industry for a number of years. As mentioned earlier, many creative people fled; and the business elements came in quickly to fill the void. The commercial mentality superseded artistic spirit, and consequently, advertisements have become the center of most creative energy. Even today actors in commercials earn more than those in films or TV series.[63] But why not? After all, the commercials are more *important*!

INDUSTRY MEMBERS SPEAK OUT

Though many people presently involved with television do seem more than willing to sell out for the money to be gained or tell you how great it all is, there are those who work in TV who are just as dismayed by current trends as people in the general public. Not everyone is hell bent on the prostitution of his or her creative talent. The various comments below indicate that television today is not as rosy as the profit margins may infer. A common theme of disenchantment begins to assert itself and must be reckoned with because it comes from people within the industry. As one producer declares:

> The network doesn't like to rock the boat, to tamper with what works. The old studio bosses, for all their faults, had some love for film-making. But all the network people do is line up the programs on their long tables and juggle them against the competition, asking, "What will work best against that?" instead of "What are we going to do?" The network is run by salesmen. It's their business not to love the process of making a film.[64]

Another executive producer with whom I spoke echoed the same feelings:

> The money people run the ship . . . They are all network business analysis people. I'll tell you what's happened in this business . . . This business is now being run by salesmen. It used to be run by creative people.

She continued:

> The creative control of things has gone out of the hands of the creative people. It now belongs to the creative control of the salesmen, and it's an insidious, ugly, terrible thing . . . [the networks] are hiring a bunch of not very bright people and they're doing it on purpose because then there's no competition and then the money men can run the business.

When I asked whether her decision to leave after eight years at one network was due to what she saw happening, she responded:

> Yes . . . I want to produce my own stuff and I want to produce quality family entertainment for children. My creativity has been stifled and trampled upon here. The only consideration is the budget. I don't mind working to a budget, but I don't want to be told by someone who knows nothing about television production when to do my show, what time to do it, what time to wake up, what time to go to sleep, because they do not know as much as I do about the medium. And besides: they don't care. I don't want

to work with people who stand up in front of community groups and say they are concerned when they are not. I'm just tired of it. I think the time has come to put an end to that kind of hypocrisy.[65]

Two producers of children's shows whom I met said they refused to do programs for one of the networks because "it's very difficult to come up with what they want on the air." One continued:

I literally hope that there comes a day very, very shortly when people really do pay for what they want to see. Then they'll be able to see what they really want instead of what's fed to them.

He went on:

This way independent producers and companies would be able to provide more varied original material as opposed to the same old stuff on network TV season after season . . .[66]

Writers, producers, and directors are not alone in these criticisms, either, because entertainers are also speaking out. One actor declares that television will "self-destruct" and adds:

The only thing you could do to save television is start all over. You'd have to fire everybody in a position of responsibility— that's how bad it is . . . The network executives don't even look at [the shows]. They are usually attorneys. They'll tell you their kids love your show, but all they themselves watch is the ratings.[67]

Another actress left CBS because she was dissatisfied with the trends she saw occurring in her series:

I was unhappy about the changes that were coming about . . . If there is no quality; if there is no integrity, then I don't need to do it.[68]

She felt some of the scripts presented the character she portrayed in an equivocal light; yet when she voiced her concern, *nobody listened.* She then received word that not everybody would be present on the first day of shooting, so she decided to stay at home, relax, and get a more positive attitude toward work. As a result, the producers put her on suspension that very evening after six years of working on the program.

How symptomatic are these episodes of Hollywood and TV as a whole? One cannot talk about television today without taking these various criticisms into account because they come from people who are directly involved with making TV happen. The montage they represent is one of disappointment and dissension that individual creativity—whether writer, producer, director, or actor—is being squeezed out by those who do not care or who are willing to hang around for the money and power they feel the broadcasting industry provides. Certainly, there are responsible, concerned people within the broadcasting community, but is the energy they expend just hopelessly wasted? Should they simply abandon TV and let it self-destruct as the one actor suggests? That television would do so is highly unlikely, for the 1980s promise more riches to come, especially with all the advancing video technologies on the horizon (see Chapter Six).

PROGRAMS AND ADS: A FINAL LOOK

There you have over a half century of broadcasting history compressed into a few dozen pages: only a brief glimpse of our TV creators and their special brand of television combat. Yet I feel one final image of our classroom rival must be presented by drawing upon industry ads and the programs themselves. In many respects, they provide the best single statement of how this one-of-a-kind business functions today. The motivations and attitudes which they reflect paint the most honest picture available of American TV, for they are the "raw" television experience.

Since a concern for young people is how I got started on all this in the first place, I want to begin with a few excerpts from random Saturday and Sunday morning programs. What follows is how a large percentage of kids in America spends their weekend leisure time and gives some indication of the informal TV twin being nurtured, both in program content and style. First of all, my strange encounter of a crazy kind about 9:00 a.m. one Saturday morning. (Many children begin the ritual around 6:30 or 7:00.)[69]

Break: Movie plug, "The People That Time Forgot."

Show: Starring Frank N. Stein, Dracula, and Bruce Wolfman in an on-going serial revolving around a young man trying to put himself through school. He works as a night janitor at the local Horror Museum, recreates the above three monsters, and brings them back to life. Reason: To fight crime and help humanity.

Break: Movie plug, "Herbie Goes to Monte Carlo." Blow Pop
candy suckers with chewing gum inside.

Back to show: Bruce Wolfman is trying to comb his dandruff-
ridden hair . . . on face, neck, and shoulders. Frank N. Stein is "in
stitches." College boy tells them all to stop joking around, or
"Dracula will be at your throats." Crazy astrologist predicts
massive California earthquake. State will break away and fall into
ocean. Newscaster *á la* Barbara Walters gives the story. Canned
laughter as astrologer and his goons, Castor and Pollux, bounce
around their hideaway. They start playing with atom bomb, which
the astrologer has stolen and which is supposed to cause the
tremendous earthquake. Astrologer vows to make his prediction
come true. Villainous laugh. Switch back to Horror Museum and
boy's Home Built Crime Computer to check on astrological
forecast.

Break: Tony the Tiger for Sugar Frosted Flakes.
Wizard of O for Spaghetti-O's.
PSA on nutrition.

Back to show: Enter Officer McMacMac. Boy quickly hides
Crime Computer in burial casket. Officer McMacMac tells about
the stolen atom bomb and then leaves. Off goes Monster Squad to
the rescue in a big, black van, cruising the streets for crime. Rock
music in background. The Mad Astrologer gives Frank and Bruce
some Knock-Out Smoke Drops and then proceeds to feed them to
his giant pet, Carlo the Clam.

Break: Corny Snaps sweet cereal with Snappy as a take-off on
Zorro. (Snappy goes around making the sign of "S"
rather than "Z.") Lone Ranger Action Heroes. (Disclaimer: Tonto sold separately.)

Back to show: Dracula reports back to Chamber of Horrors in
museum with help of his wrist communicator. His code name is
"Night Flier." Reads book entitled *How to Disassemble a
Thirty-Year-Old Atomic Bomb*. Good guys eventually win. Canned
laughter. Castor and Pollux go around with wastepaper baskets on
their heads, stepping into buckets, etc. Show ends with three
monsters receiving "This Wonderful Country's Great Honor
Award."

Break: Dairy Queen dispenser for sweet drink with Mr. Misty
Machine.

Cherrios cereal.

Then this blurb: Next week on Monster Squad: The Washington
Monument disappears, and the heroes try to find it.

There were more commercials, then another cartoon with a girl
and boy involving ghosts and money. Then back into the fray.

Break: Mini Ravioli Chef Boyardee with animated cartoon
figures.

Big Yellow Sugar Pops cereal.

Micronaut Toys. (Disclaimer: All sold separately.)

"Be a Time Traveller so you can stage your own Make
Believe Battles!"

Back to show: Frankie Frankenstein, Jr. in "The Spooktaculars."
Dr. Spectro, the bad guy, has ghost-maker machine from which he
produces his monsters. Opponents are a father and son do-gooder
team. Dr. Spectro wants to take over Pennsyltrania. Sends in three
ghosts, the Spooktaculars, or "Snooper Heroes," as Dr. Spectro
calls them. Dialogue includes such lines as, "Haven't a ghost of a
chance." Canned laughter. Frankie Frankenstein has battering ram
which comes out of his head and frost mist which emanates from
his nose à la Bionic heroes. Revenge and greed abound. Good guys
win.

Break: Same Cheerios ad as earlier.

Nestle's Quik drink.

Repeat of earlier PSA.

Back to show: Jan, Jace, and Blip (a monkey) in an escape-and-
chase sequence entitled "Great Galaxy." Battle of spaceships with
the Cyclo Centinnels and Cyclo Terror. Space Ghost offers this
moral: "Things have a way of evening out for poor, misguided
creatures like Cyclo . . ."

Break: Oscar Goldman Secret Agent with Exploding Briefcase.

Marathon Man plugging Marathon Candy bars, "The
candy you can't eat quickly!"

PSA on emphysema from the American Lung Association.

Trailer: Next week Space Ghost to the Planet Vector; giant locusts are the game. Called "Locar's Metal-Eating Space Locusts." Tune in, kids!

Can the reader possibly imagine how jellified my brain was after four hours of this? I spent nearly half an hour just walking around outside to *calm down* and regain my equilibrium. Thinking (or hoping, at any rate) that Sunday morning might be somewhat different, I switched on the set. Naturally, it all started out with a commercial.

Break: Astronauts selling chewing gum.

Back to show: This time it's about a talking shark. Shark is complete with Brooklyn accent. Comments, "I don't get no respect." Combination of comedian Rodney Dangerfield and Curly Joe of The Three Stooges.

> *Break*: Lucky Charms sweet cereal with animated leprechaun bouncing around.
> Plug for "Hardy Boys Mystery" show later that night.
> Plug for "Six Million Dollar Man," with Flip Wilson guest star as a programmed killer.

Back to show: This week's segment opens in the Swiss Tyrolian Alps. The villain (Skeleton or Skull Cap . . . I never could make out his name) is after Professor Thorston's Time Machine. Meanwhile, Jabberjaws and friends are playing in a rock band. While gigging, one band member suggests, "Let's slap on some skis and boogie down those slopes." Jabberjaws complies. The villain's stooges then come for the Professor with an immobilizer ray gun, but they get the wrong guy. Switch scene. Jabberjaws is skiing with jet-propelled skis. Later he dresses up as a computer and tries to fool the bad guys. Bad guys try to perform an operation on so-called computer. One girl comments, "Give it chicken soup and put it to bed."

> *Break*: Kellogg's Sugar Smacks with animated frog jumping around and saying, "Dig 'Em!"
> Mr. Magico Magician selling Blow Pop candy suckers.
> Plug for "Donnie and Marie Osmond Show."
> Plug for YMCA.

Back to show: Shark goes around sniffing for friends like a dog while exclaiming, "Jubber Jelly Fish!" Girl in cartoon is stereotyped dumb blonde. We finally learn why the villain wants the Time Machine: to travel back through time and plunder the riches of the past. Comes the inevitable chase scene. To hide, shark and friends get into Time Machine and are transported back to 1,000,000 BC. Then there is another chase scene with dinosaurs. Jabberjaws keeps saying, "I get no respect." After defeating the villain with the aid of the dinosaur, which the good guys transported from days of yore to help in present, show ends with rock song and people skiing back down the hills in another chase sequence. Good prevails, and the dinosaur is sent back through time.

> *Break*: Cheerios for that POW POW POWERFUL/GOOD GOOD FEELING from CHEER CHEER CHEERIOS!
> Plug for "Blanksy's Beauties."
> PSA.
> Plug for "Hardy Boys."
> Plug for "Six Million Dollar Man."
> Plug for "Happy Days."
> Plug for "Laverne and Shirley."

Enough! These examples are but an inkling of what goes on every Saturday and Sunday morning for hours on end. Not all the programs are like the ones above. There are a few which attempt to provide a certain amount of challenge to young people, but they are exceptions to the rule. Today a child's TV twin generally exists at this low level.

Now, turning to so-called adult prime-time hours on American television. The excerpts here are taken from the opening 1978/79 Fall Season, and the first selection is from the opening "block-buster" from ABC: "Washington: Behind Closed Doors." (It started off with four commercials, including one for the Bank of America, reassuring me that I too "can have CLOUT!")

> *Show*: President Griffin is in the Oval Office talking about TV while monitoring three screens. Men talking money and politics— in that order. Kids outside protesting war. President talking with aides while going to the john. Big question: Who will be the next President? Talking power and passion with CIA director, whose wife is a former lover of the President's.

Break: A-1 Steak Sauce, "A steak without A-1 is a 'misteak'."
Mother's aide in school plugging Wonderbread.
Single girl talking about taking care of herself and her car. That's why she goes to Sears Automotive Center: so they can take care of her car for her. Go to Sears. Where America shops. Sears celebrates Kenmore vacuum cleaners, freezers, etc. Save at Sears!

Back to show: CIA director cancels appointments and goes back to CIA. Looks mad. Counterspy routine. Whole role of media and press. Politicians becoming smiling don Juans before the camera's eye. Booze and pills to sleep. All tough nuts in Washington.

Break: Oil of Olay. Women around the world praising this lotion. Catch phrase is: "You can look younger, too!"
Jolly Green Giant still ho-ho-hoing. This time for frozen steaks instead of frozen vegetables.
Network plug: The Magic of ABC.
Plug for "Three's Company."
Plug for "SOAP." Disclaimer: "If you miss 'SOAP,' " you'll be the only one." (Parental discretion advised.)

Back to show: Political fustian and folderol. Impression of egotistical men dressed up in fancy suits. Image-conscious, vain-glorious people pushing others around. $250,000 "friendship" donations.

Break: Young couple saying, "Five years ago we just used to watch TV after dinner. Now we play tennis, jog, eat less." Then they go on to advertise a food product high in carbohydrates and processed sugar.
Top Choice for dogs. "Looks like hamburger!"
Lysol spray toilet bowl cleaner.
Sears: Towels.
Plug for "Happy Days."
Pele plugging American Express card: "Don't leave home without it."
Plug for 11:00 p.m. News. Trying to capitalize on special by having an "exclusive interview" with John Dean.

Fortunately, I was spared the rest of the evening because my television quite literally went on the blink. A few days later, however, after I had it repaired, I tuned in again to this soap opera set in Washington, and what I saw was virtually indistinguishable from the opening night.

    Break: Vicks Sinex cold medicine.
               Snackin' Cake. Ready-to-make quick sweet treat.
               Plug for "Welcome Back, Kotter"—Sweat Hogs in a Back-to-School Special.
               Plug for "Hardy Boys." (This was the same plug shown on kids' weekend programs.)
               Plug for "Six Million Dollar Man." (Also same as on kids' weekend TV.)
               Plug for Tuesday night viewing: "Three's Company," "SOAP," "Family."
               Allstate Insurance. "You're still in good hands with Allstate."
               Peter Pan peanut butter "is everything it's cracked up to be."
               Gillette razor blades.
               TV interviewer asking football player to test the relative merits of Right Guard vs. Ban Basic deodorant.
               Benny Goodman, The King of Swing, plugging American Express Card.
               United Airlines.

Twelve interruptions in a matter of seconds! Watching the program seemed inconsequential compared with all the commercials. I actually found myself taking notes on the breaks and missing the show. "Behind Closed Doors" went on for almost a week, with virtually the same scenario every evening. I watched some other new-season specials, caught "SOAP" because, Lord knows, I did not want to be counted among those backwoods boobs who missed the cultural event of the season; saw a few drama series, the latest edition of "Starsky and Hutch," complete with its bubble gum commercial at 10:00 p.m., when, of course, no kids are watching, and so on. Then I viewed this new program, if one can call it new, seeing as how it was the third or fourth or fifth spin-off from another successful series. An ex-husband-and-wife acting team were giving each other a hard time. Such jokes occurred as, "Is that a moustache or did you have anchovies for lunch?" A stereotyped dumb blonde appears—just like the one in the children's program—only live, not animated. When asked where ex-wife had met the blonde, the reply was, "I met her at the unemployment office before they let her go." Then this exchange:

Woman: "I respect you as a director but despise you as a person."

Man: "Your father wears panty hose."

This week's theme: old enemies become friends again for the sake of the show. Sexual banter and allusions back and forth between divorced, middle-aged couple. Then . . .

Break: Free Spirit Bra.

Arthritis Pain Formula.

Back to show: Female lead returns in mini-skirt. (All this is really a hooker disguise to cover her status as a secret agent, which is all part of the plot of the pilot series she is acting in.) Her ex-husband is directing. Stuntman is dressed in same getup as woman. Her directions are to smash him with the bust (statue), NOT bust (boobs). Ex-wife finds out ex-hubby has not remarried after all, which she had supposed. Hurt pride results in a temper tantrum in which she breaks everything on the set. Very broad slapstick à la Roman comedies and exactly the same sort of stuff as Pollux and Castor on Saturday morning kidvid. Get news that pilot is terrible—and that the network *loves* it! Want twenty more. Big party to celebrate in which stuntman comes dressed in same cocktail dress as hostess. Ex-husband and wife reconcile. He stays, and they all live happily in the house that Jack built.

And *that* is only a *taste* of what usually parades across the screen night after night, day-in and day-out, on and on and on. The seasons may come and go, but the general tone and tenor remain the same. One year there is an emphasis on adolescent comedy and sexual innuendo; the next season more crime and police programs. Docudramas are on the wane, but prime-time "soaps" are "in." And, undergirding it all, the commercials keep rolling on!

Now a look at some ads. First of all, from *Variety*:

> HEADLINE: THE AMERICAN SYSTEM OF BROADCASTING
> DOESN'T EXIST . . . Not if by a system you mean a rigid,
> unchanging set of rules . . . The American system of broadcasting
> changes almost every day. Congress passed the Communications
> Act in 1934, but broadcasters—through their ingenuity and
> through competitive pressures—change the way the system works
> every time they make a decision.

That is not exactly what I have learned about the nature of our
opponent. Nevertheless, the ad continues:

> The changes aren't going to stop. When you look at it that way,
> the American system of broadcasting is what *Variety* is all
> about . . .

Leading to the real purpose of the *spiel*:

> And what *Variety* is all about makes your advertising in its pages
> so much more effective . . . Team up with us. You'll find that our
> strengths combined with yours will create an effective selling
> combination.
>
> 70

In other words, not necessarily variety and innovation, but
advertising and successful selling offensives.

An advertisement shown on the following page plugs the new
technology and all the hardware/software which will make the
viewing of Christmas Future so much more fun. We Americans are
now the lucky recipients of Brave New World-type feelings right in
our own homes because we can lose ourselves to the image.
Imagine! Now we can watch even *more* TV!

Man's Testimonial: I used to sleep until noon. But since I bought Video Beam, I get up at 8:00 a.m. to watch "Tom and Jerry."
AD: Record executive, video freak, young man on the way out, talks about his $3,000.00 Video Beam Television and the programs he likes best.
Testimonial: It's high fidelity television. I have a videocassette recorder plugged into the Beam so I can tape programs I like. I watch them over and over, and always see something new . . . It's not passive like ordinary TV; it's a much more active medium. You feel things . . . I mean FEEL . . . And like I used to fall asleep in front of my regular TV set. I have never fallen asleep in front of the Beam. I get too involved . . . It gets you up . . . you know, ordinary TV can sometimes bring you down . . . The Beam becomes a whole environment. I love it . . .

At the bottom comes this blurb:

ADVENT'S VIDEOBEAM TELEVISION: IT'S BEYOND TV . . . [71]

Then we have this full-page ad taken out by *TV Guide* which puts the television scene in America into proper perspective. A lion is presented on the page for background graphics, then this disclaimer:

RECORDS ARE MADE TO BE BROKEN!!! In 1977, *TV Guide's* advertising revenue reached $176 million, breaking the 11-year-old record and making it the all-time revenue leader in magazine publishing history . . . In 1977, *TV Guide* again led all magazines in circulation, selling more than 1 billion copies for the fourth consecutive year! THE CHALLENGE: TO SURPASS OUR OWN RECORDS IN 1978!

[72]

Then '79, '80, '81 . . . The ad then ends with this statement:

TV Guide: AMERICA READS *TV GUIDE* . . .

Does America read anything else?

And last, but not least, is this advertisement for MIP TV. If American TV circa the 1970s and into the 1980s is about anything, I think this ad captures it all. The backdrop is the heavens, stars, galaxy, and universe beyond, and the lettering superimposed on it reads:

> GOD PROGRAMMED THE WORLD IN SIX DAYS. MIP TV OFFERS YOU 7 DAYS FOR YOUR PROGRAMS. MIP TV IS A MUST!

73

Too bad. God has finally been outdone by TV! What else can anyone say regarding the combat zone of American commercial television and the manufacturers of our TV twin?

VI

Television, Education, and the Future

THOUGHTS AND DIRECTIONS

Television in the United States has been called by some economists only an average-sized industry. This seems a curious comparison because broadcasting appears as such a vast and profitable enterprise. In reality, however, the combined annual revenue of studios and networks is similar to that made from the manufacture of cardboard boxes, cotton fabrics, or canned fruits and vegetables.[1]

Such a comparison does put the American broadcasting system and public education in a bit more perspective and makes one wonder whether all the furor over violence, advertising, and television's other effects is nothing more than a tempest in a teacup. Has TV merely become one of the more convenient scapegoats in educational circles? Are we merely bad-mouthing TV to divert attention from our own inadequacies as teachers and educators? Will panning television fade with the passage of time? Or will railing against the medium remain just something for teachers to complain about, with no hope of it ever really changing? In light of the preceding chapter, each of these alternatives would certainly seem to be anticipated.

Nor should we be unduly surprised by the mentality behind the present television industry and the way it functions as a whole. Large institutions—including as well the more conservative elements of the educational establishment—seek to perpetuate the status quo and their position of power in society. Whether TV, government, or the learning business, they strive to preserve control and influence—even if it is sometimes at the expense of individual growth and freedom. The broadcasting system in

America functions no differently from this aspect of society in general, and it would be socially and politically naive not to take this view into account.

The trouble, however, is that television is an institution which has more of an effect on our lives than cardboard boxes, canned fruit, *or even government.* We are talking about a product which interacts directly, intimately, and with relentless consistency on the individual mind and the process of learning and human communication as a whole.

This is especially true in America, where broadcasting has evolved quite differently from most other systems in the world. Over seventy percent of the TV stations outside the United States and over eighty percent outside the US and Canada are government or non-profit operations.[2] Ostensibly, they exist for the people, *not* to make money. (Of course, in many countries, the government-run TV operations are merely propaganda outlets for dictatorial regimes.) The standard American defense of government control, censorship, and violation of the First Amendment has been used time and again to defend our current system of broadcasting. We do not want a government-run industry. But perhaps we merely have traded the spectre of government regulation for that of control of the airwaves by big business. In many respects, broadcasters command a more influential position in today's society than teachers and schools *because* they have the power to decide what we do or do not see and hear over the air. And that makes them a very elite group indeed.

But the information provided earlier in this book suggests that we need to think long and seriously about our most pervasive of mass media because our TV twin has now had thirty years to spawn and grow. A lot has been taking place in the informal learning domain which we are only beginning to discover and understand, and certainly a great deal needs to be more fully questioned and explored.

Yet, merely discussing or reviewing the negative aspects of television exposure or the struggle the medium presents to teachers is only one side of the overall fight. What about a positive direction for television in the future? What can we do to lessen the adversarial role between teaching and TV? Once we do become serious and want to talk about these educational issues—as well as philosophical ones—where can we turn for constructive action? As indicated previously, the broadcasting business generally has been unresponsive to the needs of children or the audience as a whole outside of their role as consumers. Members of the industry are not going to change—really, they are *not*—unless some economically expedient or advantageous alternatives are presented to them. We cannot afford to wait for the TV business to alter its way of doing things.

Where to next? Congress and the legal system? There is the possibility of forging a more compelling legal statement regarding television, learning, and communication. But though the much needed rewrite of the 1934 Communications Act is finally coming to light, we must ask whether this will in fact help change the imbalance currently evident in our present situation. The bill calls for less regulation and more marketplace competition, thereby hoping to stimulate diversity through free trade, spurred on by the competition from cable TV and videodiscs, but it remains to be seen whether this actually will be the case. Furthermore, radio stations would immediately receive indefinite licenses after enactment, and television licenses would become permanent in ten years. This would effectively eliminate ascertainment requirements and the public's recourse to voice opinions regarding the local broadcaster's service. Instead, licenses could be vetoed for technical violations only, and the FCC has yet to rescind many licenses even on those grounds. At least, the 1934 Act called for regulation to be in "the public interest, convenience, and necessity"; but in the proposed new bill, regulation would be necessary only "to the extent that marketplace forces are deficient."[3] From the public's point of view, this is dubious and untested improvement at best—if any improvement at all. In effect, it would give the broadcasters everything they ever wanted! Even the *pretense* of licensure in the public interest would be gone.

So, where *can* we go to next? Consumer action groups? Yes, there is that alternative, but as yet the TV consumer movement in America lacks a genuinely comprehensive and coordinated strategy with which to approach the networks and government. People *are* lobbying in Washington; but the contest between public advocates and the TV business as a whole is not an even match. The advocates, too often, are portrayed as "kooks" or professional gadflies not serious-minded, level-headed individuals.

Consumer action groups, however, do provide a vital function: educating and informing the general public about the effects of television and how the broadcasting industry goes about its business. It is extremely important that we teachers and professionals in education, as well as parents, be alerted to this tremendously influential part of contemporary life. Such groups also prove that there still are people who will devote time and energy because they care, and there is some comfort to be gained by knowing that there are individuals who have not yet abandoned hope.

Where to next? Moving somewhat closer to the mark, how about coping with the problem of television more in the home? There are some fine programs available on the educational channels, and *even* occasionally on the networks themselves. America is not totally devoid of an alternative point of view. Moreover, a judicious reading of *TV Guide* by parents, teachers, and schoolboards alike could benefit children very much by helping them become more selective and critical. This is the most common-sensical approach to the matter, because it would put the responsibility of dealing with TV in the home where it belongs. The courts and broadcast industry are quick to reaffirm this and declare they are loathe to make laws and restrictions which should be under the domain of parental control. And, to a large extent, they are absolutely right.

But the truth of the matter is that if the majority of parents in this country were coping successfully with television, many children in America would not be watching five or more hours a day. As indicated in Chapter One, it seems many adults have abdicated their responsibility for monitoring what and how much their children are exposed to, especially from TV. This shift reflects a great deal about our society in personal, social, and educational terms. Yet, how are we teachers to react to people who sincerely ask: "You mean TV is *bad* for children!!??" Have grown-ups allowed television to become the child's third parent? One which gives no real formal training but merely minds Junior and keeps him quiet? Have women, as they enter the work force to pursue careers and alternative life styles, turned to TV to fill the void? And as pre-TV families diminish, how will post-TV families, those raised not knowing life without a TV, deal with their young people and this third eye in their multi-media homes?

So, where does this leave us in our side of the television/teaching fight? The general public cannot be expected to understand the nuances of communications law nor the internal workings of the broadcast industry, and many people simply do not have the time, energy, and money it takes to join or run public service groups. And parents . . . well, many parents are going to have to confront much more seriously and thoughtfully their approach to television and children.

As we stand on the brink of even more technological change, we cannot begin to fully comprehend the ramifications of Xerox Corporation's new data transfer system; cable and pay TV; superstations via satellite hook-ups; England's new Prestel videotex system; QUBE, two-way interactive TV; computers* at home and in school; keyboards to print out on seven-foot wall screens our grocery lists and banking statements; and so on. Moreover, this worldwide change in information flow will know no racial, national, or educational boundaries as countries around the world go after the viewer/learner/consumer marketplace. We are being thrust by technology with little consultation or comprehension into a media revolution which is altering rapidly and radically the way we learn about ourselves and other peoples and nations of the

---

*Computers, interestingly, while using the same cathode ray tube displays as the TV industry, may not act the same on our nervous systems. Indeed, computers may prove to be an educational ally rather than antagonist. It is too early to tell, at this point, and much research needs to be done on interactive student-computer learning. Even with video games, for example, the learner/viewer must *respond*. Despite some of the criticism waged against them, these games require the participant to be actively involved with both hand/eye movement coordination and various cognitive decisions, which makes them different from "normal" TV viewing.

world. Yet, whether this revolution will bring us greater tolerance and understanding or further individual subjugation remains to be seen. We are indeed on the threshold of a new age, but it is uncertain whether the equality of man will be realized on a low or a high level. The point is: as we approach this leap into hyper-technology, how will we cope and respond on a human plane?

As always, there are more questions than answers, but one thing that should be very clear and very real now, especially to those of us in education, is the growing role of broadcaster as social engineer. After all, psychologists use the word "programming" too, and they do not mean entertainment, but the manipulation of behavioral response. Those of us involved with learning and young people must consider what this programming means to us as teachers and to our multi-media students. What will be the function of the up-coming generation of viewers in relationship to this upheaval? How will they react to this new social engineering? The information in this book provides only a brief glimpse of what has happened already, and there is the possibility that these forces and influences will accelerate as we become more and more media oriented. So, if we have little or no satisfactory recourse through the legal system or the broadcast business analyst or the advertiser, the home or through public service groups, where are we to go? Should we simply "turn the damn TV off," as more and more people suggest?

Less mindless consumption would help, certainly, but pretending that the problem of television or other new technologies and how we are to approach them does not exist is an equally dangerous alternative. By acting that something once out of sight ceases to threaten, we might be in for even more trouble. To give up before we have even started to deal with television in a constructive manner would be an admission of defeat prior to entering the battle itself. In our quest to understand more about the nature of our classroom antagonist, we must have faith in our side of the fight; otherwise, the battle between television and learning truly will be lost before we even have the opportunity of arming our young people for constructive combat with TV. What can we do *now* to meet this pressing challenge without undue retreat or capitulation? What can we do to change from a defensive to an offensive mode?

Though I accept a certain bias on my part, it seems that one of the few choices we have left to deal with these vast changes in the way we learn and communicate is through a systematic and thorough education, one which takes into account the reality of these technological advances and the alteration in the way we learn informally, formally, and technically. This is where a committed and cohesive philosophy of thought and action in education at all levels—from kindergarten to graduate research and curriculum planning—is so critical today. We teachers in particular must grapple with this shift in information acquisition, and we must ask ourselves as another set of social engineers how we will combat the social engineering instigated by the broadcasters. H.G. Wells once said that future history will be a race between education and catastrophe, and it may very well be that the most crucial battle which takes place in the last two decades of this century will be within learning institutions themselves, trying to cope with this remarkable change.

TELEVISION AND THE CLASSROOM TEACHER

This is not to imply that educators and other professionals have been unaware of television and its effect on students and what happens in the classroom. Far from it. The past thirty years have witnessed numerous efforts to provide alternative prosocial, educational, and instructional programming to the American people. Studies and surveys conducted since the fifties both here and abroad reveal numerous advantages which television can offer. Slow learners in elementary school, medical and dental students viewing operations on closed circuit TV, and businessmen broadcasting corporate policy to branch offices around the world can all profit from the positive use of the TV screen. Today noncommercial stations, the Public Broadcasting Service, Children's Television Workshop, the Corporation for Public Broadcasting, National Educational Television (NET), independent producers, local stations, and school districts present many fine selections and provide the viewing public with choices regarding television content and style.

Yet, in spite of such efforts to use the medium in a more constructive way, which eliminates at least some of the deleterious effects of TV, we have not succeeded in implementing a thoughtful and cohesive approach to the use of television at home and in school. There are, of course, many ways of tackling the problem of television once it has been acknowledged and recognized as an important issue in education today. The individual style and focus of the teacher will determine much of what is presented regarding television communication and young people. It must also be remembered that five-year-olds, as well as high school or college students, can discuss topics about broadcasting and new technology. Just because a child is in kindergarten does not mean he is incapable of reasoning and questioning. As a matter of fact, the younger the child, the more crucial the need for awareness regarding television consumption, because often they are its *prime users*.

The following thoughts regarding television represent only a fraction of the possibilities available to the concerned and innovative teacher. These suggestions could be handled in a variety of ways, depending upon teacher/student preferences and the needs of the individual class. Impromptu discussions, surveys, panel debates, written essays, the development of critical viewing skills, or more individualized projects are all different methods for approaching the issue of teaching, television, and today's students. The important thing is that we start *some* positive action. The TV medium *is here*. It is not going to go away—far from it! Teachers, then, will have to begin to come to terms with it and to try to do the best for the students of America, within the limits imposed by the nature of TV, and recognize that *too much* TV—even "high-quality" TV—is in the end harmful both intellectually and socially.

Visual/Media Literacy
One hears more and more today of the need for developing

visual/media literacy in the young; that is, helping them to manipulate more effectively their new learning environment. After all, they will be the ones to receive this Brave New World of technology and information flow. They will require greater understanding of how to use the tools of this media revolution; and, more importantly, how to *judge critically and objectively* what they see and hear.

The National Institute of Mental Health states that an interest in teaching about television is one of the most important aspects of the research done on the medium during the last decade. Though the field of critical viewing skills is still new, it reflects a trend toward placing television in perspective with a young person's general cognitive and emotional development. The 1982 Report declares:

> ... one of the most significant developments of the decade is the rise of interest in television literacy, critical viewing skills, and intervention procedures. 'Television literacy' is a way to counteract the possible deleterious effects of television and also to enhance its many benefits ... Use of educational and intervention procedures has demonstrated that parents, children, and teachers can achieve much greater understanding of television and its effects...[4] [See Appendix D for more suggestions in this area.]

In attempting to ameliorate somewhat our antagonistic position *vis-a-vis* television, what can we do to help our young people become more media literate? One of the most straightforward starting points is for students to keep a record of what they watch. Like a person trying to diet, writing down everything he or she eats sometimes offers startling surprises. A typical viewing chart might look something like this:

Personal Viewing Habits					
Day	Program Title and Amount of Viewing Time	Theme or Subject Matter	Opinion- Like or Dislike	Watched Alone or With Someone	Other Comments
Monday Etc.					

Such an activity could then be used to facilitate further classroom discussion. A teacher might, for example, want to explore some of the following questions based upon student viewing results.

(1) What roles does television play in your life? What influence or effect do you notice from TV exposure? What have you learned from TV as opposed to your family and friends?

(2) Were you surprised by the amount of time you spent viewing? Was it more or less than you imagined? How does it compare with your fellow classmates?

(3) Do you ever just leave the set on without really watching closely? Why?

(4) Do you watch more by yourself or with family and friends? Do you talk about what you watch?

(5) Do you use the newspaper listing and *TV Guide* to select special programs, or do you just switch on the set and watch whatever is on at the time?

(6) Would you change your TV viewing habits? If so, how?[5]

This sort of activity can be accommodated to any grade level. The teacher could encourage students to read *TV Guide* alone or with their parents and try to select different types of programs, specials, documentaries, and news. This could foster the development of their own discrimination and judgment and is another way of building media literacy. More attention should be given to preschool and elementary school children; the teacher might want to offer more assistance by keeping a close look-out for quality children's programming and pointing them out to the youngsters. If specific viewing assignments are suggested by the teacher, it is important that some form of follow-up activity be carried out, such as group discussions, projects, questions and answers, or writing assignments about the program. With older students, preparatory reading prior to a special presentation could be useful to compare written versus audio-visual treatments. Teachers might also want to encourage older students to take notes while watching the news or documentaries. Being able to get the gist of a presentation and recording it on paper are important learning skills. This sort of TV activity can also aid listening and concentration. Students could be encouraged to exercise their own critical tastes by reviewing programs and writing to local stations or networks expressing their views. Being able to formulate an opinion regarding content and presentation is precisely the kind of education today's students need, for they must learn that they are capable of expressing a point of view, that they can be *active* viewers rather than passive recipients. Through all of these approaches, teachers can turn TV's hold on our youth into the motivational backdrop for more constructive and creative activities.

Program Content and Analysis

Another way of approaching television and helping young people to become more visually articulate is to formulate units on program content and analysis. Since tomorrow's young people will be watching more and more over their home TV/computer screens, they should be encouraged to develop their own critical viewing criteria. For example, they might want to consider these points regarding content and style:

(1) How are individual and group images handled? Are stereotypes used? Why?

(2) What kind of language is used in various programs such as news, documentaries, commercials, and drama? How is language manipulated to convey different messages? What is your opinion of this?

(3) How are various cultures and races presented, and what tone is employed? What type of life style is suggested by the program, and how does this fit into normally accepted patterns of behavior? Are we being informally programmed to accept only a limited range of views?

(4) How are plot and theme handled? Is the story carried forward primarily through action or ideas? If there is conflict, how is it employed? Is it physical, verbal, or psychological? Toward whom is it directed? In what context is it used, and is it truly necessary to further the plot?

(5) Artistic style could be discussed and characters analyzed for development and motivation—or lack thereof. How does TV treatment compare with novels and short stories?

The above suggestions represent only a minimum regarding content and analysis. Students themselves might come up with different ways of reviewing and discussing TV presentations or even writing their own shows for possible in-class presentation.

Commercials and Advertising

Another important aspect of media literacy involves commercials and advertising. Indeed, these two areas play perhaps the most significant role in current television business practices. The following could be useful starting points for launching classroom and student activity.

(1) What images do advertisements give of our society and ourselves? What do they reflect of our basic attitudes and aspirations? Of our wants and desires? Of what we hold important in our culture?

(2) What is your personal opinion of TV commercials? List their pros and cons.

(3) Keep a commercial record sheet similar to your TV program diary. Analyze techniques of mass persuasion, psychology, and social behavior based upon specific examples of commercials manipulation. This area is extremely important because American television, more than any other country in the world, exists of, by, and for, the advertising community. Why is this so? How does this attitude compare with other nations around the globe?

(4) Students could look at how television commercials are handled in other countries and what they reflect of different life styles, values, etc.

(5) Students might also discuss the problem of conservation and consumption and how this relates to TV. Do we really need to consume as much as television tells us to? How does this philosophy of consumption relate to the Third World and the global ecology movement as a whole? How should we react to commercials which tell us to consume more and more when three-quarters of the world is poor and starving? What are the philosophical and/or moral questions involved in all this? Explain.

News Analysis

Another vital aspect of television broadcasting which should be taken into account is news. This is particularly important because the dominance of American TV by entertainment—the idea of news *AS* entertainment or a commodity to be sold and rated along with other programs—is frightening indeed. For example, there are now instances of commercials "selling" specific news programs to the public. Phrases such as "best news you'll get all day," "news that gets to where you live," and "the news that cares about people" are appearing on the air.[6] What does this type of news salesmanship imply?

Other thoughts to consider in relationship to news analysis might include:

(1) How is news handled? What is presented? Why? Is there a balance between disaster and crime reporting (i.e., floods, bombs, fires, murders, etc.) and coverage of political events, breakthroughs in science and technology, or discussion of international affairs?

(2) Why do superficial events and personalities often receive greater attention than in-depth discussions of important national or world events?

(3) Whose views are we actually receiving: the technician's or a salesman's idea of what news will *sell*? Students might question whether broadcasters, in their quest for ratings, are misjudging what people want to hear. For example: a recent survey of American viewers revealed that newscasters totally misrepresented what the public truly wanted. Newsmen at one of the major networks estimated that only thirty-four percent of the public wanted national news, whereas in reality some sixty percent wanted such coverage. They calculated that only five percent of their viewers wanted international news when in fact forty-one percent did, and they grossly overcalculated interest in sports—so-called entertainment fare. The newsmen thought some seventy-five percent of their viewers wanted extended sports coverage when in truth only thirty-four percent wanted such news.[7] What do these actions imply? What kind of attitude does this reflect about us, the audience?

(4) Students might also scan newspapers and magazines to compare how the print media deal with news as opposed to

broadcast journalism. Radio and TV news could also be compared in a similar manner.

(5) Young people could be encouraged to write their own news presentations and give them to the class as part of current events or social studies units.

Ideas for General Discussion

Analyzing viewing patterns, program content, commercials, and the news are specific topics that can be used to begin nurturing media literacy in our students. There are many other ways, however, of approaching the problem of visual/media literacy in the young. Some general topics for classroom discussion might include such questions as:

(1) How would you define TV entertainment? How would you define education? Are the two necessarily different? If so, why?

(2) What is broadcasting, and why is it important in today's world?

(3) What is the role of government in broadcasting, the function of the FCC and FTC? What is Congress doing to legislate new broadcasting laws? What about worldwide broadcasting codes?

(4) How does American broadcasting compare with other systems in the world?

Other possibilities for encouraging media literacy among students include:

(1) Collecting information regarding trends in the industry, new technology, and discussing these in class.

(2) Having industry people speak about the medium; what goes on behind-the-scenes in production and decision-making; what opportunities there are for employment.

(3) Getting students to write industry people requesting information.

(4) Reviewing the history of radio and television broadcasting from both a scientific and commercial point of view.

Again, it is important to remember that these suggestions can be used at any grade level. Obviously, the scope and sequence of study will depend upon age and the general interest and ability of the class. Undoubtedly, the caliber and depth of discussion will vary from elementary school to high school students and beyond, but the topics and issues remain important at *all* grade levels and should become an integral part of school curriculum planning today.

In conjunction with this, teachers should also encourage students to use a variety of media and to put television in perspective with other forms of communication. Children need to learn how to use a spectrum of learning tools, and how to get the most out of each. Developing a balance between various sources is crucial for achieving visual literacy. Parents too must become involved, for without parental support, much of the effectiveness of classroom instruction will be lost. This is an extremely important part in our attempt to help youngsters become more media literate individuals. Parents have children during the most formative years of their lives. The systematic development of adult education courses and media training groups to educate grown-ups about their children and their TV twins is vital. School administrators and counselors should consider instigating inservice training for both parents and teachers along these lines. A united effort between school staff, teachers, and the community is very important in our teaching/TV combat.

Be on the Lookout

I am aware of a certain dilemma here. Teachers and educators definitely do need to come to grips with the immediate problem of kids and their fascination with TV. But by bringing *more* television into the classroom—either through discussion or viewing—we must be careful that we do not give the activity of unlimited watching further implicit sanction! Kids today watch *enough* TV, more than enough in fact; even many commercial broadcasters admit that. Ideally, we want them to watch *less* and to be more critical and selective of what they do see. Ideally, we want them to learn how to handle more effectively an important learning tool in their lives. A lot of television need not be watched in order to do this. We should attempt to look at one thing in depth rather than give only superficial attention to a great deal. Only by taking small segments at a time and giving them a thorough investigation can a critical outlook and thoughtful approach to using television be developed. Yet, taking the time to discuss these issues and topics is crucial in our efforts to negotiate a constructive alliance between teaching, children, and television. Special class time for activities in media literacy should constitute an important part of today's education. Such discussions can help our young people to develop their own capacity for judgment and understanding. Hopefully, some awareness of the vast changes in the field of communication as a whole will also be provided.

There are other things we should be aware of, too. We teachers must be on guard that we do not make our instructional day any "easier" by using games and ideas based upon television. To use TV programs, films, or discussions merely as time-fillers in our teaching day is as bad as abandoning children to the television in their own homes. If we do not make TV in the classroom an active and positive endeavor, how can we possibly expect our students to approach it actively and critically outside? Again, it lessens and cheapens what should be a thoughtful experience. It also points to the vital importance of teacher attitudes about the use of television in school and at home. The importance of genuine teacher interest, knowledge, and enthusiasm cannot be over-emphasized. We must concentrate on active choice and deliberate participation rather than passive audio/visual receiving.

Obviously, there are as many ways of dealing with the medium in a constructive manner as there are individual teachers, students, and administrators. The important thing to remember is that action is needed *now* to help students and their parents cope with a large part of their world. Is this a naive view or a very pragmatic one? One would think the best defense any nation could support is a sturdy educational system and free-thinking, media literate individuals. The only alternative is to believe that education ceases to have any real value in a society devoted to the kind of consumptive, fantasy world view generally espoused by American TV.

TEACHER EDUCATION: PRACTICAL TRAINING

Yet, discussing specific examples of how classroom teachers can motivate students to use television in a more thoughtful manner is a little like putting the cart before the horse. For instructors to help young people be more literate in media, we must first have media literate teachers and teacher training institutions which acknowledge this shift in the way people learn and communicate. The comments and suggestions in the previous section are only immediate steps for classroom use to deal with the phenomena of TV and media in general. But this does not alter the fact that those of us in education today must look *beyond* momentary remedial action to the purpose and thought behind the action itself. If we do not define more specifically where we stand in relationship to the whole process of information flow and the social engineering taking place now, we may not have the luxury of formulating a stand in the future. There is the possibility that this media/technology revolution will reach a point of fission where there will be no turning back to question and analyze what we ought to be doing now. This only stresses the need for a new philosophy and aim in education to confront an age of technological upheaval.

Technology of Learning

This technology of learning, as I call it, is a vitally important aspect of training today's teachers and school administrative staff. Indeed, what good is it to have a vast array of television sets, broadcasting equipment, dial-access systems, quality programs, computer consoles, and video material, if we do not know how to use them properly in the classroom or place them in the broader context of society as a whole? School librarians, audio-visual technicians, communication specialists, and district media directors should not be the only ones with this knowledge. *All* teachers, administrators, and school personnel should have some understanding of how to use these various tools in the context of a full and rich classroom environment. How many teachers in America today have gone through reputable education schools and never once heard anyone mention TV, whether or not it is an important aspect of education, or how to use it in the classroom? Doctoral programs provide training in these areas, but such people generally do not go back into the classroom, and that is precisely where the greatest need exists.

When I asked one school media director if many teachers even know how to set up and operate a TV set(!)—let alone other audio-visual or computer equipment—he answered:

> I'm glad you asked that. That is a joke. If all you have to do is just turn it on, 30% of the teachers are not going to be able to do even that . . . It's not that they muddle it up, it's just that most of them become frightened before they even start.[8]

Why is this? Generally, the teachers have not been properly taught how to use these learning tools as classroom aids. When I asked a professor at a graduate school of education whether there were any required courses at the teacher training level regarding TV's, computers, and so forth, his straightforward answer was "no."[9] Why? Surely this kind of training is as important, if not more so, as learning to write behavioral objectives! We cannot possibly remain successful classroom communicators unless our practical teacher training addresses these various learning materials. Otherwise, we will fall farther and farther behind in our efforts to help young people cope with their rapidly changing learning environment.

It has been estimated that some $400 million would be needed to provide basic, practical training in the use of television for instruction to every teacher, principal, and school superintendent who had not had such training.[10] Yet, a 1977 study found that only seventeen percent of all teachers had had any training whatsoever in the use of television for teaching purposes.[11] Teachers should be demanding this kind of "how to" instruction. Not only should schools of teacher training start requiring such classes for their would-be teachers, but also instructors who are already in school could benefit from on-going, professional inservice workshops to keep abreast of these changes. Schools of education need to instruct teachers how to handle the range of media that the technology of learning involves. We need to learn how to analyze the strengths and weaknesses of each medium, what its unique capabilities are, and which ones we feel the most comfortable using.

Teachers and administrators also need to be taught more about programming computers and retrieving data so we can in turn teach our students how to do the same. Indeed, how many teachers now look on in dismay as their own students "play" with small-screen computers? Young people today are already moving out into the sea of technology, while many of us are only just reaching the shore. A strange rip tide is in the making which must be dealt with and rectified. Those of us in education should not be afraid of these advancements or worried that they will take away our jobs. On the contrary: a whole new field of learning and instruction is going to flower over the next few decades concerning just these areas and topics. The challenge facing our side of the battle will be to stay familiar with these technological developments in microprocessing and television-computer-based information systems. Otherwise, we will risk being less knowledgeable and sophisticated than many of our students. Rather than being frightening, this challenge affords us the opportunity of demonstrating how to manage and manipulate the potential of these learning tools. More and more, our role in the classroom should be one of showing young people how to go about solving problems and processing information.

Again, the question is not *if* we meet this challenge but *how*. Hopefully, nothing will ever supersede the intimacy of the student/teacher relationship, but we teachers *do* need to learn more about this technology of learning as it relates to decisions we make in school. At present, much of this need is not being properly fulfilled by our teachers colleges.

TEACHER EDUCATION: THEORETICAL TRAINING

The process of transforming television from antagonist into a classroom teaching ally is more complex than simply using the medium more often in school. Learning about all the hardware itself is only the beginning of tackling this change in information retrieval and dispersal. Not only do teachers colleges need to address themselves to the mechanics and variety of media, but also much thought should be given to how these various items will affect learning and the assimilation of data by young people. We need to confront a much more comprehensive view in this area.

In the preceding chapters, I have given some indication of what influence television has had in the realm of involuntary/incidental learning; formal and technical learning; attention spans; Piagetian developmental stages; and so on. Certainly, these topics need to be explored in greater detail for us to gain better understanding of our TV twin and some of the forces facing teachers and educators today. But much discussion is also needed in schools of education and among teaching professionals about how television affects specific aspects of teacher training curriculum, such as the various taxonomies of learning behaviors, the internalization of language, and perceptual and remembering skills—all of which constitute important parts of teacher education courses.

Television and Language

A rich vocabulary, for example, and the ability to manipulate language are associated with an individual's basic intelligence, learning potential, and the ability to engage in abstract thought. The development of this language potential, however, is closely related to childhood play and how much social interaction a youngster has. The growth of language itself is stimulated by early interaction with family and peers, since the most vital period in language acquisition is between twelve to eighteen months and three to four years. By the time the average child enters kindergarten, he should be able to speak in simple sentences and phrases, and have a vocabulary of several thousand words. Yet this achievement is actually the culmination of many intricate learning mechanisms; such as the control and understanding of rhythm patterns, linguistics, syntax, spatial relationships, memory, and logical reasoning.

But now that many young people watch hours of TV each day, how is this altering the pattern of language acquisition and human communication as a whole? If language is a portrait of the mentality of the race which fashioned it, how are our students reacting to the following incongruities:

BE NATURAL!! (Dye your hair!)

FOR THE NATURAL LOOK (Use this artificial spray, deodorant, toothpaste, etc.)
SPEND NOW AND SAVE!
SAVE NOW BY SPENDING!

Clearly, the above examples represent exercises in contradiction and doublespeak and reveal a great deal about us as a society and what we are currently educating our young people *for*. Aside from the slang and street language heard on many programs, advertising, in particular, plays havoc with language patterns and words themselves. Meanings are twisted and new words formed indiscriminately. In such a context, language becomes artifice. It capitalizes upon the receptiveness of the human mind in informal learning situations. Superlatives, exaggeration, and hyperbole become the norm, and words themselves begin to lose their power to objectify experience. For example: "stroft" has been coined to describe both the strong and soft attributes of a new toilet paper. "Crunchewy" is now a word, used to detail both the crunchy and chewy properties of a certain dog food. What is a teacher to do with a preschooler or kindergartener who comes to class talking like this?

In such a language environment, the whole value of an individual's cognitive structure as symbolized by words is undermined and can lose significance. We literally may be programming young people to be less able to think about and articulate what they see because our language itself is undergoing such changes. By narrowing and/or destroying the use of words or by substituting commercial jingles for thought, our rational capacity is brought into manageable bounds. This is particularly important to consider in relationship to young TV viewers, who are just beginning to go through the process of internalizing a language structure. The way they are apprehending language through television exposure is something we must be more aware of in school. Teacher training institutions should alert their student teachers to these trends, because the importance of language and vocabulary as they relate to education, thought, and the development of a self-concept are crucial for all.

Television and the Four Learning Domains

Aside from television's potential impact on language, there are other factors we should consider. Over the last few decades, attempts have been made to organize the various aspects of learning into specific domains covering a wide range of activity, all of which influence an individual's growth and development. The principal domains are the cognitive (intellectual), affective (emotional), psychomotor (physical), and moral. They all are constructed along a hierarchy of tasks, generally starting from an easy level and working toward greater and greater difficulty. Once again, now that television has brought with it new styles of learning and competes with education in the total time spent with youngsters, how has this affected the various learning domains? Most of America's teacher training schools teach their students how to write a good lesson plan or behavioral objective, but how many of them address this aspect of the technology of learning and teaching in the future?

Cognitive Domain. The cognitive domain, for example, structures intellectual activities along a continuum, covering such areas as information recall, thinking and problem solving, and creating new ideas. This domain stresses the importance of the higher levels of intellectual work and developing individual cognitive skills. The categories in this domain cover six areas ranging from basic knowledge to evaluation.

Recall is the lowest level of the learning domain, whereas comprehension or being able to paraphrase information, is the lowest level of understanding. The next stages include such learning activities as applying information to new situations, analyzing content and structure, and formulating new patterns of ideas, such as writing an essay. The final stage involves learning at its highest level because it contains elements of the other five categories. More than anything else, the last level demands *conscious* value judgments based upon clearly defined criteria, and it stresses the nurturing of an individual critical outlook. It should also be noted that of the six levels in the cognitive domain, the last two concentrate on what is called divergent thinking, i.e., the ability to expand, create, and see different aspects of the whole.

This type of thinking requires greater cognitive effort, more "mental sweat" as it were, because the brain is taxed into making new material. Above all else, the last level involves a greater consciousness of self.

One must ask which levels of cognitive learning behavior even moderate television viewing reinforces. Naturally, much will depend upon the caliber of program presented, the amount an individual consumes, family influences, and so on; but what does TV mean to this aspect of education?

Clearly, the majority of television in the United States concentrates on sub-conscious recall; what one might say is the learning level *below* Level One! Program content appears basically as filler; it is secondary to advertisements. With commercials, however, information is stored within the brain and is elicited in a highly patterned way: presentation, reiteration, and emotional appeal. There is a great emphasis upon feelings and desire, *not* upon cognitive or intellectual response. This, coupled with the fact that TV viewing increases relaxing brain waves, means that our minds rarely are taxed at all. On the contrary: we are being fed. News, certain documentaries, and dramatic specials may call forth higher levels of cognitive activity, but generally, the viewer as individual self and potential thinker is left completely untouched. Instead, the lowest level of learning behavior is reinforced informally over and over again, and the individual is discouraged from having his own point of view. He is not allowed to, because he constantly is being told what to do, how to feel, what to wear, eat, buy, and think. It is a rote, mechanical response. This contrasts sharply with the goal of divergent thinking and of education as a whole, which stress the development of personal judgment and opinion. Perhaps we teachers should spend more time emphasizing the latter levels of the cognitive domain in the classroom which require longer periods of thought and analysis. Perhaps we need to encourage those areas which elicit more active thinking to counteract the non-thinking pattern many of our students may have acquired or fallen into by the time they enter school.

Affective Domain. Teacher training institutions should also discuss what effect television is having on the affective domain, the domain of feelings and sensations. The levels in this domain emphasize tone, emotional acceptance or rejection, and beliefs, and the activities range from simple attention of external objects to qualities of character and conscience. The behaviors here are more difficult to assess than those in the cognitive domain because they are subjective in nature, but there is a similarity in structure and organization in both domains from low to high. As with the last level in the cognitive domain, the final stage in the affective area, characterization, requires greater thoughtfulness and the development of some kind of personal philosophy or world view.

If a child or adolescent watches TV three to five hours a day during his early growing years, how much will this subtract from his ability to characterize or judge external events? Will he be able to *judge* at all, or will he simply stare at outside stimuli as if they were on TV? Again, television as we know it and generally approach it today encourages only the lowest level of the affective domain: simple receiving. This does not mean that many moving and moral issues cannot be presented. Watching the funeral of John F. Kennedy, for example, had a profound effect on many people's sense of characterization, but opportunities for such response are rare. Yet, this lack of emotional experience due to unthinking television consumption may be one of the reasons why teachers, school psychologists, and social workers are having to spend more and more time dealing with problems and feelings among their students. This was not the case thirty years ago, and it could be that many youngsters now are missing out on one of the most significant areas of healthy affective development: vital human contact.

Psychomotor Domain. The next area of consideration is the psychomotor (sensory-motor) domain. This taxonomy involves various levels of physical and motor skills from the earliest stages of growth. Proper sensory-motor development is extremely important, because the motor functions which take place during the first few years of life form a crucial basis for future learning. Indeed, the entire development of subsequent mental processes rests upon proper psychomotor stimulation. Lack of exercise and physical exploration at an early age quite literally affects all later growth.

For example: a youngster's first movement patterns help him, among other things, to understand spatial location, time sequences, and order. This type of learning in turn affects the acquisition of language because language itself (oral, written, and printed) *is* sequential. It is hard to conceive that there are over 600 distinguishable muscles in a young child and over 40,000,000 muscle fibers which all need exercise and use.[12] Yet, for the infant who watches TV from a highchair day after day, or the preschooler who spends a large portion of his time in front of the tube, how can this vitally important sensory-motor system develop at its optimum rate? Areas in this domain include:

I. *Sensory-Motor Training*
   A.   Manipulation—starts before preschool and kindergarten; by handling objects, the child learns how to differentiate between textures, forms, sizes; also helps to develop fine motor coordination.
II. *Body Awareness*—combination of:
   A.   Feelings about the body (body image).
   B.   Adjustment of bones and muscles necessary for posture and movement (body scheme).
   C.   Factual knowledge about the body (body concept).
III. *Training Movement Skills* (elementary school)
   A.   Coordination and Rhythm
      1.   gross motor—simultaneous and coordinated use of several muscles or muscle groups.
      2.   rhythm—flowing, measured, balanced movement.
   B.   Agility
        The ability to initiate movement, change direction, or adjust position quickly.
   C.   Flexibility
        The ability to move parts of the body easily in relation to each other with maximum joint extension and flex.

D. Strength
    The force exerted by the body or its parts.
E. Speed
    Tempo achieved during a movement sequence.
F. Balance
    The ability to maintain a position with minimal contact with a surface.
    1. Static—balance stable.
    2. Dynamic—maintaining position on a moving surface.
    3. Object—ability to use minimal surface to support an object without letting it fall.
G. Endurance (Note: should not be rated for children under eight)
    The ability to sustain physical activity and resist muscular fatigue.[13]

Once again, now that television consumes hour upon hour of many children's time, how will this aspect of growth and development be altered? How many five-year-olds today cannot run, jump, or skip properly because they have not had enough purely physical experiences? How many lack just a certain animal joy and exuberance toward life because they have not had enough exercise and play interaction with friends? These are questions which should be openly discussed among teachers, administrators, and physical education instructors in teachers colleges today.

Moral Domain. Finally, aside from the cognitive, affective, and psychomotor domains, attempts have also been made to organize moral behavior along specific lines. Studies with children around the world indicate that they learn morality in the same basic way, just as Piaget's findings indicate there is a tremendous commonality in the way children grow and apprehend in general. Lawrence Kohlberg, who developed the moral domain structure, sets forth his hierarchy as follows:

Level 1—decisions are based upon deference to authority in avoidance of punishment. What is right is what somebody tells you to do.

Level 2—decisions are based upon self-interest. What is right is what gets you what you want.

     Level 3—decisions here are made on the basis of conformity
           and social approval. What is right is what others are
           doing; what society considers nice or acceptable
           behavior.
     Level 4—decisions are made according to the rule of law.
           What is right is what has been decreed by established
           order.
     Level 5—decisions are made on the basis of social utility.
           What is right is what is best for all men; i.e., the
           democratic principle.
     Level 6—decisions are based upon high moral principles such
           as the sanctity of life, brotherhood of man, and
           common humanity.[14]

Level Six of the moral domain stresses orientation to one's own conscience. It emphasizes a system of personal ethics behind individual action and a sense of mutual respect and trust for others. It is similar to the higher levels of the affective and cognitive domains in that it encourages an individual point of view and the ability to judge for oneself. Yet, once again we must ask: how does television affect moral learning and education today?

Most television in America—both in programs and commercials—concerns itself with the lower levels on the Kohlberg scale: greed, conformity, and law and order. Unfortunately, concepts such as brotherhood and humanity are in scant supply in the majority of TV offerings.

Aside from themes of retribution and vigilantism which appear frequently on the screen, there are other reasons for concern. Many child psychologists agree that a young person's sense of moral judgment has its foundation in a feeling of respect for others and that this respect is formulated by contact with people, *not* in isolation. But what happens to a child's moral learning process if he spends a fair amount of his leisure time communing with TV and not interacting with real people? How does this alter his sense of respect for others and in turn his moral development? A youngster's concepts of right and wrong should be fairly well set by the time he enters school. Yet for those who spend a large portion of their early growing years watching television, it is more than likely that their TV twin may have acquired some fairly lopsided moral views.

Are our TV screens informally teaching the idea of urban bounty hunters and the notion of "get them before they get you"? The problem of desensitization discussed in Chapter Two may be related to this type of incidental instruction and a corresponding lack of moral training from real people. Also, as mentioned in Chapter Four, some of the research indicates that respect which previously has been given to parents and people from day-to-day life has been transferred to television personalities. If this is indeed the case, at what level of moral behavior do these TV people generally function? By watching TV, it is quite possible that children will simply miss out on important social experiences and group discussions which are necessary if they are to become aware of themselves in relationship to others. This is the very basis of moral training! Without this direct, human contact, a person in many ways remains perpetually immature; he learns to respond only to himself. He is never encouraged or expected to look beyond his own egocentrism and learn respect for other people and property. And, finally, if morality itself stems from a modulation of restraint and self-discipline, imagine what effect hours of TV, which emphasize quick gratification and ever-shifting reference points, have on this area of human development!

In relationship to the various taxonomies which attempt to build upon growth, learning, and communication skills, television today functions at the other end of the continuum. It works at the plateau of being told what to think and how to be. We are asked to function at a mere stimulus/response level. Television as we know it and have approached it in the past divides our world and reality into minute segments rather than structuring it as a whole. It comprises informal messages entering the mind at an out-of-awareness level with almost total disregard for the concept of individual self. This, coupled with the fact that television viewing involves only a figurative, not an operational process, should give educators even more cause for concern. When watching TV, mental images are produced which merely duplicate a precise copy of what is seen rather than a flexible two-way-communication process. We are not asked to create something new, only to absorb what is given. Again, this need not be the case depending upon how the medium is approached and used, but generally, television emphasizes this type of rote learning response. If a youngster watches several hours of television a day during his preschool years and becomes conditioned to respond primarily to this rote learning, it may be difficult to get him to tackle higher learning functions later on.

The problem, however, is that the higher levels in all four domains are infinitely more crucial in developing a critical self-consciousness, personal morality, and physical well-being—elements which should be the ultimate goal of any and every education. Teacher training institutions should initiate courses of study which probe television's relationship to these various learning domains and what the implications are for instructing students in today's classroom. Our teacher training curriculum needs this critical review so we can function more efficiently with our students.

FURTHER EDUCATION AND ADVANCED RESEARCH

The preceding discussion of language and the various learning taxonomies represents only general criteria for educational development in teacher training institutions. The various thoughts and suggestions in the previous sections must also be augmented with additional information from other branches of science and advanced research, such as biology, physiology, and psychology. We educators need to be exposed to more data outside our specific field in order to better understand what changes the *mind itself* may be going through in all this media fallout. Only recently have people begun to explore the psychological and physiological effects of television exposure on our neurological system.

Indeed, one of the most important areas of investigation stressed by the National Institute of Mental Health in their 1982 report is that of further exploration in biomedical research regarding television and the psycho-physiological implications of viewing. There is some indication, as mentioned earlier, that our brains learn differently from TV and are affected differently by TV, and the media choices we make in the classroom may have to be governed by the *type* of learning we want to encourage in our students. Clearly, we need more information from other areas of science in order to help aid these decisions in school.

The Mind and Perception

One area in particular which should be explored in detail is how the mind itself works when exposed to television and other media sources. We need to investigate in greater depth perception itself as we become increasingly immersed in our electronic communications sea. In all likelihood, media literacy and the technology of our learning future will demand that our young people be able to assimilate vast amounts of material over home media centers. We will therefore need to understand more about reading, remembering, and perceptual skills; how the eye and brain filter data, and how these in turn relate to the TV/computer console. Teachers will need to learn more about perception and how the memory functions, as well as memory techniques to better absorb TV processed data. We will need to find out more about the eye scans across a TV screen for taking in both written and pictorial materials. In conjunction with this, it would be helpful to know more about speed-viewing and speed-reading techniques as well as auding, a fast-listening technique currently used by blind people. Perhaps these aids could be used in new ways with our TV screens.

In addition, we need to learn how to extend the eye's capacity to zero in on key words and multiple word clusters in order to reduce the time fixation. By doing this, the human eye can learn how to register more and more quickly. If we can learn about training the eye and brain for high-speed perception, then we might be able to extend the eye's capacity to send increased amounts of material and information to the brain. We *can* be trained along these lines; we teachers and educators must meet this challenge, or our students will simply sink beneath all the data they will be required to absorb. This increased mental/visual capacity may well play an important role in media literacy. We need to look to advanced research in these areas to help us formulate more effective curriculum planning and teaching techniques in school today.

Brain Physiology

In addition to the above, we need more information on brain physiology and what chemical and/or electrical changes may be taking place in the brain from exposure to material presented on cathode ray tube screens. It has been thought for quite some time now that the human mind functions in a linear fashion, i.e., making lists and categories. Now, however, recent evidence suggests that this may not be so; that in fact the brain is much more multi-dimensional and non-linear in nature. Scientists are discovering rather that it works by a system of key concepts in an integrated pattern of linkage and association, jumping around and making random, disparate connections.

How does this apply to learning from television as well as learning in general? In many respects, TV has captured this associative property of the brain beautifully: it presents information in a haphazard, pictorial manner. The problem with this, however, is that the vast majority of television in this country channels thought along predetermined lines. Commercials and programming content are packaged and arranged in a highly sophisticated manner; they certainly do not allow for the divergent playfulness of the mind itself. Advertisers on Madison Avenue probably know more about words and concepts, music, rhythm, and the associative power of the brain than most of today's teachers. But this must change if we educators are to remain useful social engineers.

We also need to learn more about the left and right hemispheres of the brain and how each responds to TV. We know that the left hemisphere deals generally with verbal and logical activities, whereas the right hemisphere works with spatial concepts and visual/affective responses. How does moderate to excessive television exposure affect these two areas of the brain? Does TV stimulate the visual right portion of the brain while neglecting the verbal left as some people suggest? Is this one of the reasons why literacy scores have dropped so drastically since the advent of TV? Will too much exposure at an early age thwart or inhibit normal right/left hemisphere development? All these questions need serious consideration.

It is sobering indeed to think what television may be doing to the basic pattern of human learning. It has been calculated, for example, that the brain itself has a neuron connection capability of 10^{800}.[15] Is it possible that TV has altered this capacity to some degree? Television may have more power in real, immediate human terms over growth, learning, and behavior than the atomic bomb. We may have unleashed a more subtle form of fallout than we ever dreamed possible. For instance:

(1) How have brain waves been altered?

(2) How have eye movements and patterns changed?

(3) How have the right and left hemispheres of our brains been affected?

(4) How do we link and make mental associations while watching?

(5) Does TV thwart the mind's natural tendency to work toward closure rather than diffusiveness?

(6) How has higher cognitive functioning been affected?

This actually is not as farfetched as it may at first seem. The channel capacity of the eye/ear is fixed, but the channel capacity of the eye/brain and ear/brain *can* be changed as time goes on.[16] Man's visual system is capable of transmitting instantly 10^7 bits of information to the brain, but the brain itself has the ability to transmit only 27 bits of information per second.[17] Could the exposure we now have to the visual media, and TV in particular, cause some alteration in these physiological processes as man tries to adapt himself to his new media sea? Perhaps some very minute, yet extraordinarily profound, changes are occurring within the brain which we simply do not know about yet. Perhaps some subtle evolutionary process is going on within the human organism in order to survive in this new communications world. Is some kind of technological selective breeding taking place which favors the lower levels of the learning domains while phasing out the higher?

On the other hand, there are some exciting and intriguing possibilities suggested by all this as well. Perhaps we can learn how to turn the quick shifts in focus and subject matter so typical of television to our students' *advantage*. Perhaps being able to follow a number of various, random topics at the same time could be the basis for the development of a multi-layered consciousness, more dialectical thought, and so on—the kind of training tomorrow's students will need to cope successfully in their multi-media world.

All this may sound more like science fiction than education, but science fiction and education seem to be moving closer and closer together these days. One person has said you cannot put television into people's homes, have them use it, and then expect them ever to be the same again. It is quite possible that a new breed—a mutant or hybrid—will evolve in both a literal and figurative sense.[18] We may just be seeing the results of all this now.

These areas of perception and brain physiology must be explored in greater depth. If we teachers and administrators can learn more about these things, then perhaps we can grapple with the changes and work them for the *good* in school. If our practical and theoretical training were made more relevant, maybe we could do the same for our students. These thoughts only underscore the necessity for schools of education and research disciplines related to education to tackle these issues head-on. After all, it is we who are having to meet this revolutionary change. More than anything else, education today needs to stress the *how* of thinking and the retrieval of facts and information as they relate to the process of *being* and *becoming*.

THE SELF, PLAY OF TOLERANCE, AND THE EDUCATOR AS ENTERTAINER

Discussing classroom activities and what teacher training colleges can do or encouraging new research across a variety of interrelated fields is only the beginning. We must strive at this time for an even broader vision of education and man's position in the twenty-first century. The process of being and becoming—to which all education should ultimately address itself—will assume greater and greater significance as this century draws to a close. Technology will provide us with more and more gadgets to tinker with and greater amounts of leisure time to pursue various interests and to play. Yet, how will we utilize our new-found freedom if we do not have a sturdy sense of self with which to guide thought and action in the first place? To paraphrase Bertrand Russell: what good will the conquest of time and health be to us and our media students if we forget how to think and be now? Will man simply vegetate when he no longer has to produce? Will the media, and especially television, merely become easy ways of group management? Expedient means of dealing with people who will not die or who do not work or who have too much time on their hands? The producer/consumer inversion has already begun, but where does this leave the released worker and the generations ahead? The reality of these changes only accentuates the importance of education dealing with what effect the technology of learning and leisure will have on individual self-definition, tolerance, and our role as teachers in tomorrow's world.

The Self and Concepts of Being

In the course of this book, I have discussed a variety of research regarding the effects of television as it relates specifically to children and how they grow and learn. Regardless of the rightness or wrongness of any individual experiment; whether they really test the right thing; whether they come to the right conclusion for the wrong reasons or the wrong conclusion for the right reasons, the fact remains that a war is being waged for individual attention and an approach to life.

My main concern as an individual and especially as a teacher is precisely this attention of the will and the establishment of a personal point of view, without which no one can really begin to communicate. The questions of violence and advertising, the problems of government and industry, and other effects must be looked upon from the broader philosophical context of how they relate to the development of a self and an independent mind and personality. John Dewey once wrote that the only freedom of enduring importance is freedom of intelligence, the freedom of observation and judgment. This means helping train the will to attend selectively, to be conscious of itself and others, to evaluate and weigh opposing views. In a word: to *be*.

Yet, it is precisely in this most important area of selfhood, this attempt to deal with the totality of the individual, not just the parts, that television as currently used presents the greatest challenge. This matter is even more urgent when one considers how vital a role early life plays in starting the whole process of education. For the child who spends hours with TV, this process of developing a unique sense of self may very well be permanently impeded or even retarded.

But as twentieth century life moves toward greater complexity, the need for more consciousness of self and individuality in relationship to education in particular and society as a whole becomes critical. We will need a much more profound way of dealing with the self because the multi-faceted self, as an educational goal or a philosophical concept, is being lost. Every individual today, and this is especially true in the West, is becoming more and more a product of TV culture.[19] In a very real sense, broadcasting and television have reduced the possible range of patterns and choices an individual can make simply by filling up such large amounts of his time, regardless of any other consideration. As we move toward greater amounts of technology, this project may become more rapid still, unless we start thinking about the *way* we approach and use the medium now. In twenty or thirty years' time, will most of our selfhood be a media-made twin? Will we become increasingly isolated and marginal selves, unable to decide what to do or what to think without the aid of television or some other voice telling us how to react? Will we merely become composites of what we have absorbed and been fed rather than what we have actively and deliberately chosen? We Americans seem to place far greater importance on production and consumption than on thinking and feeling. Very little significance is attached to the process of being in a larger context, and it is to this area that education must address itself today.

We need to realize how important this direction is. To be sure, television offers numerous images of selfhood, but in its present state of usage, it does not allow an individual to develop his *own* self. Rather, it allows him—encourages him—to rely on others. This in turn inhibits the process of developing a real identity and substitutes an easily assumed one. People may play many roles or assume various postures, like actors on the screen, without confronting the uniqueness of their own being and the necessity of grappling with their own personality. Furthermore, by denying or ignoring that a self exists, responsibility for individual choice and action is abdicated. One can become so absorbed in the facade, the false image, that he loses sight of who he is and what he stands for.

This is partially due to the fact that the bulk of television in America, as indicated earlier, presents some other world, a world we pretend we live in but which in fact we do not. It tells us virtually nothing of life itself and who we are in relationship to the *real* world. An American historian wrote some years ago that one of the miracles of television was its remarkable power to give experience such a new vagueness. Through television we learn to see "something-or-other happening somewhere-or-other at some-time-or-other."[20] In this context, the distinction between live and taped, real and simulated becomes blurred. At the same time, this exposure to something other prevents people from coming to grips with real life. The individual today seems to forget that he is (or should be) his own actor; he need not substitute TV roles for developing and choosing roles of his own.

Yet, because television removes this vital human contact, it removes active, two-way participation. It gives instead something else: symbols, sounds, images, and gestures, but not real people and life. Television allows us to remain in an early pattern of taking without giving. We are not asked to be concerned about sharing and thinking. We need only satisfy our own desires. Television maximizes the need for immediacy while it minimizes, as the discussion on the various taxonomies indicates, true intellectual, emotional, and physical effort. It excuses viewers from confronting themselves in either a personal or a social context. While watching TV, they can cease being selves having to cope with other selves because the individual eye/I is always channeled along predetermined lines. This all-pervasive vagueness may be one of the reasons for the growing sense of hopelessness and hardness many teachers and other professionals see in today's students. The young simply may not have learned about dealing with emotions in real life.

There are other issues regarding these concepts of self. For example: I have had a number of students who assume the posture of a particular TV character rather than deal with a difficult problem as themselves. This kind of occurrence is strange to the point of being unsettling. I realize that children play-act, for it is a part of growing up and learning about the world, but what I am referring to is somehow different in tone and degree. Under the influence of the TV screen, they seem to become someone else, dissemblers but not themselves.

This difficulty in confronting one's self also manifests itself in other ways. I have found many students, though superficially quite talkative, curiously inarticulate when asked to communicate personal feelings and opinions. Sometimes I have wondered if they had any. Or, they make fun and sarcastic remarks about emotions because they do not know how to respond sincerely. This may be due in part to having so much placed before them which denies their character testing. Or, perhaps they just have not had enough practice being people with feelings.

In relationship to this, we should also remember how much current television advertising practices tell us to be dissatisfied with who and what we are. We constantly are told that we need to change our hair color or our brand of toothpaste; to be younger, more athletic, slimmer; or to use a different detergent, drive a special car, and so on. We are reminded again and again that our real self simply is not good enough, that we lack something somewhere and must change into something else NOW! Is this not the ultimate infringement of rights: taking away from an individual the challenge of finding out and answering questions of style and taste for himself? Without the tools of learning and an education which develops a strong sense of self and personal character, how will young people in particular assume independent roles in a technological future?

Not only are some people finding it more difficult to discover their own character behind all the admonitions to do or be something else, but a definite trend away from individual choice to group standard is becoming more and more apparent. Many students today, unlike their counterparts only ten short years ago, want to conform. They do not want to rock the boat or change the world. Independent questionnaires of high school and college students reveal that involvement with television has been associated with this syndrome of conventionality and conservatism. And this holds true for younger and older adolescents; males and females; and for samples of students from markedly different backgrounds.[21]

Is this the type of social engineering we have in mind? For children to be conventional, for them to copy other selves and not extend their own self to the fullest possible extent? Do we Americans truly have so little imagination that we are baffled by the face of genuine non-conformity? We certainly have the illusion of variety and change through all the products available to us, but do we have the *substance*? How can we educators work toward a better integration of the self and the whole man in a society whose sole purpose at present seems to keep man insecure, confused, and buying? How can we stimulate the creative imagination and a balanced, confident self rather than the neurotic imagination, stimulated in many ways by television which says we are not whole, that we constantly are lacking, and that we are not good enough as we are? Education at all levels should concentrate on this process of becoming a unique entity and learning how to answer questions of style and taste for oneself. Education at this time must work harder than ever to help youngsters discover their individual capabilities and to employ their television screens in a positive mode. If people in the future are going to have more time on their hands, better they should know who and what they are in order to enjoy themselves to their fullest capacity. We educators need to teach the self to be a self and not any number of false selves. We need to stress the union of the interior and exterior realms, not their separation. We need to use television to join emotion and intellect, not tear them apart. We are not trapped, by any means, in a negative picture regarding TV's past. There is much we can hope for if we look to manipulate the medium for personal development and critical analysis. Indeed, television has great, untapped potential for achieving this goal if we work to implement it in a constructive fashion.

Education and the Play of Tolerance

In conjunction with this need to emphasize concepts of self and being are the broader issues of tolerance and understanding. As the individual learns to appreciate his own uniqueness, he can then be encouraged to translate this into a larger group context. But without regard for strong personal identity first unencumbered by an unthinking TV twin, such concepts as tolerance and reciprocity lose meaning. There simply is no basis in subjective experience with which to acknowledge another's point of view. Yet, it is precisely this play of tolerance, this give and take in classroom communication and in life, which is so desperately needed today. Education and broadcasting both share the enormous responsibility of helping people live together in a rapidly changing world. The importance of developing real tolerance—respect for the individual and the race as opposed to mere non-interference—is absolutely crucial.

There is a possibility that the changes occurring within broadcast technology will provide an opportunity for new avenues of expression which will help to promote this play of tolerance—*if* advertising does not become the primary focus of these new channels of communication and *if* new media do not remain luxury toys for those who can afford them. It is feasible that the creative and educational communities will find greater freedom as various developments, such as pay TV, cable, video recorders, and so on, begin to gain momentum across the land and around the world. As more and more people buy sets and more and more nations become televised, the relationship between program creators, educators, administrators, and distributors will become much more influential. Distribution will play a key role in all this, and could affect the domain of education a great deal. As distribution widens, so, too, does the marketplace, which need not be looked upon in mass terms functioning at the lowest levels of the learning domains but as diversified audiences capable of a spectrum of thought and feeling. It may well be an important time for the educator as communicator, because he has the capability of bridging the gap now arising between people. He may have greater chances for expanding a vision of man, and his role in developing programming for the new broadcasting age may be profound. As the marketplace grows, the need for software may offer educators many avenues for nurturing the sympathetic eye/I and building a play of tolerance and understanding between nations as well as individual people.

The Educator as Entertainer

Our attitude will be crucial here, not only in relationship to the way we approach the use of television, but also how we come to look upon ourselves and define our role as instructors in tomorrow's world. At present, we still have a tremendous imbalance in America between so-called educational and entertainment programming, between reality and fantasy material. Why education and entertainment must be looked upon as mutually exclusive commodities and why we tend to view these two aspects of life as conflicting activities is curious to say the least. For some reason, reality is looked upon as either too bothersome, or less compelling, exciting, intriguing, stimulating, and/or fun as escapist subject matter. We have developed over the years—or more appropriately our commercial broadcasting community has developed—a separation between these two aspects of programming which need not exist. Consequently, we have little experience in blending the two. Entertainment can be educational, and education can be entertainment of the highest order depending upon how one presents a topic. The popularity of many BBC productions based upon science, biology, drama, and history demonstrates only too clearly that audiences can be drawn to a variety of reality subjects which are also quite entertaining, fascinating even. It proves that people can be active viewers, at least as active as the television medium will physically permit, as well as passive recipients. It also points to the necessity of teachers to consider a new style of teaching and instruction. We need to confront the idea of the teacher as educator/entertainer; teaching *AND* entertainment as opposed to teaching *VERSUS* entertainment.

Furthermore, we may soon have the opportunity of approaching our various learning audiences from a different frame of reference. Perhaps we can change from the concept of mass education and entertainment to that of myriad individuals capable of response and feeling far greater than many people think, especially current broadcasters. We may have greater opportunities for developing and providing concept orientation material because people genuinely want to learn more about each other. The innate curiosity *is* there. Perhaps we will be able to provide a larger and broader spectrum of dramatic entertainment as well. Artists, independent directors, producers, and educators working together may be able to exercise more influence than ever before because they have the potential of trying to keep on top of all the technological growth by reaffirming the human element. The possibilities of all this in terms of education are profound because people in the near future may be able to learn virtually anything via their home TV screens.

We must also remember that as we enter a new phase of economic growth based upon production and distribution, entertainment and education undoubtedly will move closer and closer together. The dichotomy between the two which we see at present may grow less and less distinct as time goes on. A country that can produce a balanced output and quality in a variety of fields may find new areas for economic expansion without the subjugation of individual response. On the contrary: perhaps the widening of that response. There is some indication that the American broadcasting industry is beginning to consider the ramifications of these changes, and the educational establishment is developing its own software for the coming education/entertainment era. Right now the American broadcasting industry has a monopoly of sorts over worldwide TV because it manufactures quantity. But as other nations begin to jump into the global broadcasting scene, America could lose its commanding position in this area because other countries may demand and/or provide more quality product, a product dealing with real men in real life. Again, the opportunities in terms of education are great because the marketplace for learning *and* entertainment will expand drastically in the decades to come.

FINE TUNING FOR THE FUTURE

What we are left with finally are the moral and philosophical questions involved with communication, education, and how they relate to the instruction of children. Much now rests with us as teachers and educators and how we handle this upheaval; what stances we take in curriculum planning, classroom activities, and graduate research centers in relationship to this issue as a whole. This is especially true, since we have not been prepared for these sweeping changes in our own formal education, and we do not seem to be handling them all that successfully with our students. As a teacher and an individual living in a growing technological age, I find this change in human learning and communication patterns one of the most demanding issues of our day, one which has the greatest repercussions for both schools and society at large.

The tremendous shift from formal to informal learning patterns—with television as the vanguard of the New Wave—should be regarded by educators with great concern, for it is in the informal domain that most behavioral programming takes place. Yet the unconscious nature of this incidental learning at the same time allows for a high degree of patterning. Uncertainty and nervousness can also result simply because people are being trained to react emotionally rather than conceptually. Individuals are being taught informally to *feel* they must behave or think a certain way or want a certain object without consciously knowing why. This certainly does not bode well for any society which asks its citizens to make rational choices, because the emotional nature of informal learning may generate a populace quick to react but slow to think and to consider. But, with the future promising ever-increasing amounts of leisure time and with technology releasing more and more people from the labor force, the need for more conceptual thinking processes becomes critical. Without this new direction in conceptualizing, the growing world population could merely become a ready target for even more political and economic exploitation via the home screen/learning center.

On the other hand, a stronger foundation in conceptual thinking might help to counterbalance some of the pull of our informal TV twin. And, again, it is the youth growing up under television's expanding gaze who need this training and direction. Otherwise, the final purpose of these technological changes may be nothing more than unrelenting pressure for them to think and feel certain things in certain ways and to accept material persuasion or a specific view of life as the final purpose of their existence. Is this what we truly want for the young: more informal/involuntary behavior which relies upon eliciting pre-ordained, emotional responses, or more formal/voluntary behavior which asks the individual to be a unique self, to question, to judge, and to ask why?

All this is closely tied to what expectations we formulate in the field of education regarding our media and young people; whether we desire primarily emotional or cognitive responses or at best a balance between the two. Much depends upon how we teachers approach television in the classroom; what kind of subject matter is presented and how; the emphasis on products (things) as opposed to processes (thought). Because it is precisely in the informal domain of attitudes and expectations that television exerts its strongest pull, and where we teachers must exert the greatest counterbalance today.

The only alternative we have to all this is to accept the possibility that curiosity and education or the concept of individual selfhood are not that valuable anymore. Perhaps they will only cause more trouble in the future than good. Perhaps the uninformed circus goer, who seems so willing to be led, is exactly what this Brave New World needs. It is possible that broadcasters as social engineers truly will make our students' lives like child's play and take away—or at least modulate informally—their freedom of selection and the burden of individuality. Perhaps freedom itself will no longer be appropriate in the world of technocracy where techniques of control will become progressively swift and subliminal, drawing upon stores of information and emotion within our minds with lightning speed.

Ultimately, we cannot divorce ourselves from the fact that morality and human fate will become more and more involved with technology and education as the century draws on; it will be harder and harder to separate the two. This is particularly true in the area of television and broadcasting because they will assume an even greater role in our lives. Make no mistake. The network generals, their lieutenants, and sergeants—all those social engineers—take this game very seriously, and so should we. Time and again the phrase "realities of the marketplace" is heard in defense of current business philosophies and practices. Yes, business *is* business; but there is another business which concerns itself with the realities of the human mind and heart which are subjected to all these images and impressions. Teaching and education in very broad terms work upon the principle that the up-coming generations should be encouraged to bring as much curiosity and imagination into the world as they possibly can—products and commodities which are hard to assess in dollars and cents or on profit and loss sheets but which are invaluable nevertheless.

We need to initiate a renaissance of thought *and* action behind the use of our television screens. The possibilities for a stunning new creativity and imaginative playfulness are available to us and our students if we meet the reality of television in a constructive way. The challenge rests with us as teachers, educators, and administrators to inform ourselves of the various technological advances and deploy them to our advantage. Both education and ignorance can be powerful weapons; the question is which side we choose to enhance. A choice must be made regarding curriculum planning and educational budgeting at the local, state, and federal levels concerning television; its role in the future of linking home learning with the educational establishment; of training teachers and other school staff how to cope with television in the most positive manner. No one institution, no single faction can possibly hope to accomplish all this. We need an orchestrated approach within each section of society and between various groups— parents, teachers, schools, research centers, government, and industry—a cooperative chain of interaction based upon the needs of our children and their learning future.

Notes

CHAPTER I

1. Nat Rutstein, *Go Watch TV!*, Sheed & Ward, Inc., New York, 1974, p. 21.
2. Charles Spokin, *7 Glorious Days, 7 Fun-Filled Nights*, Simon & Schuster, New York, 1968, p. 13.
3. Statistics on TV consumption by children compiled from the following sources:
    (a) Rutstein, *Go Watch TV!*, p. 165.
    (b) Jack Lyle and Heidi Hoffman, "Explorations in Patterns of Television Viewing by Pre-School Children," in *Television and Social Behavior, Reports and Papers Vol. IV Television in Day-to-Day Life*, Eli A. Rubenstein, George A. Comstock, and John P. Murray (Editors), Washington, D.C., 1972, p. 269.
    (c) Math conference held at Beverly Hills School District, September 22, 1976.
4. For additional comparisons, see David Littlejohn, "Communicating Ideas by Television," in *Television as a Social Force: New Approaches to TV Criticism*, Douglass Cater (Editor), Aspen Institute for Humanistic Studies, Praeger Publishers, New York, 1975, pp. 65-67.
5. Statistics about lowering literacy scores compiled from "Why Johnny Can't Read," *Newsweek*, December 8, 1975, pp. 58-65.
6. *Los Angeles Times*, June 11, 1981, Part I, p. 3.
7. "Video's New Frontier," *Newsweek*, December 8, 1975, p. 52.
8. First two quotes from Robert T. Bower, *Television and the Public*, Holt, Rinehart, and Winston, New York, 1973, pp. 157-158. Next three quotes from Gary A. Steiner, *The People Look at Television*, Alfred A. Knopf, New York, 1963, p. 86.
9. See Herbert E. Krugman and Eugene L. Hartley, "Passive Learning From Television," *Public Opinion Quarterly*, 1970, Vol. 34.
10. Herbert E. Krugman, "Brain Wave Measures of Media Involvement," *Journal of Advertising Research*, 1971, Vol. 11, No. 1, pp. 8ff.
11. Jean Piaget, *Play, Dreams, and Imitation in Childhood*, W.W. Norton & Co., New York, 1962, p. 62.

12. Same as above.
13. Edward T. Hall, *The Silent Language*, Fawcett Publications, Inc., Connecticut, 1951, p. 80.
14. Wilbur Schramm and Donald F. Roberts (Editors), *The Process and Effects of Mass Communication*, University of Illinois Press, Chicago, 1971 (see Introduction), p. 3.
15. Robert Lewis Shayon, *Television and Our Children*, Longmans Green & Co., New York, 1951, p. 7.

CHAPTER II

1. Chart from Shayon, *Television and Our Children*, p. 76.
2. Chart from Wilbur Schramm, Jack Lyle, and Edwin B. Parker, *Television in the Lives of Our Children*, Stanford University Press, California, 1961, pp. 139-140.
3. Same as above, p. 138.
4. Both sets of statistics from the National Association for Better Radio and TV, cited in Robert M. Liebert, John M. Neale, and Emily S. Davidson, *The Early Window*, Pergamon Press, New York, 1973, p. 23. Also see Rutstein, *Go Watch TV!*, p. 73.
5. *Variety*, April 5, 1978, pp. 50 and 70. There is some contradictory information regarding Gerbner's information. During February, 1978, the National Citizens' Committee for Broadcasting reported some different results. This group found that "blood and guts" declined during the fall season on ABC and NBC but increased sharply on CBS. According to their survey, CBS actually showed a 14 percent increase in overall violent content and a 105 percent increase during the Family Viewing Hour. ABC, however, dropped over 20 percent and NBC decreased 11 percent. Discrepancies are probably due to different rating methods and/or the number of shows monitored. See *Variety*, February 8, 1978, p. 8, and *The Wall Street Journal*, February 21, 1978, p. 12.
6. *Variety*, November 9, 1977, p. 48.
7. Mills and Kilbridge chart compiled from information in *Viewpoint*, section of *Los Angeles Times*, Sunday edition, April 18, 1976, p. 2.
8. Erik Barnouw, *The Image Empire*, Oxford University Press, New York, 1970, p. 268.
9. Eleanor E. Maccoby, "Television: Its Impact on School Children," *Public Opinion Quarterly*, 1951, Vol. 15, p. 442.
10. Hilde T. Himmelweit, A.N. Oppenheim, and Pamela Vince, *Television and the Child*, Oxford University Press, London, 1958, p. 18.
11. Same as above, p. 37.
12. Same as above, p. 119.
13. Same as above, p. 215.

14. See Albert Bandura, "Influence of Models' Reinforcement Contingencies on the Acquisition of Imitative Responses," *Journal of Personality and Social Psychology*, 1965, Vol. 1, pp. 589-595.
15. Chart from Albert Bandura, "Vicarious Processes: A Case of No-Trial Learning," in *Advances in Experimental Social Psychology*, Vol. 2, Academic Press, New York, 1965, pp. 21-22.
16. Albert Bandura, Dorothea Ross, and Sheila A. Ross, "Vicarious Reinforcement and Imitative Learning," *Journal of Abnormal and Social Psychology*, 1964, Vol. 67, p. 605.
17. Same as above.
18. Leonard Berkowitz, *Aggression: A Social Psychological Analysis*, McGraw-Hill Book Co., New York, 1962, p. 236.
19. Faye B. Steuer, James M. Applefield, and Rodney Smith, "Televised Aggression and Interpersonal Aggression of Pre-School Children," *Journal of Experimental Child Psychology*, 1971, Vol. 11, pp. 442-445.
20. Alberta E. Siegel, "The Effects of Media Violence on Social Learning," in *The Process and Effects of Mass Communication*, Wilbur Schramm and Donald F. Roberts (Editors), pp. 634ff.
21. Chart from Liebert *et al.*, *The Early Window*, p. 60.
22. Robert Liebert and Robert A. Baron, "Some Immediate Effects of Televised Violence on Children's Behavior," *Developmental Psychology*, 1972, Vol. 6, p. 469.
23. Chart from Liebert *et al.*, *The Early Window*, pp. 75-76.
24. Same as above, p. 76.
25. Same as above, p. 63.
26. Same as above.
27. David J. Hicks, "Imitation and Retention of Film-Mediated Aggressive Peer and Adult Models," *Journal of Personality and Social Psychology*, 1965, Vol. 2, No. 1, p. 97.
28. Richard E. Goranson, "Media Violence and Aggressive Behavior," in *Advances in Experimental Social Psychology*, Leonard Berkowitz (Editor), Academic Press, New York, Vol. 2, No. 1, p. 97.
29. Howard Munson, "Teenage Violence and the Telly," *Psychology Today*, March, 1978, p. 50.
30. *Los Angeles Times*, October 26, 1977, part 4, p. 19.
31. Leonard Eron, L. Rowell Huesmann, Monroe M. Lefkowitz, and Leopold O. Walder, "Does Television Violence Cause Aggression?," *American Psychologist*, April, 1972, Vol. 27, pp. 252ff and 263.
32. The five supporting volumes are: *Media Content and Control, Television and Social Learning, Television and Adolescent Aggressiveness, Television in Day-to-Day Life: Patterns of Use,* and *Television's Effects: Further Explorations.*
33. Leo Bogart, *The Age of Television*, Frederick Unger Publishing Co., New York, 1956, pp. 278-279.

34. Harry J. Skornia, *Television and Society*, McGraw-Hill Book Co., New York, 1965, p. 145.
35. Douglass Cater and Stephen Strickland, *TV Violence and the Child: Evolution and Fate of the Surgeon General's Report*, Russell Sage Foundation, New York, 1975, p. 12. Also see *Surgeon General's Report Television and Growing Up: The Impact of Televised Violence*, Washington, D.C., 1972, pp. 45-46.
36. The Advisory Committee members were:
    (a) four psychologists: Thomas Coffin, Irving Janis, Alberta Siegel, Gerhard Wiebe.
    (b) three sociologists: Ira Cisin, Joseph Klapper, Harold Mendelsohn.
    (c) two psychiatrists: Charles Pinderhughes, Andrew Watson.
    (d) one political scientist: Ithiel de Sola Pool.
    (e) one anthropologist: Anthony Wallace.
    (f) one educator: Evelin Omwake.
37. Leo Bogart, "Warning: The Surgeon General Has Determined that TV Violence Is Moderately Dangerous to Your Child's Mental Health," *Public Opinion Quarterly*, 1972, Vol. 36, p. 520.
38. Cater and Strickland, *TV Violence and the Child*, p. 114.
39. The Surgeon General's Report, p. 10.
40. The Surgeon General's Report, p. 53.
41. Same as above, pp. 57-58.
42. Same as above, p. 103.
43. Same as above, p. 123.
44. Joseph T. Klapper, *The Effects of Mass Communication*, The Free Press, New York, 1960, p. 159.
45. Cater and Strickland, *TV Violence and the Child*, p. 101.
46. Same as above, p. 190.
47. *Variety*, October 5, 1977, p. 47.
48. *Los Angeles Times*, November 11, 1977, part 4, p. 18.
49. *Television and Behavior: Ten Years of Scientific Progress and Implications for the Eighties*, National Institute of Mental Health, U.S. Government Printing Office, Washington, D.C., 1982, pp. 89-90.
50. Same as above, p. 6.
51. Cited in Bogart, *The Age of Television*, pp. 275-276.
52. *Los Angeles Times*, February 28, 1977, part 4, p. 12.
53. From lecture given by novelist Jerzy Kosinski at Royce Hall, University of California at Los Angeles, October 14, 1976.
54. Victor B. Cline, Roger G. Croft, and Steven Courrier, "Desensitization of Children to Television Violence," *Journal of Personality and Social Psychology*, 1973, Vol. 27, pp. 363-365.
55. Same as above, p. 360.
56. The Surgeon General's Report, pp. 189-190.

57. "What TV Does to Kids," *Newsweek*, February 21, 1977, p. 67.
58. Marie Winn, *The Plug-In Drug*, The Viking Press, New York, 1977, p. 74.
59. See "Youth Crime Plague," in *Time*, July 11, 1977, pp. 18-28. All quotations by boys from this article.
60. Same as above.
61. "What TV Does to Kids," *Newsweek*, p. 69.
62. *Variety*, April 5, 1978, p. 50.
63. *Newsweek*, March 14, 1977, p. 90.
64. *Newsweek*, April 10, 1978, p. 10.
65. See The Surgeon General's Report, Liebert *et al.*, Leonard Berkowitz, "The Effects of Observing Violence," *Scientific American*, 1964, Vol. 210, No. 2, pp. 35-41, and Richard E. Goranson, "Media Violence and Aggressive Behavior," in *Advances in Experimental Social Psychology*, 1970, Vol. 5, pp. 1-31.
66. Max Gunther, "All That Violence: Is It Really Harmful?" *TV Guide*, November 13, 1976, p. 38.
67. George Gerbner and Larry Gross, "The Scary World of TV's Heavy Viewer," *Psychology Today*, April, 1976, p. 44.
68. Barnouw, *The Image Empire*, p. 269.
69. The Surgeon General's Report, p. 66.
70. Liebert *et al.*, *The Early Window*, p. 45.
71. Bandura, "Vicarious Processes: A Case of No-Trial Learning," p. 27.
72. Berkowitz, "The Effects of Observing Violence," p. 38.
73. First two quotes from Bogart, *The Age of Television*, pp. 286 and 277, respectively. The third quote from Charles A. Siepmann, *Television and Education in the United States*, published by UNESCO, Paris, 1962, p. 12. The fourth quote from a parent.
74. Bogart, *The Age of Television*, quotes from p. 277.
75. First quote from Liebert *et al.*, *The Early Window*, p. 2. Second quote from Norman S. Morris, *Television's Child*, Little, Brown & Co., Boston, 1971, p. 115.
76. Both quotes from Rutstein, *Go Watch TV!*, p. 57.
77. *Los Angeles Times*, February 24, 1977, part 4, p. 9.
78. First quote from "What You Can Do About TV Violence," *Reader's Digest Reprint*, July, 1975, pp. 2-3. Second quote from lecture presented by the Build the World Symposium at Marymount School for Girls, Los Angeles, California, October, 1977.
79. *Los Angeles Times*, August 19, 1977, part 1, p. 4.
80. All quotations and statistics on TV Criminals and Criminals in Real Life, see Grant Hendrick, "When Television Is a School for Criminals," *TV Guide*, January 29-February 4, 1977, pp. 4-10.
81. Barnouw, *The Image Empire*, p. 153.
82. See Thomas Baldwin and Colby Lewis, "Violence in Television: The

Industry Looks at Itself," in *Television and Social Behavior Vol. 1 Media Content and Control*, Comstock and Rubenstein (Editors), Washington, D.C., 1972, pp. 290-373. Also see National Association for Better Broadcasting *Newsletter*, "Violence Is a Saleable Commodity," Spring, 1973.

83. Muriel G. Cantor, "The Role of the Producer in Choosing Children's Television Content," in *Television and Social Behavior, Vol. 1 Media Content and Control*, p. 273 (also p. 21).
84. Cater and Strickland, *TV Violence and the Child*, p. 65.
85. See note No. 83.
86. Cater and Strickland, *TV Violence and the Child*, p. 60.
87. Same as above.
88. First and third quotes from *Symposium on Television Violence*, organized by the research branch of the Canadian Radio-Television Commission, Ottawa, 1976, pp. 131-132. Second quote from Baldwin and Lewis, "Violence in Television: The Industry Looks at Itself," p. 357.
89. Barnouw, *The Image Empire*, p. 318.
90. Baldwin and Lewis, "Violence in Television: The Industry Looks at Itself," p. 358.
91. Cater and Strickland, *TV Violence and the Child*, p. 120. Also see "What You Can Do About TV Violence," *Reader's Digest Reprint*, p. 5.
92. Marshall McLuhan, *Understanding Media: The Extensions of Man*, McGraw-Hill Book Co., New York, 1965, p. 50.
93. See *Variety*, July 26, 1978, p. 50, and *Variety*, December 6, 1978, pp. 60 and 72.
94. *Variety*, December 21, 1977, p. 1.

CHAPTER III

1. Chart from William Melody, *Children's Television: The Economics of Exploitation*, Yale University Press, London, 1973, p. 77.
2. Same as above, p. 81.
3. Same as above, p. 51.
4. Same as above.
5. Mattel story compiled from various information and interviews supplied by Douglas Spellman, advertiser, September, 1977.
6. Barbie story compiled from various information supplied by Douglas Spellman, advertiser.
7. *Seeking Solutions to Violence on Children's Television*, Committee on Children's Television (now Coalition on Children and Television), San Francisco, 1977, p. 5.
8. *Edible TV: Your Child and Food Commercials*, report from the Council

on Children, Media, and Merchandising, Washington, D.C., June, 1977, p. 11.

9. Chart information compiled from the following sources:
   (a) Rutstein, *Go Watch TV!*, pp. 121-122.
   (b) *Research on the Effects of Television Advertising on Children*, report prepared for the National Science Foundation, p. 183.
   (c) *Edible TV: Your Child and Food Commercials*, p. 11.
   (d) *Variety*.

10. As part of my research, I watched a number of children's television programs. This excerpt is taken from the weekend of June 18-19, 1977.

11. *Los Angeles Times*, September 7, 1978, part 4, p. 13.

12. The countries surveyed in this study were: Austria, Australia, Canada, Denmark, Finland, France, Britain, Ireland, Italy, Japan, The Netherlands, Norway, Sweden, Switzerland, the U.S., and West Germany. Countries allowing advertising to children were: the U.S., Canada, England, and Japan. Since this 1971 survey, however, Canada has disallowed advertising to children under certain circumstances.

13. Chart from Liebert *et al.*, *The Early Window*, p. 114.

14. National Science Foundation Report, p. 21. These time allotments are subject to frequent change.

15. *Variety*, June 7, 1978, pp. 50 and 72.

16. National Science Foundation, *Research on the Effects of Television Advertising on Children*, Washington, D.C., 1977, p. 283.

17. Herbert E. Krugman, "Impact of Television Advertising: Learning Without Involvement," in Wilbur Schramm and Donald F. Roberts (Editors), *The Process and Effects of Mass Communication*, p. 490. Also see Herbert E. Krugman, "The Impact of Television Advertising," *Public Opinion Quarterly*, 1965, Vol. 29, pp. 349-356.

18. Krugman, *The Process and Effects of Mass Communication*, p. 492.

19. Rutstein, *Go Watch TV!*, p. 11-12.

20. McLuhan, *Understanding Media*, p. 227.

21. Lawrence H. Streicher and Norman L. Booney, "Children Talk About Television," *Journal of Communication*, 1974, Vol. 24, p. 58.

22. Chart from Liebert *et al.*, *The Early Window*, pp. 129-130.

23. Same as above.

24. Bogart, *The Age of Television*, pp. 258-259.

25. Helen White Streicher, "The Girls in the Cartoons," *Journal of Communication*, 1974, Vol. 24, No. 2, p. 127.

26. Chart compiled from various information provided by Annes A. Sheikh, V. Kanti Prasad, and Tanniru R. Rao in "Children's TV Commercials: A Review of Research," *Journal of Communication*, 1974, Vol. 24, No. 4, pp. 126-136.

27. *Edible TV: Your Child and Food Commercials*, p. 12. The status referral function is also discussed in *The Process and Effects of Mass Communication*.

28. *Edible TV*, p. 13.
29. Attributed to Dr. Kenneth O'Bryan, Director of the Ontario TV Research Laboratory; cited in *To the Federal Trade Commission in the Matter of a Trade Regulation Rule on Over-the-Counter Drugs*, submitted by the Council on Children, Media, and Merchandising, 1977, p. 20.
30. National Science Foundation Report, p. 48.
31. Same as above, p. 46.
32. Same as above, pp. 68ff.
33. Same as above, p. 216.
34. Same as above, p. 264.
35. Same as above, pp. 265-266.
36. Chart from *Edible TV*, p. 75.
37. Same as above.
38. National Science Foundation Report, p. 189.
39. Same as above, p. 179.
40. See "America: Out to Eat," *Newsweek*, October 3, 1977, pp. 86-89.
41. Chart from *To the Federal Trade Commission in the Matter of a Trade Regulation Rule on Over-the-Counter Drugs*, p. 22.
42. Same as above, p. 49.
43. Same as above, p. 33.
44. National Science Foundation Report, p. 168.
45. Same as above, p. 170.
46. Same as above, p. 51.
47. Same as above.
48. Same as above, p. 346, Appendix C.
49. Same as above, p. 287.
50. Same as above, p. 247.
51. Same as above, p. 347, Appendix C.
52. Same as above, p. 181.
53. Same as above, p. 180.
54. Melody, *The Economics of Exploitation*, p. 59.
55. First quote from Liebert *et al., The Early Window*, p. 125. Second quote from William Melody and Wendy Ehrlich, "Children's TV Commercials: The Vanishing Policy Options," *Journal of Communication*, 1974, Vol. 24, No. 4, p. 118. Third quote from C. Miller, *Process of Persuasion*, cited in Rutstein, *Go Watch TV!*, p. 125.
56. National Science Foundation Report, p. 184. The original promotion appeared in *Advertising Age*, March 8, 1976.
57. *Los Angeles Times*, October 11, 1976, part 4, p. 20.
58. *Los Angeles Times*, November 25, 1976, part 4, p. 40.
59. All quotes from Melvin Helitzer and Carl Heyel, *Youth Market: Its Dimensions, Influences, and Opportunities for You*, Media Books, New York, 1970, cited in William Melody, *Children's Television: The Economics of Exploitation*, pp. 61, 63, and 80, respectively.

60. Melody, *Children's Television: The Economics of Exploitation*, p. 79.
61. Melody and Ehrlich, "Children's TV Commercials: The Vanishing Policy Options," p. 114.
62. Same as above, p. 122.
63. Same as above, p. 124.
64. *Los Angeles Times*, October 10, 1977, part 1, p. 5, and *Variety*, November 9, 1977, pp. 31 and 48.
65. *Variety*, March 8, 1978, p. 61.
66. *Variety*, August 31, 1977, p. 58.
67. Interview with John Goldhammer, Director of Programs, KABC-TV, Los Angeles, California, December 27, 1977.
68. Interview with Giovanna Nigra-Chacon, Executive Producer, KNBC-TV, Los Angeles, California, June 27, 1977.
69. Interview with Douglas Spellman, advertiser, September 14, 1977.
70. See last section of the National Science Foundation Report, entitled "Recommendations," pp. 283ff.
71. *Seeking Solutions to Violence on Children's Television*, p. 6.

CHAPTER IV

1. Rutstein, *Go Watch TV!* p. 58.
2. Erik Barnouw, *The Sponsor: Notes on a Modern Potentate*, Oxford University Press, New York, 1978, pp. 100-102.
3. Liebert *et al., The Early Window*, pp. 18-19.
4. Chart from Joseph R. Dominick, "Crime and Law Enforcement on Prime-Time Television," *Public Opinion Quarterly*, 1973, Vol. 37, pp. 245-246.
5. Same as above, p. 249.
6. Melvin DeFleur, "Occupational Roles as Portrayed on Television," *Public Opinion Quarterly*, 1964, Vol. 28, p. 68.
7. Himmelweit *et al., Television and the Child*, p. 229.
8. Hilde T. Himmelweit, "A Theoretical Framework for the Effects of Television: A British Report," *Journal of Social Issues*, 1962, Vol. 18, p. 27.
9. Himmelweit *et al., Television and the Child*, pp. 92-95.
10. Same as above, p. 408.
11. Chart from Schramm *et al., Television in the Lives of Our Children*, p. 27.
12. Chart same as above, p. 89 and pp. 103-104.
13. Chart same as above, p. 152.
14. Chart from Jack Lyle and Heidi Hoffman, "Children's Use of Television and Other Media," in *Television and Social Behavior, Reports and Papers Vol. IV Television in Day-to-Day Life*, Eli A. Rubenstein, George A. Comstock, and John P. Murray (Editors), Washington, D.C., 1972, p. 174.

15. Aimee D. Leifer, N.J. Gordon, & S.B. Graves, Children's Television: More Than Mere Entertainment, *Harvard Educational Review*, 1974, Vol. 44, No. 2, p. 239.
16. Timothy P. Meyer, "Children's Perceptions of Favorite Television Characters as Behavioral Models," *Educational Broadcasting Review*, 1973, Vol. 7, No. 1, p. 30.
17. Same as above.
18. National Institute of Mental Health Report, 1982, pp. 46-47.
19. Morris, *Television's Child*, p. 9.
20. First two quotes from Shayon, *Television and Our Children*, pp. 20 and 83, respectively. Third quote from Bogart, *The Age of Television*, p. 271. Fourth quote from Feinberg, "The Classroom Is No Longer Primetime," *Today's Education*, September/October, 1977, Vol. 66, No. 3, p. 79. Fifth quote from *Seeking Solutions to Violence on Children's Television*, p. 16.
21. Interview with Bill Porter, Director of Media, Beverly Hills School District, June 20, 1977.
22. Interview with Giovanna Nigra-Chacon, June 27, 1977.
23. Interview with John Goldhammer, December 27, 1977.
24. Chart from Schramm *et al., Television in the Lives of Our Children*, p. 36.
25. Chart same as above.
26. Chart from Lyle and Hoffman, "Children's Use of Television and Other Media," *Television and Social Behavior*, Vol. IV, p. 158.
27. National Institute of Mental Health Report, 1982, p. 80.
28. Same as above.
29. From lecture given by Jerzy Kosinski, UCLA, October 14, 1976.
30. Winn, *The Plug-In Drug*, p. 51.
31. Chart from Schramm *et al., Television in the Lives of Our Children*, p. 14.
32. Feinberg, "The Class Is No Longer Primetime," pp. 78-79.
33. "What TV Does to Kids," *Newsweek*, p. 65.
34. National Institute of Mental Health Report, p. 5.
35. Same as above.
36. Same as above, pp. 48, 89.
37. Winn, *The Plug-In Drug*, p. 84.
38. Maccoby, "Television: Its Impact on School Children," p. 435.
39. Harry J. Skornia, *Television and Society: An Inquest and Agenda for Improvement*, McGraw-Hill Book Co., New York, p. 164.
40. The Surgeon General's Report, pp. 99-100.
41. Peter H. Wood, "Television as Dream," in *Television as a Cultural Force*, Richard Adler (Editor), Aspen Institute for Humanistic Studies, Praeger Publishers, New York, 1976, pp. 21-23.
42. *Calendar Section, Los Angeles Times*, Sunday edition, July 9, 1978, p. 36.

43. National Institute of Mental Health Report, p. 5.
44. Same as above, p. 10.
45. Same as above, p. 11.
46. *Edible TV: Your Child and Food Commercials*, p. 33.
47. Chart compiled from various information presented at an adult night seminar given by the Las Virgenes School District, California, Fall, 1977, and also from an article appearing in *Los Angeles Times*, August 30, 1977, part 1, p. 3.
48. Rutstein, *Go Watch TV!*, p. 52.
49. Claire Safran, "How TV Changes Children," *Redbook*, November, 1976, p. 88.
50. Same as above, p. 91.
51. *Edible TV: Your Child and Food Commercials*, p. 79.
52. William Glasser, *The Identity Society*, Harper & Row, New York, 1972, p. 136.
53. Same as above, p. 137.
54. Both quotes from Winn, *The Plug-In Drug*, p. 17.
55. Safran, "How TV Changes Children," p. 17.
56. Chart compiled from information in Robert D. Hess and Harriet Goldman, "Parents' Views of the Effects of Television on Their Children," *Child Development*, 1962, Vol. 33, p. 415.
57. Martin Mayer, *About Television*, Harper & Row, New York, 1972, p. 128.
58. "What TV Does to Kids," p. 67.
59. See Paul Lazarsfeld and Robert Merton, "Mass Communication, Popular Taste, and Organized Social Action," in *The Process and Effect of Mass Communication*, Schramm and Roberts (Editors), pp. 565ff.
60. National Institute of Mental Health Report, p. 20.
61. Schramm *et al.*, *Television in the Lives of Our Children*, p. 119.
62. *Los Angeles Times*, July 25, 1978, part 1, pp. 1, 17, 18.
63. First and sixth quote from Shayon, *Television and Our Children*, pp. 29 and 30, respectively. Second quote from Spokin, *7 Glorious Days, 7 Fun-Filled Nights*, p. 68. Quotes three, four, five, and seven from "What TV Does to Kids," p. 67.

CHAPTER V

1. Interview with David Crippens, KCET, Los Angeles, California, July 7, 1977.
2. I have relied heavily on Erik Barnouw's trilogy, *A Tower in Babel, The Golden Web,* and *The Image Empire*, Oxford University Press, for basic information about industry history.
3. Erik Barnouw, *A Tower in Babel*, Oxford University Press, New York, 1966, pp. 107-111.

4. Same as above, p. 265.
5. Same as above, p. 283.
6. Cited in Barnouw, *A Tower in Babel*, p. 282.
7. Same as above, pp. 268-270.
8. Both quotes from Erik Barnouw, *The Golden Web*, Oxford University Press, 1968, pp. 34-35 and pp. 72-73, respectively.
9. Same as above, p. 35.
10. This was the Wagner-Hatfield Act. The reference from *Broadcasting* magazine is cited in Barnouw, *The Golden Web*, p. 26.
11. Same as above.
12. Same as above, p. 230.
13. Same as above, pp. 231-232.
14. Same as above, pp. 234-235.
15. Same as above, p. 236.
16. Same as above, p. 241.
17. Among those blacklisted were Leonard Bernstein, Aaron Copeland, Norman Corwin, Dashiell Hammett, Judy Holiday, Langston Hughes, Howard K. Smith, Arthur Miller, Edward G. Robinson, and Pete Seeger, to name but a few.
18. Barnouw, *The Golden Web*, p. 282.
19. Barnouw, *The Sponsor*, pp. 48-49.
20. See Barnouw, *The Golden Web*, for various case studies.
21. Barnouw, *The Golden Web*, p. 286.
22. Same as above, pp. 282-292.
23. Barnouw, *The Image Empire*, p. 6.
24. Nicholas Johnson, *How to Talk Back to Your Television Set*, Little, Brown & Co., Boston, 1967, p. 25.
25. Barnouw, *The Image Empire*, p. 23.
26. Same as above, p. 33.
27. Same as above.
28. Barnouw, *The Sponsor*, p. 54.
29. Same as above.
30. Barnouw, *The Image Empire*, p. 37.
31. Same as above, p. 267.
32. Same as above, p. 69.
33. Same as above.
34. Same as above, p. 123.
35. Same as above, p. 74.
36. Fred Friendly, *Due to Circumstances Beyond Our Control*, Vintage Books, Random House, New York, 1968, p. 99.
37. Les Brown, *The Business Behind the Box*, Harcourt, Brace, Jovanovich, Inc., New York, 1971, p. 65.
38. Barnouw, *The Image Empire*, pp. 197-198.
39. Same as above, p. 251.

40. Same as above, p. 268.
41. Same as above, p. 277.
42. Friendly, *Due to Circumstances Beyond Our Control*, p. 183.
43. Same as above, p. 212.
44. Barnouw, *The Image Empire*, pp. 304-305.
45. Chart from Liebert *et al., The Early Window*, p. 7.
46. *Variety*, January 13, 1982, p. 156.
47. Merrill Panitt, "Network Power—Is It Absolute?" *TV Guide*, February 26 to March 4, 1977, p. 37.
48. *Variety*, July 12, 1978, pp. 1 and 76.
49. *Variety*, July 19, 1978, p. 1.
50. These are hypothetical examples based upon information received by the Federal Trade Commission. See *Los Angeles Times*, July 19, 1978, part 2, p. 1.
51. *Los Angeles Times*, August 22, 1977, part 4, p. 14.
52. Chart from *Variety*, September 9, 1977, p. 33.
53. Same as above.
54. Melody, *The Economics of Exploitation*, p. 69.
55. Les Brown, *The Business Behind the Box*, p. 179.
56. Same as above, p. 151.
57. Same as above, p. 77.
58. First quote from *Variety*, May 10, 1978, p. 172. Second quote from *Variety*, October 26, 1977, p. 47. Third quote from *Variety*. This type of scorecard is run on a regular basis.
59. Tom Shales, *Los Angeles Times*, July 4, 1978, part 4, p. 11.
60. "The Coddled Critics," *Newsweek*, July 4, 1977, p. 78.
61. *Symposium on Television Violence*, pp. 131-132.
62. *Herald Examiner*, January 22, 1978, Section E, p. 1.
63. According to Barnouw, by 1972 members of the Screen Actors Guild were earning more from commercials than from theatrical or TV films combined. See *The Sponsor*, p. 81.
64. Cater and Strickland, *TV Violence and the Child*, p. 64.
65. Interview with Giovanna Nigra-Chacon, June 27, 1977.
66. Interview with Lou Scheimer and Norman Prescott, producers, Filmation Studios, Sherman Oaks, California, November 8, 1977.
67. *Variety*, May 31, 1978, p. 63.
68. *Los Angeles Times*, October 4, 1977, part 4, p. 12.
69. Excerpts from children's programs were taken from Saturday and Sunday morning network shows, June 18-19, 1977.
70. *Variety*, August 17 and 24, 1977, pp. 41 and 43, respectively.
71. *Variety*, November 2, 1977, p. 65.
72. *Variety*, January 11, 1978, p. 15.
73. *Variety*, February 22, 1978, p. 71.

CHAPTER VI

1. Roger G. Noll, Merton J. Peck, and John J. McGowan, *Economic Aspects of Television Regulation*, The Brookings Institute, Washington, D.C., 1973, p. 1. This comparison represents TV advertising circa early 1970's and therefore is subject to change.
2. Noll *et al.*, p. 208.
3. *Los Angeles Times*, June 8, 1978, part 4, p. 28.
4. National Institute of Mental Health Report, p. 8.
5. Suggestions taken from *A Family Guide to Television*, Far West Laboratory for Educational Research and Development, San Francisco, CA; prepared at WGBH Office of Radio and Television for Learning, by Ned White.
6. Richard Ashmore, *Fear in the Air: Broadcasting and the First Amendment—The Anatomy of a Constitutional Crisis*, W.W. Norton & Co., Inc., New York, 1973, pp. 164-165.
7. From CBS Late Night News, January 9, 1978, 11:00 p.m.
8. Interview with Bill Porter, June 20, 1977.
9. Conversation with Dr. M. David Merrill, Department of Instructional Technology, University of Southern California, July, 1981.
10. Peter J. Dirr, "The Future of Television's Teaching Face," in *Children and the Faces of Television*, Edward L. Palmer and Aimee Dorr (Editors), Academic Press, New York, 1980, p. 106.
11. Same as above.
12. Arnold Gesell and Frances L. Ilg, *The Child From Five to Ten*, Harper & Brothers, New York, 1946, pp. 224-225.
13. Marianne Frostig and Phyllis Maslow, *Learning Problems in the Classroom: Prevention and Remediation*, Grune & Stratton, New York, 1973, pp. 162-164.
14. See Kevin Ryan, "Television as a Moral Education," in *Television as a Cultural Force*, pp. 114-117.
15. Tony Buzan, *Use Your Head*, BBC Publications, London, 1974, for general information, pp. 16-17.
16. Brian Winston, *Dangling Conversations Book II Hardware/Software*, Davis-Poynter, Ltd., London, 1974, p. 36.
17. Douglass Cater, "TV and the Thinking Person," Policy Paper No. 727, Aspen Institute for Humanistic Studies, 1975, p. 8.
18. Brian Winston, *Hardware/Software*, pp. 135-136.
19. Tom Burns, *The BBC: Public Institution and Private World*, MacMillan Press, Ltd., London, 1977, pp. 40-41.
20. Daniel J. Boorstin, "TV's Impact on Society," *Life*, September 10, 1971, pp. 38-39.
21. Russel H. Weigel and Richard Jessor, "Television and Adolescent Conventionality: An Exploratory Study," *Public Opinion Quarterly*, 1973, Vol. 37, pp. 76, 83, 87.

Bibliography

BOOKS

Adler, Richard (Editor), *Television as a Cultural Force*, Aspen Institute for Humanistic Studies, Praeger Publishers, New York, 1976.

Ashmore, Harry S., *Fear in the Air: Broadcasting and the First Amendment— The Anatomy of a Constitutional Crisis*, W.W. Norton & Co., Inc., New York, 1973.

Barnouw, Erik, *A Tower in Babel: A History of Broadcasting in the United States, Vol. I to 1933*, Oxford University Press, New York, 1966.

Barnouw, Erik, *The Golden Web: A History of Broadcasting in the United States, Vol. II 1933-1953*, Oxford University Press, New York, 1968.

Barnouw, Erik, *The Image Empire: A History of Broadcasting in the United States, Vol. III from 1953*, Oxford University Press, New York, 1970.

Barnouw, Erik, *The Sponsor: Notes on a Modern Potentate*, Oxford University Press, New York, 1978.

Berkowitz, Leonard, *Aggression: A Social Psychological Analysis*, McGraw-Hill Book Co., New York, 1962, pp. 229-255.

Bloom, Benjamin S. (Editor), *Taxonomy of Educational Objectives Vol. I The Cognitive Domain*, Longman, Inc., New York, 1956.

Bogart, Leo, *The Age of Television*, Frederick Ungar Publishing Co., New York, 1956.

Bower, Robert T., *Television and the Public*, Holt, Rinehart, and Winston, New York, 1973.

Brown, Les, *Television: The Business Behind the Box*, Harcourt, Brace, Jovanovich, Inc., New York, 1971.

Burns, Tom, *The BBC: Public Institution and Private World*, MacMillan Press, Ltd., 1977.

Buzan, Tony, *Use Your Head*, BBC Publications, London, 1974.

Cater, Douglass (Director), *Television as a Social Force: New Approaches to TV Criticism*, Aspen Institute for Humanistic Studies, Praeger Publishers, New York, 1975.

Cater, Douglass and Stephen Strickland, *TV Violence and the Child: The Evolution and Fate of the Surgeon General's Report*, Russell Sage Foundation, New York, 1975.

Comstock, George and Eli A. Rubinstein (Editors), *Television and Social Behavior, Reports and Papers Vol. III Television and Adolescent Aggressiveness*, U.S. Government Printing Office, Washington, D.C., 1972a.

Comstock, George and Eli A. Rubinstein (Editors), *Television and Social Behavior, Reports and Papers Vol. 1 Media Content and Control*, U.S. Government Printing Office, Washington, D.C., 1972b.

Comstock, George, Eli A. Rubinstein, and John P. Murray, *Television and Social Behavior, Reports and Papers Vol. V Television's Effects: Further Explorations*, U.S. Government Printing Office, Washington, D.C., 1972.

De Franco, Ellen B., *TV: On/Off—Better Family Use of Television*, Goodyear Publishing Co., Santa Monica, 1980.

Elliott, William Y. (Editor), *Television's Impact on American Culture*, Michigan State University Press, Michigan, 1956.

Friendly, Fred, *Due to Circumstances Beyond Our Control*, Vintage Books, Random House, New York, 1968.

Frostig, Marianne and Phyllis Maslow, *Learning Problems in the Classroom: Prevention and Remediation*, Grune & Stratton, New York and London, 1973.

Gesell, Arnold and Frances L. Ilg, *The Child From Five to Ten*, Harper & Brothers, New York, 1946.

Glasser, William, *The Identity Society*, Harper & Row Publishers, New York, 1972.

Glick, Ira O. and Sidney J. Levy, *Living With Television*, Aldine Publishing Co., Chicago, 1962.

Hall, Edward T., *The Silent Language*, Fawcett Publications, Inc., Greenwich, Conn., 1959.

Himmelweit, Hilde T., A.N. Oppenheim, and Pamela Vince, *Television and the Child: Study Sponsored by the Nuffield Foundation*, Oxford University Press, London, 1958.

Hovland, Carl I., Irving L. Janis, and Harold H. Kelley, *Communication and Persuasion*, Yale University Press, New Haven, 1953.

Johnson, A.H. (Editor), *Whitehead's American Essays in Social Philosophy*, Harper & Brothers, New York, 1959.

Johnson, Nicholas, *How to Talk Back to Your Television Set*, Little, Brown & Co., Boston, 1967.

Kaye, Evelyn, *The Family Guide to Children's Television*, Pantheon Books, Random House, New York, 1974.

Kendrick, Alexander, *Primetime: The Life of Edward R. Murrow*, J.M. Dent & Sons, Ltd., London, 1969.

Klapper, Joseph T., *The Effects of Mass Communication*, The Free Press, New York, 1960.

Krathwohl, David R. (Editor), *Taxonomy of Educational Objectives Vol. II The Affective Domain*, Longman, Inc., New York, 1964.

Lee, Robert E., *Television: The Revolution*, Essential Books, J.J. Little & Ives Co., New York, 1944.

Liebert, Robert M., John M. Neale, and Emily S. Davidson, *The Early Window: Effects of Television on Children and Youth*, Pergamon Press, Inc., New York, 1973.

Mayer, Martin, *About Television*, Harper & Row Publishers, New York, 1972.

McLuhan, Marshall, *Understanding Media: The Extensions of Man*, McGraw-Hill Book Co., New York, 1965.

McLuhan, Marshall and Quentin Fiore, *The Medium Is the Message*, Random House, New York, 1967.

Melody, William, *Children's Television: The Economics of Exploitation*, Yale University Press, New Haven, 1973.

Merton, Robert K., *Mass Persuasion: The Social Psychology of a War Bond Drive*, Harper & Brothers, New York, 1946.

Morris, Norman S., *Television's Child*, Little, Brown & Co., Boston, 1971.

Noll, Roger G., Merton J. Peck, and John J. McGowan, *Economic Aspects of Television Regulation*, The Brookings Institute, Washington, D.C., 1973.

Palmer, Edward L. and Aimee Dorr (Editors), *Children and the Faces of Television: Teaching, Violence, Selling*, Academic Press, New York, 1980.

Piaget, Jean, *Play, Dreams, and Imitation in Childhood*, W.W. Norton & Co., New York, 1962.

Piaget, Jean, *The Moral Judgment of the Child*, The Free Press, New York, 1965.

Potter, Rosemary Lee, *New Season: The Positive Uses of Commercial Television With Children*, Charles E. Merrill Publishing Co., Ohio, 1976.

Pulaski, Mary Ann, *Understanding Piaget: An Introduction to Children's Cognitive Development*, Harper & Row, New York, 1971.

Rather, Dan, *The Camera Never Blinks*, Wm. Morrow & Co., Inc., New York, 1977.

Rubinstein, Eli A., George A. Comstock, and John P. Murray, *Television and Social Behavior, Reports and Papers Vol. IV Television in Day-to-Day Life: Patterns of Use*, U.S. Government Printing Office, Washington, D.C., 1972.

Russell, Bertrand, *Education and the Good Life*, Boni & Liveright, Inc., London, 1926.

Rutstein, Nat, *Go Watch TV!*, Sheed & Ward, Inc., New York, 1974.

Schramm, Wilbur, Jack Lyle, and Edwin B. Parker, *Television in the Lives of Our Children*, Stanford University Press, Stanford, 1961.

Schramm, Wilbur and Donald F. Roberts (Editors), *The Process and Effects of Mass Communication*, University of Illinois Press, Chicago, 1971.

Schramm, Wilbur Lang (Editor), *Quality in Instructional Television*, East-West Center Books, University Press of Hawaii, Honolulu, 1972.

Shayon, Robert Lewis, *Television and Our Children*, Longmans Green & Co., New York, 1951.

Siepmann, Charles A., *Television and Education in the United States*, series of studies published by UNESCO, Paris, 1952.

Siepmann, Charles A., *TV and Our School Crisis*, Dodd, Mead & Co., New York, 1958.

Skornia, Harry J., *Television and Society: An Inquest and Agenda for Improvement*, McGraw-Hill Book Co., New York, 1965.

Spokin, Charles, *7 Glorious Days—7 Fun-Filled Nights*, Simon & Schuster, New York, 1968.

Steiner, Gary A., *The People Look at Television: A Study of Audience Attitudes,* Alfred A. Knopf, New York, 1963.

Tarbet, Donald G., *Television and Our Schools*, Ronald Press Co., New York, 1961.

Waldrop, Frank C., and Joseph Borkin, *Television: A Struggle for Power*, William Morrow & Co., New York, 1938.

Whitehead, Alfred North, *The Aims of Education and Other Essays*, MacMillan Co., New York, 1929, 1957.

Wilkins, Joan Anderson, *Breaking the TV Habit*, Charles Scribner's Sons, New York, 1982.

Winn, Marie, *The Plug-In Drug*, The Viking Press, New York, 1977.

Winston, Brian, *Dangling Conversations Book I: The Image of the Media*, Davis-Poynter, Ltd., London, 1973.

Winston, Brian, *Dangling Conversations Book II: Hardware/Software*, Davis-Poynter, Ltd., London, 1974.

JOURNAL ARTICLES AND PERIODICALS

Arthur, Paul Allen, "Big Brother: The Pimp in Your Pad," *Players Magazine*, Vol. 3, No. 5, October, 1976, pp. 13, 38, 56, 69.

Bandura, Albert, "Influence of Model's Reinforcement Contingencies on the Acquisition of Imitative Responses," *Journal of Personality and Social Psychology*, 1965a, Vol. I, pp. 589-595.

Bandura, Albert, "Vicarious Processes: A Case of No-Trial Learning," *Advances in Experimental Social Psychology*, Vol. II, Academic Press, New York, 1965b, pp. 1-55.

Bandura, Albert, Dorothea Ross, and Sheila A. Ross, "Transmission of Aggression Through Imitation of Aggressive Models," *Journal of Abnormal and Social Psychology*, 1961, Vol. 63, No. 3, pp. 575-582.

Bandura, Albert, Dorothea Ross, and Sheila A. Ross, "Imitation of Film-Mediated Aggressive Models," *Journal of Abnormal and Social Psychology*, 1963, Vol. 66, pp. 3-11.

Bandura, Albert, Dorothea Ross, and Sheila A. Ross, "Vicarious Reinforcement and Imitative Learning," *Journal of Abnormal and Social Psychology*, 1963, Vol. 67, pp. 601-607.

Barcus, F. Earle, "Parental Influence on Children's Television Viewing," *Television Quarterly*, 1969, Vol. 8, No. 3, pp. 63-73.

Bauer, Raymond A. and Alice H. Bauer, "America, Mass Society, and Mass Media," *Journal of Social Issues*, 1961, Vol. 16, No. 3, pp. 3-66.

Baxter, William S., "The Mass Media and Young People," *Journal of Broadcasting*, 1960, Vol. 5, pp. 49-58.

Berkowitz, Leonard, "The Effects of Observing Violence," *Scientific American*, February, 1964, Vol. 210, No. 2, pp. 35-41.

Berkowitz, Leonard and Edna Rawlings, "Effects of Film Violence on Inhibition Against Subsequent Aggression," *Journal of Abnormal and Social Psychology*, 1963, Vol. 66, pp. 405-412.

Berry, Gordon L., "Television and the Urban Child: Some Educational Policy Implications," *Education and Urban Society*, Sage Publications, Inc., November, 1977, Vol. 10, No. 1, pp. 31-54.

Bogart, Leo, "American Television: A Brief Survey of Research Findings," *Journal of Social Issues*, 1962, Vol. 18, pp. 36-42.

Bogart, Leo, "Warning: The Surgeon General Has Determined that TV Violence Is Moderately Dangerous to Your Child's Mental Health," *Public Opinion Quarterly*, 1972, Vol. 36, pp. 491-521.

Bogart, Leo, "The Management of Mass Media," *Public Opinion Quarterly*, Winter, 1973-1974, Vol. 37, No. 4, pp. 580-589.

Boorstin, Daniel J., "TV's Impact on Society," *Life*, September 10, 1971, pp. 36-39.

Bryan, James H. and Nancy H. Walbek, "The Impact of Words and Deeds Concerning Altruism Upon Children," *Child Development*, 1970, Vol. 14, pp. 747-757.

Chaffee, Steve H., L. Scott Ward, and Leonard P. Tipton, "Mass Communication and Political Socialization," *Journalism Quarterly*, 1970, Vol. 47, pp. 647-659; also p. 666.

Chaney, D.C., "Involvement, Realism, and the Perception of Aggression in Television Programmes," *Human Relations*, 1970, Vol. 23, No. 5, pp. 373-381.

Clark, Cedric C., "Television and Social Controls: Some Observations on the Portrayals of Ethnic Minorities," *Television Quarterly*, 1969, Vol. 8, No. 2, pp. 18-22.

Cline, Victor B., Roger G. Croft, and Steven Courrier, "Desensitization of Children to Television Violence," *Journal of Personality and Social Psychology*, 1973, Vol. 27, pp. 360-365.

Coffin, Thomas E., "Television's Impact on Society," *American Psychologist*, 1955, Vol. 10, pp. 630-641.

Collins, W. Andrew, "Learning of Media Content: A Developmental Study," *Child Development*, 1970, Vol. 41, pp. 1133-1142.

DeFleur, Melvin L., "Occupational Roles as Portrayed on Television," *Public Opinion Quarterly*, 1964, Vol. 28, pp. 57-74.

DeFleur, Melvin L. and Lois B. DeFleur, "The Relative Contribution of Television as a Learning Source of Children's Occupational Knowledge," *American Sociological Review*, 1967, Vol. 32, pp. 777-789.

de Sola Pool, Ithiel and Barbara Adler, "Educational Television: Is Anyone Watching?" *Journal of Social Issues*, 1962, Vol. 18, pp. 50-61.

Dominick, Joseph R., "Crime and Law Enforcement on Primetime Television," *Public Opinion Quarterly*, 1973, Vol. 37, pp. 241-250.

Ellis, Glenn Thomas and Francis Sekyra III, "The Effect of Aggressive Cartoons on the Behavior of First Grade Children," *Journal of Psychology*, 1972, Vol. 81, pp. 37-43.

Eron, Leonard, L. Rowell Huesmann, Monroe M. Lefkowitz, and Leopald O. Walder, "Does Television Violence Cause Aggression?" *American Psychologist*, April, 1972, Vol. 27, pp. 253-263.

Eron, Leonard D., L. Rowell Huesmann, Monroe M. Lefkowitz, and Leopald O. Walder, "Behavior—Aggression: How Learning Conditions in Early Childhood—Including Mass Media—Relate to Aggression in Late Adolescence," *Journal of Learning Disabilities*, 1976, Vol. 9, No. 3, pp. 31-32.

Feinberg, Susan, "The Classroom Is No Longer Primetime," *Today's Education*, September/October, 1977, Vol. 66, No. 3, pp. 78-79.

Flanders, James P., "A Review of Research on Imitative Behavior," *Psychological Bulletin*, 1968, Vol. 69, No. 5, pp. 316-337.

Friedrich, Lynette K. and Aletha H. Stein, "Prosocial Television and Young Children: The Effects of Verbal Labeling and Role Playing on Learning and Behavior," *Child Development*, 1975, Vol. 46, pp. 27-38.

Gardner, Carl, "Dangerous Visions," *Time-Out*, May 4-10, 1979, No. 472, pp. 12-15.

Gerbner, George and Larry Gross, "The Scary World of TV's Heavy Viewers," *Psychology Today*, April, 1976, pp. 41-45 and p. 89.

Goranson, Richard E., "Media Violence and Aggressive Behavior," in *Advances in Experimental Social Psychology*, edited by Leonard Berkowitz, Academic Press, New York, 1970, Vol. 5, pp. 1-31.

Greenberg, Bradley S., "Television for Children: Dimensions of Communicator and Audience Perceptions," *Audio-Visual Communication Review*, 1965, Vol. 13, No. 4, pp. 385-396.

Gunther, Max, "How Television Helps Johnny Read," *TV Guide*, September 4, 1976, pp. 6-10.

Gunther, Max, "All That TV Violence: Is It Really So Harmful?" *TV Guide*, November 13, 1976, pp. 34-40.

Hale, Gordon A., Leon K. Miller, and Harold W. Stevenson, "Incidental Learning of Film Content: A Developmental Study," *Child Development*, 1968, Vol. 39, pp. 69-77.

Hendrick, Grant H., "When Television Is a School for Criminals," *TV Guide*, January 29, 1977, pp. 4-10.

Hess, Robert D. and Herbert Goldman, "Parents' Views of the Effect of Television on Their Children," *Child Development*, 1962, Vol. 33, pp. 411-426.

Hicks, David J., "Imitation and Retention of Film-Mediated Aggressive Peer and Adult Models," *Journal of Personality and Social Psychology*, 1965, Vol. 2, No. 1, pp. 97-100.

Himmelweit, Hilde T., "A Theoretical Framework for the Consideration of the Effects of Television: A British Report," *Journal of Social Issues*, 1962, Vol. 18, pp. 16-28.

Hovland, Carl L., "Effects of the Mass Media on Communication," *Handbook of Social Psychology*, Gardner Lindzey, Editor, Addison-Wesley Publishing Co., 1954, Vol. II, pp. 1062-1103.

Hyman, Herbert H., "Mass Communication and Socialization," *Public Opinion Quarterly*, Winter, 1973-1974, Vol. 37, No. 4, pp. 524-540.

Johnson, Nicholas, "The Wasteland Revisited," *Playboy Magazine*, December, 1970, pp. 229, 264, 266, and 268.

Johnson, Norris R., "Television and Politicization: A Test of Competing Models," *Journalism Quarterly*, 1973, Vol. 50, pp. 447-455.

Katz, Elihu, Michael Gurevitch, and Hadassah Hass, "Of the Use of the Mass Media for Important Things," *American Sociological Review*, 1973, Vol. 38, pp. 164-181.

Klapper, J.T., "What We Know About the Effects of Mass Communication: The Brink of Hope," *Public Opinion Quarterly*, 1957, Vol. 21, pp. 451-474.

Krugman, Herbert E., "The Impact of Television Advertising: Learning Without Involvement," *Public Opinion Quarterly*, 1965, Vol. 29, pp. 349-356.

Krugman, Herbert E., "Brain Wave Measures of Media Involvement," *Journal of Advertising Research*, 1971, Vol. 11, No. 1, pp. 3-9.

Krugman, Herbert E. and Eugene L. Hartley, "Passive Learning From Television," *Public Opinion Quarterly*, 1970, Vol. 34, pp. 184-190.

Lazarsfeld, Paul F., "Why Is So Little Known About the Effects of Television on Children and What Can Be Done?" (Testimony before the Kefauver Committee on Juvenile Delinquency), *Public Opinion Quarterly*, 1955, Vol. 19, pp. 243-251.

Leifer, Aimee D., Neal J. Gordon, and Sherryl B. Graves, "Children's Television: More Than Mere Entertainment," *Harvard Educational Review*, 1974, Vol. 44, No. 2, pp. 213-245.

Lerner, Daniel, "Notes on Communication and the Nation State," *Public Opinion Quarterly*, Winter, 1973-1974, Vol. 37, No. 4, pp. 541-550.

Liebert, Robert M. and Robert A. Baron, "Some Immediate Effects of Televised Violence on Children's Behavior," *Developmental Psychology*, 1972, Vol. 6, pp. 469-475.

Maccoby, Eleanor E., "Television: Its Impact on School Children," *Public Opinion Quarterly*, 1951, Vol. 15, pp. 421-444.

Maccoby, Eleanor E., "Why Do Children Watch Television?" *Public Opinion Quarterly*, 1954, Vol. 18, pp. 239-244.

Maccoby, Eleanor E. and William Cody Wilson, "Identification and Observational Learning From Films," *Journal of Abnormal and Social Psychology*, 1957, Vol. 55, pp. 76-87.

Mannes, Marya, "Television: The Splitting Image," *Saturday Review*, November 14, 1970, pp. 66-68.

Melody, William H. and Wendy Ehrlich, "Children's TV Commercials: The Vanishing Policy Options," *Journal of Communication*, 1974, Vol. 24, No. 4, pp. 113-125.

Methvin, Eugene, "What You Can Do About TV Violence," *Reader's Digest Reprint*, July, 1975, pp. 1-6.

Meyer, Karl E., "Television's Trying Times," *Saturday Review*, September 16, 1978, pp. 19-28.

Meyer, Timothy P., "The Effects of Verbally Violent Film Content on Aggressive Behavior," *Audio-Visual Communication Review*, 1972, Vol. 20, No. 2, pp. 160-169.

Meyer, Timothy P., "Children's Perceptions of Favorite Television Characters as Behavioral Models," *Educational Broadcasting Review*, 1973, Vol. 7, No. 1, pp. 25-33.

Murray, Randall L., Richard R. Cole, and Fred Fedler, "Teenagers and TV Violence: How They Rate and View It," *Journalism Quarterly*, 1970, Vol. 47, pp. 247-255.

Muson, Howard, "Teenage Violence and the Telly," *Psychology Today*, March, 1978, pp. 50-54.

Mussen, Paul and Eldred Rutherford, "Effects of Aggression on Children's Aggressive Play," *Journal of Abnormal and Social Psychology*, 1961, Vol. 62, No. 2, pp. 461-464.

Nayman, O.B., Charles K. Atkin, and Bill Gillette, "The Four-Day Workweek and Media Use: A Glimpse of the Future," *Journal of Broadcasting*, 1973, Vol. 17, pp. 301-308.

Noble, Grant, "Effects of Different Forms of Filmed Aggression on Children's Constructive and Destructive Play," *Journal of Personality and Social Psychology*, 1973, Vol. 26, pp. 54-59.

O'Brien, Clare Lynch, "Using Commercial TV in the Classroom," *Teacher*, September, 1976, pp. 45, 46, 51, and 52.

Panitt, Merrill, "Television Today: The State of the Art," *TV Guide*, February 19, 1977, pp. 6-11.

Panitt, Merrill, "Network Power—Is It Absolute?" *TV Guide*, February 26, 1977, pp. 34-39.

Panitt, Merrill, "Programming for Profit," *TV Guide*, March 5, 1977, pp. 35-40.

Parker, Edwin B., "Implications of New Information Technology," *Public Opinion Quarterly*, Winter, 1973-74, Vol. 37, No. 4, pp. 590-600.

Rarick, David L., "Parental Evaluations of Television Violence," *Educational Broadcasting Review*, 1973, Vol. 7, No. 1, pp. 34-43.

Rarick, David L., "Rating TV Shows," *Consumer's Digest*, November/December, 1977, pp. 37-40.

Rarick, David L., James E. Townsend, and Douglas A. Boyd, "Adolescent Perceptions of Police," *Journalism Quarterly*, 1973, Vol. 50, pp. 438-446.

Reeves, Richard, "The Dangers of Television in the Silverman Era," *Esquire*, April 25, 1978, pp. 45-57.

Riley, John W., Frank V. Cantwell, and Katherine F. Ruttiger, "Some Observations on the Social Effects of Television," *Public Opinion Quarterly*, 1949, Vol. 13, pp. 223-234.

Rossiter, John R. and Thomas S. Robertson, "Children's TV Commercials: Testing for Defenses," *Journal of Communication*, 1974, Vol. 24, No. 4, pp. 137-144.

Safran, Claire, "What's the Verdict on Sesame Street?" *TV Guide*, October 2, 1976, pp. 4-8.

Safran, Claire, "How TV Changes Children," *Redbook*, November, 1976, pp. 88, 91, 95, and 97.

Seldes, George, "Some Impressions of Television," *Journal of Social Issues*, 1962, Vol. 18, pp. 29-35.

Shayon, Robert Lewis, "TV and Radio: Mission Immoral," *Saturday Review*, November 19, 1966, p. 34.

Sheikh, Annes A., V. Kanti Prasad, and Tanniru R. Rao, "Children's TV Commercials: A Review of Research," *Journal of Communication*, 1974, Vol. 24, No. 4, pp. 126-136.

Siegel, Alberta E., "The Influence of Violence in the Mass Media Upon Children's Role Expectations," *Child Development*, 1953, Vol. 29, No. 1, pp. 35-56.

Siegel, Alberta E., "Film-Mediated Fantasy Aggression and Strength of Aggressive Drive," *Child Development*, 1956, Vol. 27, No. 3, pp. 365-378.

Smith, David M., "Some Uses of Mass Media by Fourteen Year Olds," *Journal of Broadcasting*, 1971, Vol. 16, pp. 37-50.

Smythe, Dallas W., "Reality as Presented by Television," *Public Opinion Quarterly*, 1954, Vol. 18, pp. 143-156.

Steuer, Faye B., James M. Applefield, and Rodney Smith, "Televised Aggression and Interpersonal Aggression of Preschool Children," *Journal of Experimental Child Psychology*, 1971, Vol. 11, pp. 442-447.

Streicher, Helen White, "The Girls in the Cartoons," *Journal of Communication*, 1974, Vol. 24, No. 2, pp. 125-159.

Streicher, Lawrence H. and Norman L. Bonney, "Children Talk About Television," *Journal of Communication*, 1974, Vol. 24, No. 3, pp. 54-61.

Surlin, Stuart H. and Joseph R. Dominick, "Television's Function as a Third Parent for Black and White Teenagers," *Journal of Broadcasting*, 1970, Vol. 15, pp. 55-64.

Tannenbaum, Percy H. and Bradley S. Greenberg, "Mass Communication," *Annual Review of Psychology*, 1968, Vol. 19, pp. 351-386.

Tobin, Richard L., "Spots Before Our Eyes," *Saturday Review*, February 14, 1970, pp. 67-68.

Vinovich, George, "About TV Violence," *Consumer Newsletter*, May 27, 1976, Vol. 7, No. 22, issue 170, pp. 10-11.

Walters, Judith K. and Vernon A. Stone, "Television and Family Communications," *Journal of Broadcasting*, 1971, Vol. 15, pp. 409-414.

Waters, Harry F., "What TV Does to Kids," *Newsweek*, February 21, 1977, pp. 62-70.

Weigel, Russel H. and Richard Jessor, "Television and Adolescent Conventionality: An Exploratory Study," *Public Opinion Quarterly*, 1973, Vol. 37, pp. 76-90.

Wiebe, Gerhard D., "Two Psychological Factors in Media Audience Behavior," *Public Opinion Quarterly*, 1969, Vol. 33, pp. 523-537.

Zusne, Leonard, "Measuring Violence in Children's Cartoons," *Perceptual and Motor Skills*, 1968, Vol. 27, pp. 901-902.

OTHER REFERENCES

"America: Out to Eat," *Newsweek*, October 3, 1977, pp. 86-89.

Cater, Douglass, "TV and the Thinking Person," a Policy Paper, Aspen Institute for Humanistic Studies, No. 727, California, 1975.

Chapin, Donna, "Some Aspects of the Impact of Television on Children's Formal and Informal Education," paper presented to University of Southern California Education Department, 1966.

Comstock, George A., "Television Violence: Where the Surgeon General's Study Leads," Paper 4831, May, 1972, from Rand Corporation, Washington, D.C.

Comstock, George A., "Television and Human Behavior: The Key Studies," prepared under a grant from Edna McConnel Clark Foundation, Report 1747-CF, June, 1975, Rand Corporation, Santa Monica, California.

Comstock, George A., "Television and the Young: Setting the Stage for a Research Agenda," Paper 5550, November, 1975, Rand Corporation, Santa Monica, California.

Comstock, George A., "Research and the Constructive Aspects of Television in Children's Lives: A Forecast," Paper 5622, March, 1976, Rand Corporation, Santa Monica, California.

Comstock, George A., "Television and Its Viewers: What Social Sciences Sees," Paper 5632, May, 1976, Rand Corporation, Santa Monica, California.

Crippens, David and Susan Brody, "The Future of Children's Programming for the Public TV Perspective," paper prepared by KCET, Los Angeles, California, 1976/1977.

Edible TV: Your Child and Food Commercials: A Report of the Council on Children, Media, and Merchandising, prepared by Robert B. Choate and Pamela C. Engle, Washington, D.C., June, 1977.

Federal Communications Commission: Children's Television Programs, Report and Policy Statement, 1974, Vol. 39, No. 215, Part II, Washington, D.C.

Frank, Josette, *Television: How to Use It Wisely With Children*, pamphlet published by Child Study Association of America, 1965.

Idman, Pekka, *Educational and Psychological Interactions*, bulletin from the Department of Educational and Psychological Research, School of Education, Malmo, Sweden; *Consumer Education in Schools: An Experiment in the Production of Education Material*, October, 1977, No. 63.

Jones, George William, "The Relationship of Screen-Mediated Violence to Anti-Social Behavior," Abstract of dissertation, Syracuse University, February, 1971.

National Institute of Mental Health, *Television and Behavior: Ten Years of Scientific Progress and Implications for the Eighties*, U.S. Government Printing Office, Washington, D.C., 1982.

Public Broadcasting and Education: A Report to the Corporation for Public Broadcasting, from the Advisory Council of National Organizations, March, 1975, Chairman William F. Fore.

Research on the Effects of Television Advertising on Children: Review and Recommendations, report prepared for National Science Foundation under NSF Grant No. APR75-10126, Washington, D.C., 1977.

Seeking Solutions to Violence on Children's Television, transcripts from a Strategy Workshop, May 5, 1976, sponsored by the Committee on Children's Television.

"Sex and Violence: Hollywood Fights Back," *TV Guide*, August 27, 1977, pp. 4-18.

Symposium on Television Violence, organized by the Research Branch, Canadian Radio-Television Commission, Ottawa, 1976.

Television and Growing Up: The Impact of Televised Violence, report to the Surgeon General, United States, Public Health Service, from the Scientific Advisory Committee on Television and Social Behavior, U.S. Government Printing Office, Washington, D.C., 1972.

To the Federal Trade Commission in the Matter of a Trade Regulation on Over-the-Counter Drugs, paper submitted by Council on Children, Media, and Merchandising, Roger Fitzpatrick presiding officer, February, 1977.

"Video's New Frontier" and "Why Johnny Can't Read," *Newsweek*, December 8, 1975, pp. 52, 57, and 58-65.

"Violence Is a Saleable Commodity," National Association for Better Broadcasting Newsletter, *Better Radio and Television*, Spring, 1973.

Window Dressing on the Set: Women and Minorities in Television, report of the U.S. Commission on Civil Rights, August, 1977.

"Youth Crime Plague," *Time*, July 11, 1977, pp. 18-28.

Appendix A

Piagetian Developmental Stages

Stage 1

0 to 2 years: sensory-motor activity. The child starts to attend to outside stimuli and manipulate things felt. Can have thought concepts without language.

Stage 2

2 to 7 years: pre-operational stage. Child begins to focus attention more clearly. Development of language and a very egocentric period. Cannot deal with many classification experiences or another's point-of-view. Sequential thought difficult. Uses trial-and-error.

(Part of pre-operational stage)

5 to 7 years: intuitive operational stage. Transition between pre-schooler and school-age child. Less egocentric, but still tied to concrete thinking, i.e., first-hand rather than vicarious experience. Can see whole or parts but has difficulty in combining the two. Reversing thought process is difficult.

Stage 3

7 to 11 years: concrete operational stage. Begins to "think" as opposed to relying merely on perceptual awareness only. Begins to compare feelings with others. Multiple classification and reversibility begin to develop as well as the ability to see causal relationships. Child is capable of forming a logical series, classification, recognizing equivalent parts, reversing thought, and conserving thought, i.e., knowing that one cup of water is the same whatever the shape of the container it is in.

(Part of concrete operational stage)

9 to 11 years: transitional operational stage. Begins to hypothesize but cannot exhaust all possibilities. Has finer discrimination abilities. Can solve problems effectively in situation where child has had first-hand experience.

Stage 4

11 to 16/17 years: formal operational stage. Young adulthood. Can combine thoughts into rules or variables in order to solve problems. Can analyze and synthesize. Greater power to see alternatives.

Appendix B

TVQ: Questions and Answers About Television

What's Your TVQ?

How much do you know about TV? Not about the programs—or the stars—but about the industry and the habit. Answers to some of these questions may surprise you, but they're the kinds of things that top TV executives think about when they make programming decisions.

Give yourself 10 points for each correct answer and then figure out your TVQ!

1. On a typical Sunday night, one out of every two Americans is
   A. at the movies
   B. watching television
   C. knitting sweaters
   D. reading

2. If you're a member of an average TV household, your tube is on more than
   A. 40 hours a week
   B. 50 hours a week
   C. 60 hours a week
   D. 70 hours a week

3. You're the ad manager for a new perfume called "Thirty Love," designed to appeal to active women ages 18-34 with its heady, sporty fragrance. To buy thirty seconds of commercial time on a top-rated prime time show, you will have to spend about
   A. $ 8,500
   B. $15,000
   C. $25,000
   D. $40,000

4. Which of the following is NOT usually true of the typical television hero?
    A. he resorts to violence only when he has to
    B. he is good-looking, white, and in his 30s
    C. his beliefs often differ from those with great wealth and political power
    D. he is married

5. You've just manufactured a banana-flavored soft drink called "Bingo," and you want to run a series of commercials showing everyday people comparing Bingo to other leading soft drinks. What is the position of the Federal Trade Commission (the agency that regulates television advertising) in regard to your ad campaign?
    A. the FTC encourages this kind of advertising because it believes these commercials, when truthful, let people know about product differences.
    B. the FTC discourages such ads.
    C. the FTC allows you to run the ad, as long as you do not mention your competitor's name.
    D. the FTC prohibits such ads.

6. It has been shown that watching a lot of television affects the way people look at the world. Which of the following has NOT been shown?
    A. adult heavy viewers are much more likely than light viewers to own guns for protection.
    B. heavy viewers who are children are more likely to think it's "all right to hit someone if you're mad at them" than light viewers.
    C. in Hawaii, heavy viewers are better drivers than light viewers.
    D. heavy viewers are more likely to be afraid of walking city streets alone at night than light viewers.

7. If the people listed below were in your family, who would be the most likely to watch the most TV, according to Nielsen statistics?
    A. Annie, age 8
    B. Henry, age 15
    C. Morton, age 29
    D. Rhoda, age 59

8. The A.C. Nielsen Company measures our TV viewing habits. Their Storage Instantaneous Audiometer—known to some as the "little black box"—is installed in about 1200 homes and results in "ratings" determining which shows stay on the air and which are taken off. Which of the following is NOT true about this device?
    A. it records only when the TV set is on, and to which channel it is tuned.

    B.   Nielsen pays families to have the Audiometer installed in their homes.

    C.   the identities of these families are kept secret.

    D.   the information gathered from these households measures the viewing habits in all American homes accurately.

9. If you owned a television station, your license to operate would come up for renewal every three years. The Federal Communications Commission is the regulatory agency which oversees this process. Which of the following is NOT an FCC guideline or law affecting approval of your license application?

    A.   you should devote at least one hour out of 12 to public affairs programs such as news, talk shows, and consumer shows.

    B.   you should give "reasonable" time to important community issues and treat them "fairly."

    C.   your station should produce at least two hours of its own programming daily.

    D.   if you sell a half hour of time to a political candidate, you must offer to sell a half hour of time to the opposing candidate.

10. Violence on television, cause for much debate over the past 25 years, hit its peak in 1976 and is now on the downswing.
        TRUE or FALSE

TVQ Answers

1B. In numbers, this means about 100 million people.

2A. 43 hours and 52 minutes, to be precise.

3D.

4D. Most leading male TV characters are single. Interestingly, item "C" is generally true, indicating that we find appeal in characters who are in conflict with top layers of established society.

5A.

6C. In Hawaii, heavy television viewers were shown to be more reckless behind the wheel than light viewers.

7D. Rhoda is in the heaviest viewing group—women, ages 55 and older. Women in general watch more television than men. Teenagers watch the least amount of television, compared to other age groups.

8D. The samplings can't be exact, and the Nielsen Company itself notes that ratings are really just estimates. Over a long period of time, however, a program's rating becomes more meaningful. Notice that the "little black box" can't tell if anyone's watching the set or, if they are, whether they're enjoying what they're seeing.

9C. "A" is a guideline, while "B" and "D" are strict regulations.

10. TRUE:
    Apparently, sponsors and TV executives have reacted to the public
    outcry against televised violence.

    What's your TVQ? Give yourself 10 points for each correct answer:
    90-100 points: Move over, Freddie Silverman!
    70-80 points: You've got yourself a hit show!
    50-60 points: Broadcasting may not be your "bag," but you've got good
    TV sense.
    30-40 points: A lot to learn. There's more to TV than the on-off button.
    0-20 points: Your show's been cancelled.

Far West Laboratory for Educational Research and Development, San Francisco,
California. Prepared at WGBH's Office of Radio and Television for Learning by Ned
White.

Appendix C

Let's Face It: Topics for Family Discussion

Let's Face It!

Television figures in family life in many different ways. Some of these issues appear below. Which way do you face? How does your position differ from that of other members of your family? Have each member of the family choose the number from 1 to 5 which best indicates where he or she stands. Then discuss your answers.

It's good for families to talk about the TV they watch. They can learn about each other.

It's bad. A lot of families can't talk about these things without quarreling.

| 1 | 2 | 3 | 4 | 5 |

In our house, TV is a good way for us to avoid each other. Turn on the set, sit down, and stare at the screen.

TV is a way of bringing our family together—it's fun to share something together.

| 1 | 2 | 3 | 4 | 5 |

We're careful about what we watch on TV. It's important to be selective, to know why you're watching a certain show.

TV is almost all entertainment. It's a way to escape problems, to give your mind a rest. Just turn it on and see what happens.

| 1 | 2 | 3 | 4 | 5 |

Characters on TV family shows are very real—a lot like some of my friends and their families.			Most characters on TV family shows don't seem very real to me, even though they're "realistic." They may be enjoyable to watch, but they're exaggerated.

1	2	3	4	5

On the whole, I'd say my family could do with a lot less TV. There are other things we can do with our time that would be more valuable.			TV's important in our family. If we didn't have it, we wouldn't know what to do with ourselves.

1	2	3	4	5

Far West Laboratory for Educational Research and Development, San Francisco, California. Prepared at WGBH's Office of Radio and Television for Learning by Ned White.

Appendix D

Television Literacy and Critical Viewing Skills

The following suggestions are offered by the National Institute of Mental Health for increasing television literacy and viewing competency in children. For further information, see *Television and Behavior: Ten Years of Scientific Progress and Implications for the Eighties*, National Institute of Mental Health, U.S. Government Printing Office, Washington D.C., 1982.

One set of skills criteria includes helping young people to:
    (1) understand the various types of television programs;
    (2) understand how programs are created;
    (3) understand the electronics of television;
    (4) learn what aspects of a program are real and what are fantasy;
    (5) learn the purpose and types of commercials;
    (6) understand how television influences our feelings and ideas;
    (7) become more aware of television as a source of information and how stereotypes are used on TV;
    (8) understand the difference between violence on television and violence in real life;
    (9) become more aware of personal viewing habits; and
    (10) use television in language arts and writing programs in school.

Other suggestions for television literacy among children and adolescents include encouraging the ability to:
    (1) describe why a program is selected, i.e., the decision-making process behind selection;
    (2) describe the consequences of viewing and other activities for entertainment besides television;
    (3) identify program content characteristics;
    (4) identify the various uses of different programs; and
    (5) identify the significance of television in one's personal life.

Ways parents can contribute to more effective TV training include:
  (1) monitoring the amount or number of hours of television exposure;

(2) supervising viewing and deciding what can and cannot be seen;
(3) viewing television with children and discussing what is seen;
(4) engaging children in alternative family activities;
(5) encouraging purposeful viewing, i.e., selecting specific, special programs;
(6) offering direct mediation, i.e., explanatory comments about what occurs on TV;
(7) offering indirect mediation, i.e., parents themselves modeling critical viewing skills by discussing program pros and cons; and
(8) using television as a springboard for applying information to other situations.

For further information on critical viewing skills and television curriculum, the following sources may be consulted:

Anderson, J.A. and Ploghoft, M.E. *The Way We See It: A Handbook for Teacher Instruction in Critical Receivership*, Salt Lake City, Media Research Center, 1978.
Dr. Charles R. Corder-Bolz, Southwest Educational Development Laboratory, Austin, Texas 79701.
Dorr, A., Graves, S.B., and Phelps, E. "Television Literacy for Young Children," *Journal of Communication*, 1980, Vol. 30, No. 3.
National Institute of Education, *Schooling and Leisure Time Use of Television*, March, 1978.
O'Bryant, S.L. and Corder-Bolz, C.R. "Tackling 'the Tube' with Family Teamwork," *Children Today*, 1977, Vol. 7, pp. 21-24.
Singer, D.G., Zuckerman, D.M., and Singer, J.L. "Helping Elementary School Children Learn About TV," *Journal of Communication*, 1980, Vol. 30, No. 3, pp. 84-93.
Walling, J.I. "The Effect of Parental Interaction on Learning from Television," *Communication Education*, 1976, Vol. 25, pp. 16-24.
Withrow, J.B. "Objectives for Critical Television Viewing Skills Curricula," *Television and Children*, 1980, Vol. 2, pp. 32-33.

Appendix E

Resource List of Organizations and Addresses

The following organizations and groups may be contacted for further information about various aspects of television and how the public can become more involved. The addresses have been sub-divided into categories for easy reference.

Government

Federal Communications Commission
Public Information Office
1919 M Street NW
Washington, DC 20554

Federal Trade Commission
Pennsylvania Avenue & Sixth Street NW
Washington, DC 20580

House Subcommittee on Communications
Rayburn House Office Building
Room B333
Washington, DC 20515

Senate Subcommittee on Communications
Russell Senate Office Building
Room B333
Washington, DC 20515

Networks/Broadcasting

ABC Network
1330 Avenue of the Americas
New York, NY 10019

CBS Network
51 West 52nd Street
New York, NY 10020

Corporation for Public Broadcasting
1111 16th Street NW
Washington, DC 20036

NBC Network
30 Rockefeller Plaza
New York, NY 10020

Public Broadcasting Service
475 L'Enfant Plaza West, SW
Washington, DC 20024

Public Service Groups

Action for Children's Television
46 Austin Street
Newtonville, MA 02160

Citizens' Communication Center
1914 Sunderland Place NW
Washington, DC 20036

Coalition for Children and Television
10906 Rochester Avenue
Los Angeles, CA 90024

Committee on Children's Television
1511 Masonic Avenue
San Francisco, CA 94117

Council on Children, Media, and Merchandising
1346 Connecticut Avenue
Washington, DC 20036

National Association for Better Broadcasting
P.O. Box 43640
Los Angeles, CA 90043

National Citizens' Committee for Broadcasting
1028 Connecticut Avenue NW
Washington, DC 20036

National PTA
TV Action Center
700 N. Rush Street
Chicago, IL 60611

Television Research/Information

Center for Early Education and Development
Institute of Child Development,
Room 226
51 East River Road
Minneapolis, MN 55455

Center for Science in the Public Interest
1779 Church Street NW
Washington, DC 20036

Center for Understanding Media
267 West 25th Street
New York, NY 10001

Children's Television Workshop
Community Education Services Division
One Lincoln Place
New York, NY 10023

Far West Laboratory for Educational Research and Development
1855 Folsom Street
San Francisco, CA 94103

National Association for the Education of Young Children
Attention: Media Committee
1834 Connecticut Avenue NW
Washington, DC 20009

Prime Time School Television
120 South LaSalle Street
Chicago, IL 60603

Teachers' Guide to Television
699 Madison Avenue
New York, NY 10021

Television Awareness Training
Media Action Research Center, Inc.
475 Riverside Drive
New York, NY 10027

Television Information Office
745 Fifth Avenue
New York, NY 10022

Television Resources, Inc.
Box 6712
Chicago, IL 60680

TV Information Center
Gessell Institute in Child Development
745 Fifth Avenue
New York, NY 10022

TV and Movie Facts for Parents
Box A-4
1345 Third Avenue
New York, NY 10021

Yale University Family Television Research/Consultation Center
Box 11A
Yale Station
New Haven, CT 06520

Index